**case studies in
ARCHAEOLOGY**

SERIES EDITOR

JEFFREY QUILTER

Ripon College

TOWARD A SOCIAL
HISTORY OF ARCHAEOLOGY IN
THE UNITED STATES

Toward a Social History of Archaeology in the United States

Thomas C. Patterson
Temple University

Harcourt Brace College Publishers

Fort Worth Philadelphia San Diego New York Orlando Austin San Antonio
Toronto Montreal London Sydney Tokyo

Publisher	Ted Buchholz
Acquisitions Editor	Christopher P. Klein
Developmental Editor	Linda Wiley
Project Editor	Daniela Raynes
Production Manager	Cynthia Young
Art Director	Nick Welch
Electronic Publishing Coordinator	Cathy Spitzenberger

Cover Image: The 'Gateway of the Sun' at Tiahuanaco, Bolivia

ISBN: 0-15-500824-2

Library of Congress Catalog Card Number: 94-75895

Address for Editorial Correspondence:
Harcourt Brace College Publishers, 301 Commerce Street, Suite 3700, Fort Worth, TX 76102.

Address for Orders:
Harcourt Brace & Company, 6277 Sea Harbor Drive, Orlando, FL 32887-6777. 1-800-782-4479, or 1-800-433-0001 (in Florida).

Printed in the United States of America

5 6 7 8 9 0 1 2 3 4 7 1 9 8 7 6

About the Series

These case studies in archaeology are designed to bring students in beginning and intermediate courses in archaeology, anthropology, history, and related disciplines insights into the theory, practice, and results of archaeological investigations. They are written by scholars who have had direct experience in archaeological research, whether in the field, laboratory, or library. The authors are also teachers, and in writing their books they have kept the students, who will read them, foremost in their minds. These books are intended to present a wide range of archaeological topics as case studies in a form and manner that will be more accessible than writings found in articles or books intended for professional audiences, yet at the same time preserve and present the significance of archaeological investigations for all.

About the Author

Tom Patterson is professor of anthropology and history at Temple University. He attended the University of California and the Universidad Nacional Mayor de San Marcos, and received a Ph.D. in anthropology from the former in 1964. He was a Fulbright Scholar in Peru and a Research Professor at the Center for Research in the Humanities at Copenhagen University in 1987. In 1993, he received a Certificate of Recognition from the National Black Graduate Students, the Distinguished Alumnus Award from the University of California at Riverside, and the Temple University. Great Teacher Award.

He is a trade union activist and member of numerous professional organizations, such as the World Archaeological Congress. A former secretary of the Archeology Division of the American Anthropological Association and assistant editor of *American Antiquity,* Patterson is currently on the editorial board of *Critique of Anthropology.*

During the last three decades, he has written more than a dozen books and one hundred articles, notes, and reviews dealing with archaeology, class and state formation, contemporary social theory, and the historical development of archaeology and anthropology as professions in the United States and Latin America. He is currently writing a book about civilization and its multicultural critics for Monthly Review Press.

About this Case Study

When I mentioned to some of my colleagues that one of our first case studies was a history of archaeology in the United States, I often met a blank stare or a questioning look. But such a book, especially this one, belongs in this series for a number of reasons.

First, the concept of a "case study" broadly includes any well-written work that offers a succinct presentation of some aspect of archaeology. This may be a narrative of research carried out in a laboratory, at a site, or in a library; a summary of the most up-to-date history of a particular archaeological culture or region; an ethnoarchaeological study; a topical work, such as the analysis of mortuary practices; or the latest techniques to examine artifacts or other residues. So long as they are written in a style that is accessible to undergraduates, theoretical works or even technical manuals may also serve as case studies. The objective of this series is to provide an opportunity for archaeologists to present a wide range of viewpoints.

Second, this book offers a clear presentation of how to understand changes in archaeological theory and practice. Simply put, archaeologists have not done a very good job discussing the history of their own discipline. This is rather surprising, given that archaeologists study the past. Some may see the author's approach as controversial, but he provides a distinct point of view to be supported or challenged in the classroom and beyond.

Finally, this work offers a radically different approach to the history of archaeology in the United States than the few accounts currently available. The "internalist" histories, as Patterson calls them—those that recount events from within the discipline, with little regard for the larger social contexts—abound with references to leading archaeologists of various historical epics. But discussions of the pioneering thoughts and deeds of a few professionals who shape the course of archaeology until the next great theorist or excavator comes along are quite ironic. Most anthropological archaeologists who work and teach in the United States today emerged from an intellectual milieu that left little room for the role of direct human agency in cultural and social development, yet in discussing the processes that shaped their own discipline they refer to the "great men" of the past!

Toward a Social History of Archaeology in the United States offers a significant contribution to the discussion of why archaeologists do what they do. It examines the discipline within larger social contexts as well as recognizes the importance of human agency. Whether readers find the author's unique perspective depressing or hopeful, they will not look at archaeology in quite the same way as before.

Jeffrey Quilter

PREFACE

This book began over a cup of coffee. Actually, it was several thousands of cups of coffee consumed throughout the years over a dining room table strewn with books, student papers, and notes scribbled on pads of yellow paper. These appeared every evening after the dinner dishes were removed and the family members retired to other parts of the house to pursue various activities—drum practice, homework, or preparing a legal brief. For more than a decade, I have regularly drunk coffee in the evening with my historian colleague Peter Gran. Together, we have maintained a running commentary on what we are writing and thinking, what is happening in the world, and what is going on at Temple University, where we teach.

During this period, Peter was working on a book concerned with Eurocentrism and the practice of history in states with different forms of hegemony—that is, political domination, leadership, and consent. About ten years ago, he asked me some rather pointed questions about archaeology in Peru, Mexico, and the United States—states which, in his view, have fundamentally different forms of hegemony. I couldn't answer them. They were important questions, and, over the years, I tried to formulate answers or at least clarify the issues involved. When I thought I had an idea or argument, I would put them on the table for discussion. They would undergo a regular process of dissection, examination, rejection, refinement, and reassembly.

As a result, I dedicate this book to Peter Gran, without whose thought-provoking questions and persistent interrogation, it probably would not have been written. I want to thank Judy Gran, who launched her career as a public interst lawyer during this period. Her questions about what I was thinking were every bit as provocative; they forced me to think more clearly about the contexts in which archaeologoy has been practiced both here and abroad. I also want to thank Stephen and Nora Gran who initially welcomed me into their home as only an eight- and five-year-old can do. I felt adopted, privileged to interact with them, and fortunate to watch them grow into truly exceptional young adults. They taught me a lot with their unswerving candor, honesty, and integrity.

This book is a sketch map, a guide that points out major features of a complex terrain. The landscape is still poorly known, and what seem to be major features still appear hazy on the horizon. As a result, other studies are desperately needed to clarify our understanding and appreciation of lands we are just beginning to traverse. A few of the many immediately come to mind: critical intellectual biographies; investigations of patronage, patron-client relations, and the construction of theory groups; and greater appreciation of the shaping effects of religion and the media.

While writing the book, I continually benefited from the instantaneous and constructive criticism of colleagues: Elizabeth Brumfiel of Albion College, Robert Paynter of the University of Massachusetts, Mark Leone of the University of Maryland, Jeffrey Quilter of Ripon College, Bruce Trigger of McGill University, and Alison Wylie of the University of Western Ontario.

Recently and over the years, many people have shared insights and observations that have enhanced my understanding of the history of archaeology and its relationship with the world around us. I especially want to express my gratitude to

Robert McC. Adams, Bassey Andah, Larian Angelo, Talal Asad, Lee Baker, Martin Bernal, Michael Blakey, Elizabeth Brumfiel, Carole Crumley, Stephen Dyson, Don Fowler, Christine Gailey, Peter Gran, Donna Keren, Mark Leone, Mary Ann Levine, Barbara Little, Richard S. MacNeish, Randall McGuire, Frank McManamon, Donald McVicker, William Marquardt, Juan José Ortiz Aguilú, Robert Paynter, Peter Rigby, John Rowe, Karen Sacks, Mario Sanoja, Paul Schackel, Peter Schmidt, Douglas Schwartz, Karen Spalding, Neil Silberman, Frank Spencer, Jalil Sued-Badillo, Daniel Tompkins, Bruce Trigger, Iraida Vargas Arenas, Kathy Walker, Gordon Willey, David Wise, Martin Wobst, Richard Woodbury, Henry Wright, Alison Wylie, John Yellen, and Larry Zimmerman.

I also want to thank Daniela Raynes of Harcourt Brace for her assistance in the final preparation of the manuscript.

I also want to acknowledge the contributions of Temple University, which has provided both support and a climate that demands clear, critical thought.

CONTENTS

CHAPTER 1

An Introduction

This book examines the historical development of archaeology in the United States. In it, I want to make two arguments. The first is that scientific activities such as archaeology are more thoroughly understood when we not only consider their accomplishments but also examine them in light of the shifting social and cultural contexts in which they developed and to which they are responses. The second is that the historical development of archaeology in the United States must be understood in the context of the making and remaking of the United States itself.

The first argument acknowledges that intellectuals, scholars, and technicians conduct their studies against a background where their practices and conclusions have meaning. Internalist accounts of the history of archaeology, written by professional archaeologists, such as Gordon Willey and Jeremy Sabloff's (1993) *History of American Archaeology* or Glyn Daniel's (1981) *A Short History of Archaeology,* concentrate almost exclusively on the scientific works: methodological, theoretical, and interpretive problems as they come to be defined by the scientific community. As a result, such accounts strip the practices from the social and intellectual milieu in which they formed and stress instead their independent development through the formation of ideas or methods or the adventures of the great. In their view, the interaction of scientific ideas or of intellectuals provides sufficient explanation of the dynamics of the science. However, what gets left out in the internalist accounts is the background: the social and cultural contexts in which the activities took place and acquired meaning. This omission ultimately impoverishes our understanding not only of the circumstances in which the practices came to make sense but also of the practices themselves. As Sandra Harding (1991, 10–12), the feminist philosopher of science, has observed: Science is created in political struggle; it is politics by other means. Science has social origins, and the knowledge it produces is socially situated. Therefore, one challenge in this book is to describe and explain the socially situated character of archaeological practice and knowledge in the United States.

The second argument contends that U.S. society has undergone a series of significant structural and cultural transformations. These have been profound enough that an accurate understanding of the social relations and cultural practices of one period does not automatically or naturally provide guidance for appreciating the institutions and activities of another period. This is particularly true of common-sense perspectives, like those rooted in neoclassical economic models. The common-sense views incorporated in neoclassical economics naturalize and universalize

1

contemporary capitalist social relations and cultural practices. Social theorists who have adopted them proclaim that neoclassical models adequately represent and explain the social relations and cultural practices of both earlier phases of capitalist development and precapitalist or noncapitalist societies! Besides potentially distorting the content and meaning of past practices and relations, they also leave us in a vacuum if we are trying to explain why changes occurred. They obscure the processes that are actually involved in the dissolution of past relations and practices, in their reorganization and reconfiguration, and in the emergence of new relations and customs that are frequently described as both rooted in and preserving tradition. Thus, a second challenge in this book is to describe and explain the structural transformations that have occurred in U.S. society and how these are reflected and refracted in the historical development of archaeology in the United States.

The challenges presented by the two arguments require that we take seriously the relations among society, the individual, and intellectual trends at particular moments in time. They also require that we specify how they are connected. Archaeologist Joan Gero (1985, 343) has sketched one possible way of doing this: (1) view the present as a narrow band of time and identify the political events and short-lived fashions that enter archaeological interpretations; (2) view the present as having a duration of forty or fifty years and see how structures of rewards and constraints are revealed in archaeological interpretation; and (3) recognize that contemporary archaeology is practiced in a state-based society and examine how the activities of archaeologists both justify and reinforce existing hierarchical relations and distinctions.

In approaching these challenges, I adopt a materialist conception of history—which treats complexities—rather than one or another overly deterministic formulation that attributes massive causality to demographic, environmental, technological, economic, or other factors. Such views ultimately yield "no-fault" histories, in which individuals are passive, so completely constrained by existing structures and extenuating circumstances that they are never confronted with options or the task of choosing between alternative courses of action (Haskell 1979).

Like the historian R. S. Neale (1985, xiii) and others who have explored the complexities of Marx's materialist conception of history and its problems, I am increasingly aware that "... the determination ... it asserts ... actually relates structure to agency in interactive 'un-determined' ways." Moreover, it also places "human agency of a powerfully creative kind" at center stage. As Neale (1985, xvii–xviii) proceeds to point out, the labor and productive activities of people, including scholars,

... always take place within definite sets of socially produced property relations. These property relations grant powers of control and decision-making and, therefore, of appropriation of the social product. Property relations, whether they be familial, communal, national, cooperative, corporatist, absolutist, communist, or private, and as they generate class relations, determine what can be produced and when, and how much, and who gets what and when, and how much. They both structure societies and create conditions for conflict within and between them over power and control and appropriation of social product. One cannot envisage a human society apart from these crucial structures and relationships.

As each cohort of people enters into the pre-existing set of propertied and class circumstances they... are also always constrained by the traditions of their dead

generations. They work out their own destinies using and developing the range of symbolic forms, including language, available to them.... The conflicts and struggles people enter into, structured by property rights and encrusted by tradition and symbolic forms, sometimes lead to social structural change, sometimes nowhere....
Consciousness and cultural production, although imbricated in the whole productive process, immersed in relations of production, are shaped by it—there are no innate ideas, no gods, except people make them, no spirits of the age, except historians conjure them up, no 'arts' apart from human definition of them; yet everywhere there is creativity, conscious human labour, trapped and liberated by relations of production.

As individuals, we come into contact with all the trappings of culture and class, first through empathy and then through deliberate indoctrination. We learn them gradually and from varied sources—family members, peers, school, church, or the media, to name only a few obvious ones. Consequently, there are subtle distinctions in how different individuals in the same class position experience, learn, incorporate, and reproduce the social relationships and cultural symbols and traditions associated with that position. Furthermore, there are often subtle differences of understanding and interpretation when, later in life, they reflect on the meaning of those earlier, formative relationships and experiences and act in light of their refracted impressions. Although we often assume that we are self-contained individuals, relatively untouched by contact with the outside world, we are, in reality, the sum of our experiences, our interpersonal relations, and our subsequent reflections on them.

This is a realist view of the linkages between the social and the individual. The generative forces and relations of society, known by inference from their effects and empirically from their diverse expressions in the everyday life of diverse communities, correspond to the theoretical conceptions many psychoanalysts have in mind "... when they postulate 'internal worlds' and states of 'internal relations' as formations shaping and constraining [the] everyday experience" of a given individual (Ruskin 1991, 126).

WHAT IS ARCHAEOLOGY?

Contemporary archaeologists describe what they do in different ways. Most claim their goal is to recover and reconstruct the development of past forms of human society and to explain the processes of their transformation up to their union with modern societies. They achieve these aims by locating, excavating, and analyzing the remains of past societies and the contexts in which they are found. Other archaeologists assert different goals: the study of the archaeological record for itself, the examination of the material remains of past societies, the formulation of general laws of human behavior, or the analysis and critique of the interpretive practices and theories they use to relate the past to the present. This diversity of aims subtly reflects the historical development of archaeology itself.

However, if we shift our lens from what archaeologists say they are doing to some of their actual practices, a slightly different image gradually comes into focus. We see the excavation of ruins and raise the following questions: Which ancient peoples dug up ruins, and why did they do so? The list of ancient societies that pursued the past in this manner is already long: various dynasties in Egypt, Andean peasants in the Ica Valley during the time of Inca rule, landlords and merchants in China at different times in the first millennium B.C., the inhabitants of Europe during the Middle Ages, or the Pilgrims on the Massachusetts coast a few days after they arrived in mid-November 1620. Although this is far from a complete listing of known instances, the examples reveal that people dug up the remains of their predecessors for a variety of reasons. The Andean peasants and Middle Kingdom and Saite Dynasty rulers in Egypt used old objects as models to be emulated as well as to establish or reaffirm their linkages with the traditional peoples of the region (Patterson 1991, 105–106; Lloyd 1983, 289). Looting tombs of their contents in China during the third century B.C. and in medieval Europe provided landlords and merchants with potentially vast hoards of wealth that could either be used or exchanged for other luxury goods (Greenhalgh 1989, 145–201; Swann 1934, 191). On November 15, 1620, the Pilgrims stole a kettle and cache of corn, which they uncovered in an abandoned house; the next day, they looted a burial, taking "the prettiest things away" with them. After that, they "... digged in sundry like places, but found no more Corne, nor anythings els but graues" (Mourt 1622, 6–7, 11). All of the examples listed above resonate with the discovery of King Tut's tomb or the salvaging of the *Atocha* or some other shipwreck graphically portrayed in the pages of *National Geographic;* these grade almost imperceptibly into the activities of today's professional archaeologists. They show decisively that the practices most commonly associated with archaeology are neither modern nor exclusively Western. The practices as well as the primitive accumulation associated with them are often coincident with the formation or disintegration of civilizations—that is, state-based societies.

If we turn our lens in still a different direction, another image comes into focus when we consider the history of the word *archaeology* itself and reflect on the significance of shifting meanings and the different contexts in which it has been deployed. In *Hippias Maior,* Plato (429–347 B.C.) wrote a dialogue that allegedly took place a century earlier between Hippias, a traveling teacher, or sophist, and the noted philosopher Socrates. In the dialogue, Hippias used the classical Greek word *archaiologia* to refer to those inquiries into the ancestral traditions and customs of peoples and city-states, stories about the origins and ancient histories of cities, genealogies of heroes and others, and lists of archons, or rulers. Thus, in the early fourth century B.C., *arche* meant both "beginning" and "power." It is the root of words such as *archaiologia* that refer to ancient or origins, and of other words, such as *monarch* (ruler) or *hierarchy* (belonging to a ranked order), that involve the idea of power. In Plato's time, the two meanings were connected. Powerful individuals and city-states and pervasive customs and practices were those with historical roots.

People used accounts of the origins of cities or customs to legitimate and explain the existing social order or the changes that occurred when the positions and power relations of different states changed. Thus, *archaiologia,* the study of beginnings and power, involved something more than the pursuit of antiquarian knowledge. The word *archaiologia* continued to be used into the first century A.D., when Flavius Josephus used the word in a book about the history of the Jewish people from their origins to the present, and Dionysius of Halicarnassus used it in the title of another book that dealt with the archaic history of Rome. Their accounts were based on oral traditions and legends as well as classical and biblical texts.

The sophist practitioners of *archaiologia* were not the only individuals in the ancient Greek world who wrote about power and the past. Herodotus's (484–420 B.C.) *History* describes wars and revolts that occurred a generation before he was born and the contemporary barbarians—that is, non-Greek-speaking foreigners—who lived in Egypt, Babylonia, and around the Black Sea. The *History of the Peloponnesian War*, written by aristocrat Thucydides, describes a series of military expeditions that occurred during his lifetime and emphasizes the roles of individuals in the events, power politics, and imperialism of the period between 431 and 404 B.C. The emphasis Herodotus and Thucydides placed on current events or those of the recent past distinguished their writings from those of the *archaiologists*, who dealt with the more distant past.

There was a resurgence of archaeological and historical scholarship on both sides of the Mediterranean during the fourteenth and fifteenth centuries. It coincided with the massive reorganization of commerce in the Mediterranean world, which was accompanied by important shifts in the distribution of wealth and political power throughout the region. These changes left the inhabitants of Mediterranean North Africa and Europe with the problem of having to explain what had happened to the traditional social order of their world (Abu-Lughod 1989; Heller 1978). In the *Muqaddimah*, Ibn Khaldun (1337–1406), the North African diplomat, historian, and social theorist, tied the social and cultural transformations of his day to changes in mercantile trade and the structures of everyday life (Rosenthal 1952).

Clerics, curial officials, judges, politicians, and merchants, schooled in humanist thought at the all-male universities and ecclesiastical academies, began to study ancient texts and monuments in Rome, Padua, Verona, and the other city-states of northern Italy from the fourteenth century onwards. They sought to provide new accounts of their place in a changing world (Rowe 1965; Weiss 1988). They borrowed heavily from earlier writers, constructing new worldviews that incorporated elements of the classical and Judeo-Christian perspectives that were already familiar or that they had discovered buried away in the copyists' archives of medieval monasteries. From their standpoint, the new social order was dynamic, constantly in flux. For the humanists, people could begin to regain the freedom lost during the Middle Ages by retrieving and developing the capacities possessed by the peoples of classical antiquity. Thus, ancient Rome became a standard of excellence and an object worthy of investigation.

Fifteenth-century European humanists identified and examined various kinds of objects or monuments that had survived from antiquity for information about the past societies of the Mediterranean world and beyond. They and their successors combined these studies with information culled from historical texts, inscriptions, coins, traditions, genealogies, and place names. This combination of sources came to constitute a well-established domain of knowledge or discipline called *antiquarianism*, which thrived from the fifteenth to the nineteenth centuries (Levine 1987). Its early development coincided with the scientific revolution.

Western science began to acquire a recognizably modern form in the male enclaves of the late medieval universities. As historian of science David Noble (1992, 151–71, 220–237) observes, Western science was steeped from its inception in the monastic culture of Western Christianity; it was essentially a religious calling, rather than a secular enterprise that was practiced in the context of universities. Latin, the language of everyday discourse in the schools, was sex-linked and used mainly by males. Consequently, science in early modern Europe was largely a "world without women," and many of its leading practitioners at the time were gay. Scientific academies, such as the Royal Society of Fellows, established in the seventeenth century were also male bastions where clerical ascetic culture slowly mutated into a kind of scientific asceticism. Many members, Isaac Newton for instance, believed that personal purification—living an austere life, avoiding women, and suppressing private thoughts because of the political inconvenience they could cause—was essential to the success of their activities.

Francis Bacon and René Descartes, both from families of elite Crown servants, challenged the dominant philosophy of nature in the early seventeenth century. Bacon, one-time clerk of the infamous Star Chamber, wanted to reform the apparatus of government to create the conditions for an imperial monarchy. His project included legal reforms that redefined and diminished the role of judges. He also proposed using natural philosophy to solve the problems confronting statesmen; science should become a royal enterprise concerned with the conquest of nature. He made two broad proposals in *Novum Organum:* The first was a set of procedures, now called scientific methods, which resembled those of a judge and jury sifting through piles of information to establish the facts of a particular case; and the second called for creation of a set of state institutions, involving large numbers of individuals, some engaged in the systematic collection of information and others who created the facts and interpreted their significance (Martin 1992). Bacon's work is a blueprint of capitalist labor processes and the organization of work, characterized by a hierarchically organized technical division of labor, that precipitated and crystallized during the seventeenth century (Dickson 1979).

In the 1630s, Descartes laid the foundations for a mechanical philosophy of nature. He made nature mathematical, arguing that matter was inert and passive. In effect, he proclaimed the "death of nature" because matter lacked active powers (Merchant 1980). Following Plato, he claimed that highest reality was intellectual form or pure ideas embodied perfectly in mathematics and imperfectly in physical objects. As a result, it was possible to describe nature as a mechanism, which perhaps resembled some gigantic clock or pendulum (Deason 1986; Kubrin 1981). Descartes also drew an absolutely unbridgeable distinction between matters of faith and matters of fact. Whereas the former were determined by revelation, the latter were the domain of observation and reason. By separating the Creator from his creation, Descartes implied that nature was a divinely ordered realm that was fixed and operated according to externally imposed natural laws, which could be discovered by properly educated authorities (Noble 1992, 218–19).

By the 1670s, the ideas of the scientific revolution were impinging on antiquarian studies in both France and England. Jacob Spon (1647–85), a physician and antiquary from Lyon, and English naturalist George Wheler traveled to Greece and Asia Minor in 1675 and 1676 to make firsthand observations and studies of their antiquities. Spon coined the Latin word *archaeologia* to describe what antiquarians did when they studied objects and monuments rather than other sources of information about the past (Daniel 1981, 14–15; Stoneman 1987, 56–83). This implied that antiquarians practiced archaeology when they studied ancient remains and antiquarianism when they directed their efforts toward legends, place names, relics, curiosities, topographies, and even natural histories.

Spon drew this distinction against the backdrop of the scientific revolution, which incorporated the influences of the commercial revolution, gave primacy to mathematics as both a basis of truth and a method of inquiry, and adopted a worldview that incorporated a mechanistic philosophy, which claims nature is composed of inert matter in motion and can be understood in terms of the mathematical relationships governing that motion. The scientific revolution also promoted ideas about the systematic destruction and conquest of nature and embraced procedures for gathering information (Shapiro 1983, 119–62). Spon was distinguishing these practices of antiquarians from those activities they pursued when they focused on the other kinds of information. He viewed archaeology as a set of procedures or practices that could be used to collect information and establish facts about the past. Conceptualizing archaeology in this fashion made it possible to focus exclusively on monuments and to study them independently from the people who made and used the objects (Levine 1977). The antiquarians who belonged to the Royal Society and wrote in its *Philosophical Collections* and *Philosophical Transactions* during the 1680s began to employ Spon's distinction (Hunter 1971, 1975). They also began to write in vernacular languages instead of Latin.

By the end of the seventeenth century, the activities and writings of antiquarians were already beginning to mirror and blur subtle differences of class, religion, and nationality. In the main, the antiquaries were educated men from the professional and administrative middle class rather than the landed gentry or the court nobility (Casson 1939, 143; Trigger 1989, 46). Although not especially wealthy as a group, they had both the leisure and the opportunity to pursue antiquarian interests. Their firsthand observations of ancient remains were the activities of technicians, the lowest-level personnel in Bacon's hierarchical organization of scientific inquiry. This practice undoubtedly made them aware and enhanced their appreciation of the significant contributions made to the development of utilitarian and scientific knowledge during the preceding century by other of Bacon's low-level technicians—notably the naturalists, artisans, printers, and miners who came from a fraction of a different class (Zilsel 1942, 1957). Inventions and observations credited to members of this group—compasses, clocks, pumps, and innovations in printing—put to rest the idea that quality of life had been better in ancient times than in the present. They also established solid foundations for accepting the idea of progress: the belief that knowledge and the control over nature were cumulative, that significant advances had occurred in recent times and were continuing to take place, and that this was a natural rather than a socially constituted process.

Those antiquarians with the inclination, opportunity, and resources to travel on the continent to study ancient monuments did so; others, whose circumstances or interests prevented them from journeying to the continent, contented themselves with monuments and ruins found in their own countries. In broad terms, the Vatican and French Catholics with close ties to the court and state were particularly interested in Roman antiquities and largely responsible for the renewed interest in classical themes in the seventeenth and eighteenth centuries; in fact, their activities were often supported and channeled by the power and authority of both the Church and state (Bondanella 1987, 90–151; Bowersock 1978). English, Dutch, and German antiquaries, overwhelmingly Protestant, were drawn increasingly to Greece by the end of the seventeenth century as merchants from those countries extracted trading privileges from the Ottoman officials who controlled the region (Tsigakou 1981, 16). In the eighteenth century, their work simultaneously resonated with classicism and the image of ancient Rome and provided underpinnings for Romanticism and renewed interest in the Hellenic world (Bernal 1987, 189–223; Piggott 1937). The Spaniards, although aware of Roman antiquities in their country and of classical authors, focused a great deal of attention on the Aztec and Inca civilizations, which had been incorporated into their overseas colonial empire (Padgen 1982).

This meant that the Spaniards, like the northern antiquaries whose countries were largely devoid of Roman monuments, used literary sources, both ancient and modern, to flesh out the details of these societies. While the Spaniards were concerned mainly with their colonial possessions in the Americas, the northern antiquaries focused their attention on the peoples who resided in their homelands at the time of the Roman Empire. As a result, the Spaniards and particularly the English began to employ the same analytical categories to describe their subjects in the Old and New Worlds; the categories derived their meaning in large part from the colonial experience in the Americas and Ireland.

They distinguished three kinds of individuals and societies during the seventeenth century: civilized, barbarian, and savage (Rowe 1964, 16–19). After 1600, the English adjective *civil,* which meant "belonging to citizens" and "orderly and educated," added new meanings. The verb "to civilize" indicated "making a criminal case a civil matter, or bringing into a particular form of social organization." This involved two contrasts, as Raymond Williams (1983, 57–60) noted: one between civil and criminal and the other between orderly and educated and their opposites—disorderly and uneducated. The nouns "civility" or "civilization" referred to a state of social order and refinement that could, by the nineteenth century, be achieved by education. The English and Spanish gentry were civilized; their commoners and the indigenous peoples of their colonies were not. By 1600, according to *The Oxford English Dictionary,* the latter were already being described as "barbarians" or "savages." Barbarians were uncultured, uncivilized, unpolished, uneducated foreigners who moved from place to place and whose language and customs differed from those of the gentry. Savages were even more remote from civilization than barbarians. They were fierce, cruel, and untamed; lived in a state of nature as part of the landscape or scenery; and existed at the lowest stage of development.

By the early 1760s, Enlightenment writers such as Adam Smith and his contemporaries were conceptualizing the development of human society as a progression through a series of stages characterized by different modes of subsistence (Meek 1976). In their view, the first societies were composed of small numbers of men and women who provisioned themselves by hunting and foraging; they lived in small communities, were satisfied with their circumstances, and had neither property nor viable forms of government. As their numbers increased, they domesticated animals and became herders; when their population grew even further, those communities occupying favorable environments turned to agriculture. These barbarians, who had communal notions of property, exhibited diverse forms of government. Barbarism was followed by a significant advance in the division of labor as some individuals found it advantageous to leave the land and settle in towns to pursue craft production and exchange goods with other members of the community and with those of different nations. Civilized societies, which represented the highest stage of human social development, had a number of characteristics that distinguished them from savagery and barbarism: cities, social classes, state institutions and practices, commerce, money, writing, continuous wars, and, most importantly, private property. In their view, the highest stage of social development resembled the kinds of societies that were emerging in the rapidly industrializing regions of Europe, whereas the earlier stages evoked images of various native peoples in the Americas, the South Sea islands, Africa, and Asia. By 1800, the northern antiquaries sometimes attributed archaeological monuments to peoples mentioned by classical writers; in other instances, however, they referred them to the generic ancient inhabitants of the country, peoples whom they believed represented precivilized stages of development.

The antiquarians and their contemporaries employed two powerful metaphors in the seventeenth and eighteenth centuries (Piggott 1976, 101–32). One was the idea of ruins—what remains after the decline and fall or decay of a society or thing. The other was the idea of a wilderness. Originally a wild, uncultivated, and uninhabited tract of land, the term had already added the meaning of a mingled or confused collection of things by 1600 (Nash 1982, 1–43). In the context of societies, whose centers of gravity were becoming increasingly urban, ruins dotted the landscape, and wildernesses were forming outside the cities as manorial estates were abandoned and old customs gave way to the new (Maravall 1986; Springer 1987). For those layers of the old gentry that lost ground and power in the palace intrigues of the royal courts of increasingly absolutist states in the West, the decay represented by the ruins in the wilderness was a time when life was more predictable, if not better. For the Vatican and the courtiers who thrived on the court intrigues of the seventeenth century, the monuments and remains scattered across the landscape were survivals—symbols of continuity that linked the past and present, that bore witness to the material progress of civilization, and that pointed toward the future, albeit one that was contested. While these and other metaphors and images were brought to North America during the seventeenth century, their meanings were soon modified by local circumstances and aspirations.

U.S. SOCIAL HISTORY AND THE ORGANIZATION OF THIS BOOK

Let me outline, schematically for now, how I have periodized the historical development of U.S. society and organized the book. I hope the reasons for this approach will become apparent and satisfactorily explained as the text unfolds.

The making and remaking of the United States began shortly after 1500. It involved isolated Spanish entradas from Mexico and the Caribbean colonies into the Southeast and Southwest; the seasonal fishing stations of Basque, Portuguese, and French fishermen scattered along the coast from Cape Cod to Nova Scotia and Newfoundland; sporadic slave raids; the penetration of merchant capital up inland waterways such as the Hudson River Valley and the construction of trading posts;

and numerous unsuccessful attempts to establish settler colonies from North Carolina to Nova Scotia before 1607. Waves of European settler-colonists, almost exclusively from the middle and lower classes, successfully established remote colonies in the seventeenth century. By the 1660s, an agrarian-commercial economy—dominated by merchants, large landholders, and speculators—was firmly entrenched along the littoral, with the new or emerging urban commercial centers at Boston, New York, Philadelphia, Charleston, and French New Orleans serving as the hubs of regional trade networks. The colonies, however, remained relatively isolated, separated from each other by stretches of sparsely inhabited land, distinctive class structures, and cultural differences. Because the colonies were tied to England and not to each other, there was little common political life before the 1760s (Greene 1988, 176–98; Nash 1986, 3–34).

The adoption of the U.S. Constitution in 1789 signaled the formation of a strong central government designed to protect the economic interests of wealthy merchants, landholders, and speculators and to discipline discontented farmers, slaves, Indians, artisans, unskilled urban workers, and women. In the 1790s, most of the country's four million residents—a figure that included seven hundred thousand slaves but no Indians—lived on the Atlantic seaboard and gained their livelihood by working the land. The English flooded the national market, which crystallized in the wake of the constitutional convention, with cheap goods; this stimulated cotton production and made slavery profitable in the South. It also inhibited industrial expansion, even though legal restrictions on manufacturing had been lifted several decades earlier in the wake of the revolution. Industrial production grew rapidly during and after the War of 1812, especially in New England and the Middle Atlantic states; it also coincided with the rise of U.S. imperialism accompanied by westward expansion and the removal of Indian peoples from their traditional homelands. These processes promoted new forms of sectionalism and the development of new regional cultures and class structures. Oversimplified, these included Baptist and Presbyterian small farmers in the West and South, who opposed Anglican slaveowners; the domination of petty commodity producers in New England by Congregationalist and Unitarian merchants and speculators; and the arrival of Irish Catholics in the burgeoning cities of the eastern seaboard and German immigrants in the Ohio River Valley in the 1830s and 1840s (Anbinder 1992; Franklin 1943; Cross 1950; Pessen 1985; Sellers 1991).

The Compromise of 1877, which signaled the collapse of Reconstruction, marked a major episode of class and state formation in the United States (Du Bois 1935). It involved the dominance of East Coast corporate and finance capitalism over the national capitalism of other regions (Kolko 1963; Sanders 1987); the reconfiguration of sectional political interests and struggles as well as regional cultures, especially in the South and West (Bensel 1984; Hahn 1983; McNall 1988); and the emergence of a regulatory state with an increasingly professionalized civil service (Higgs 1987; Skowronek 1982). The rise of capital- and labor-intensive industrial production—centered initially in the Northeast, Middle Atlantic, and Great Lakes states—brought renewed concerns over non-English-speaking immigrant workers in the cities and underpinned new forms of racism, nativism, and xenophobia (Higham 1981). The expansion of U.S. industrial production from the late nineteenth century onwards has coincided with continued U.S. imperialism in Latin America and the Pacific—for example, the Spanish American War of 1898, the annexation of Puerto Rico and the Philippines, and the opening of the Panama Canal (Williams 1961, 1972). In the wake of World War II, the United States emerged and reigned briefly as the world's dominant political-economic power. The sustained economic growth of the postwar era broke down around 1970, and attempts to resuscitate it have been largely unsuccessful, although the burden of its demise has been shifted to the Third World (Harvey 1982, 373–445; Wolfe 1981).

The 1870s also witnessed the rise to prominence of a new, secularized historical consciousness, which took seriously the ideas "... that society must be understood as a product of continuous historical change,... [that] earthly causes were sufficient to explain its motion, and those causes were seen to operate in a succession of qualitatively different historical contexts" (Ross 1984, 909–10). This signaled the decline, but not the demise, of two earlier forms of historical consciousness. One saw change as the inevitable consequence of immutable laws associated with transcendental divine power and understood the development of U.S. society in terms of Judeo-Christian history. The other saw historical change as the destruction or decay of those agrarian conditions, that underwrote the virtues of the republican ideal, in the face of liberal progress; it linked those conditions and virtues with the past and understood that their recovery meant resurrecting and refurbishing institutions and practices marginalized by progress (Ross 1984).

This periodicity does not turn on events commonly used in introductory U.S. history texts. Although the American Revolution or the Civil War, for example, were episodes of change, both the form and long-term meaning of the changes they signaled were contested and not immediately apparent. Superficially, the periodicity I employ appears to turn on events defined largely in political terms—the adoption of the U.S. Constitution, the end of Reconstruction, or World War II. At one level, this is true. At another level, however, the events were forged in complex ways by the precipitation and crystallization of underlying economic processes and relations. At still another level, the activities set in motion by these events were part of everyday life. Consequently, the struggles they provoked were waged partly but not exclusively in cultural arenas. Archaeology, because it is a relatively expensive activity, continues to be sensitive to the interests of institutions—the state, public and private museums, philanthropic organizations—and individuals that provide financial support. These sources typically have educational, cultural, or scientific aims in mind and rarely, if ever, define their goals directly in political or economic terms. However, the different levels of a society are not autonomous; they are linked by complex, continually shifting and changing relations, so that a development in one can have profound consequences in the others. This also means that the systemic character of U.S. civilization is historically contingent; that is, certain changes or developments were confined to particular periods and could not have occurred earlier or later.

Chapter 2 deals with archaeology in the United States before 1877. Preprofessional archaeologists such as Thomas Jefferson used Enlightenment categories and viewed history as a storehouse of lessons. The archaeology of classical Rome and Greece provided symbols of civilization for the emerging nation-state. Biblical archaeology examined the roots of Christianity, the civilizing process. American Indian archaeology contrasted civilized and noncivilized societies in a context shaped by Locke's notions of worked land as property, of westward expansion, and of the displacement of the native communities. Local and national organizations—such as the American Philosophical Society, the American Antiquarian Society, the American Oriental Society, and the Smithsonian Institution—appeared and published the results of archaeological inquiries. By the 1840s, the distinction between civilized and non-civilized societies was often conflated with the idea of a hierarchy of races, which drew inspiration from the ideologies of Manifest Destiny and scientific racism. Archaeological data were frequently used to provide evidence of a society's or race's position in the various racial hierarchies that had been proposed and to sustain claims of innate superiority or inferiority.

Chapter 3 examines the professionalization of archaeology between 1877 and 1932. The discipline was professionalized, along with other social sciences, in the wake of the Civil War, Reconstruction, and the reorganization of capitalist production relations. During the 1870s and 1880s, the so-called Gilded Age of U.S. history, the ruling class attempted to construct and impose a genteel cultural tradition based on European standards and a greater appreciation of the European past. The custodians and entrepreneurs of culture scheduled regular world's fairs and expositions. Philanthropists established and financed museums in various cities, many of which supported archaeological research. The period witnessed a long recession; continued U.S. imperialism; the passage of the Dawes Act (1887), which linked citizenship with land and property issues on Indian reservations; and the crystallization of distinctive regional cultures. Racism, nativism, and Social Darwinism were dominant ideologies during the formative years of the profession, when most professional archaeologists were trained either in Germany or with German immigrant scholars. The discipline became more differentiated as the interconnections of traditional practices weakened and new linkages and identities, such as Egyptology, were forged.

The remaining chapters in the book are in a triple sense more internalist than the earlier ones. They devote more space, examine in more detail, and critically assess particular developments in the emerging discipline and profession as they juxtapose and link them with the underlying processes and relations structuring the wider society.

Chapter 4 examines the development of archaeology from the relief programs of the New Deal during the Depression years through the era of sustained, corporatist economic growth that lasted into the late 1960s. Like other social scientists, professional archaeologists worked in various capacities for the U.S. government during and after World War I. Professional archaeology expanded significantly during the interwar years. The federal government employed archaeologists to supervise Tennessee Valley Authority (TVA) and Civilian Conservation Corps (CCC) projects in the 1930s. The University of Chicago's Oriental Institute and Johns Hopkins University sponsored research in Egypt and the Near East; oil and mining interests and ultimately the Good Neighbor Policy underwrote research by U.S. professionals in Latin America. In Guatemala and the Yucatán Peninsula their work was sustained mainly by the Carnegie Institution of Washington and the United Fruit Company. Professional archaeologists again worked in various capacities for the government during World War II.

The idea that human society had developed progressively through a lineal succession of economic or political stages from primitive origins to the modern nation-state became the dominant interpretive perspective for all but classical and biblical archaeology by the early 1950s. The profession's centers of gravity shifted to the universities after World War II, and its social composition was subtly transformed by the GI Bill and other state subsidies to higher education. The profession grew unevenly from the late 1950s onward as new graduate training programs appeared, mainly in the West, and as the established ones at certain Eastern universities continued to influence investigations in particular geographical areas. As a result, regional "styles" of research became more firmly entrenched. Parts of the profession received increasing levels of federal support through the late 1960s from various federal agencies—notably, the River Basin Survey in the Midwest and the National Science Foundation.

Chapter 5 is concerned with the privatization of archaeology. Federal legislation—The Historic Sites Preservation Act (1966), the National Environmental Policy Act (1969), and the Archaeological and Historical Conservation Act (1974)—combined with declining state subsidies to higher education, provided public- and private-sector employment for archaeologists and shifted the center of gravity of archaeological research in the United States into the private sector. This legislation also promoted further diversification and the consolidation of the profession into a more complex mosaic of various historic, prehistoric, and regional specialities, which facilitated land and real estate development during the 1970s and 1980s. The increasingly fragmented discipline underwrote various pieces of legislation phrased in the logical positivist idiom and tropes of the "New Archaeology," which emphasized scientific methodology, hypothesis testing, and value neutrality. The results of research in the United States were appropriated and recast to sustain heritages that portrayed everyday life at particular times and places and provided backgrounds for development projects and commemorations—the restorations in Williamsburg and Santa Fe, the battlefields at Gettysburg and the Little Big Horn, and Philadelphia's Society Hill and its Bicentennial celebrations.

Chapter 6 examines the interplay between archaeology and multiculturalism. Third World states that gained political independence in the wake of decolonization and social movements with diverse concerns developing since the 1970s have presented U.S. archaeologists with a range of issues: demands for the repatriation of objects and skeletal remains and challenges to dominant views from feminist, Afrocentric, neonationalist, and neopopulist groups seeking to have their own understandings of history and heritage taken seriously. This is the complicated terrain of multiculturalism, which demands a close examination of the multivocality produced by differences in power relations and the intersections of class, region, race, and gender. These viewpoints actuate a variety of essentialist, racialist, Social Darwinist, rationalist, and relativist perspectives that often recuperate and refract arguments heard during earlier episodes of class formation and cultural conflict, such as the 1880s and 1890s. Proponents of these perspectives have recast their views in terms of Enlightenment categories, metaphors, and images; they have rooted their explanations of contemporary social relations in human nature and history. Archaeologists have contributed to and are beginning to confront the powerful, often contradictory, images emanating from voices that were muted in the past and that express diverse perceptions and sensibilities.

In sum, this book is concerned with the historical development of different kinds of archaeology in the United States. It will examine the circumstances that facilitated their formation, the shifting social and political conditions in which archaeological knowledge is produced and deployed, the appearance of practices that have centers of gravity in particular regions or groups in the wider society, the relationships of archaeological discourses to structures of power, and the ideological role the profession has played in creating and perpetuating heritages and graphic images of past and contemporary peoples.

Because U.S. archaeology is now a set of diverse, loosely related practices and discourses, my aim is to explore how U.S. archaeologists have viewed the past as a contested terrain and how they have organized various understandings of it in terms of categories and images that have added and lost meaning since the Enlightenment. In their debates, they have used the past to put forth alternative explanations of current institutions and practices, which provide different understandings of the present and of what might be possible in the future. Their explanations offer competing loci for the crystallization and development of national consciousness in a country whose citizens and residents, as well as the state itself, are preoccupied with their heritage, destiny, and allegedly exceptional or exemplary role in human history.

By shedding light on (1) the ideas, metaphors, and images evoked by archaeologists in their accounts of what happened in the past and their explanations of how human society came to be the way it is and (2) the implications they have for both understanding and social action, I hope to illuminate why the historical development of archaeology in the United States must be understood in terms of the shifting contexts in which it occurred.

CHAPTER 2

Archaeology in the United States
before 1877

The inhabitants of the anglophone colonies established along the Atlantic seaboard had little sense of a shared American identity before the mid-eighteenth century. This identity was forged in circumstances shaped by the increasing repression, violence, and political debate that preceded and provoked the American Revolution in the 1770s. To reveal that identity at different moments and how it formed, it is necessary both to peel away later additions and to identify what has been erased. Thus, this chapter begins with a discussion of various class fractions, which had different concerns and therefore appropriated or incorporated the past in different ways. While examining how this identity was constructed and subsequently contested, it is useful to keep four observations in mind.

First, the original colonies were settled by diverse groups for diverse reasons. Inmates released from debtors' prisons were sent to Georgia to serve as a frontier garrison that would confine Spanish interests to Florida. Anglican speculators, who believed civil society was established by human action instead of divine will, went to Virginia and the Chesapeake, where they grew tobacco for export. By the 1670s, they were shipping fifteen million pounds of tobacco each year to England and the Continent. Their plantations were worked by indentured servants at first and increasingly by slaves as the seventeenth century came to a close. Calvinist Puritans, who believed the existing social order was predetermined by God, flocked to Massachusetts and then Connecticut, its offshoot, where they established a rigid, hierarchically ordered society of families in small farming communities (Nash 1986, 3–34).

Second, the doctrinal disputes and political struggles waged in Europe during the seventeenth century also occurred in the American colonies: Putting witches to death in Salem or Languedoc was not unrelated to the idolatry trials in Peru or the execution of disobedient children in Geneva. Religious orthodoxy, rationalism, and pietism repeatedly spilled over into the political arena, where wars were fought, leaders assassinated, and losers imprisoned or worse. The fortunate ones fled to avoid persecution; for the Pilgrims and Puritans, this meant a self-imposed "errand in the wilderness": migration from the Old World to a new Canaan, a metaphorical pilgrimage into the desert wilderness to rebuild the kingdom of God (Bercovitch 1993, 32–34). For others, it meant bitter armed conflict. The Seven Years' War, waged on the American frontier by England and France from 1754 to 1763, has come to be known in the United States as the French and Indian War (Jennings 1988; Nash 1979).

Third, by rule of law, the colonies were forced to maintain closer political relations with England than with each other until the 1750s and 1760s, when the metropolis uniformly imposed the same tariffs and taxes on each of its possessions. Although these acts promoted greed and ambition among some, they fomented resistance and debate among others who gradually came to recognize that they occupied similar positions in a system of colonial exploitation and repression they found oppressive. Local newspapers—such as the *American Magazine* printed in Philadelphia—rapidly found audiences in the other colonies and increasingly identified the English as foreigners. For their part, the English acknowledged the distinctive features of American English and recognized them as part of an emerging and uniquely colonial culture (Aptheker 1966, 140–41; Curti 1964, 74).

Fourth, the colonies were class-stratified societies that exhibited significant political-economic and cultural differences. The tensions that already existed or developed between classes and regions before and immediately after the American Revolution were subsequently written into the Constitution. Furthermore, there was little sense that a new nation—the United States—had actually been forged before the Constitution was ratified in 1789 and the original thirteen colonies had ceded significant powers to the newly constituted, strong central government. This signaled a victory for the ruling classes—the merchants and the slave owners. Property qualifications for voting were advantageous to the ruling class of every state. The federal character of the new government and the provision to count three-fifths of slaves in determining congressional districts reflected compromises between different regional ruling classes. The system of checks and balances was a compromise between the ruling class and landholding small producers (Aptheker 1976; Wiebe 1985).

During the 1790s, this was particularly beneficial to the Federalists—a fraction of the ruling class composed of the Northern merchants and Southern slave owners who trafficked with England—and their allies, the Congregationalist small producers in the increasingly depressed areas of western New England who profited from English imports (Fisher 1975; Kerber 1970). The War of 1812, which pitted England against the United States, marked the demise of the Federalists. It also strengthened patriotic and nationalist sentiments and marked the consolidation of power by the commercial farmers and merchants who did not gain their livelihood through trade with England. These were the Jeffersonian Republicans, who stressed the importance of continued access to land and agricultural production and encouraged the development of transportation systems and new commercial and financial institutions (Banning 1980).

By 1800, small farmers and producers, mainly from the South and the Middle Atlantic states and to a lesser extent from New England, were pouring in large numbers into the newly opened territories west of the Alleghenies—Tennessee, Kentucky, and the Ohio and Mississippi River valleys (Cayton 1986). They saw virgin land in the interior of the continent and imagined transforming it into the "Garden of the World" (Smith 1950, 138). Westward expansion marked the increased economic importance of commercial agriculture. By the 1830s, western New York and the Ohio Valley were the nation's breadbaskets, and cotton production for export had risen exponentially in the South. At the same time, the small farmers of western New England were plunged into an economic depression and driven into the woolen mills and foundries built next to waterfalls. The factories and, particularly, steam engines were increasingly seen as signs of progress—greater control over nature as well as greater productivity. Machines—steamboats, railroads, and telegraphs—began to appear in the Garden of the World in the 1830s (Marx 1959).

The United States was a civilization in flux, and its class structure became even more complicated after 1800, as new regional hierarchies crystallized in the wake of westward expansion and the old established ones on the Atlantic seaboard were reconstituted to take account of the new realities. They acknowledged the rise to prominence of speculators who invested capital in industry and mining and the arrival of new immigrants from Europe, many of whom were Catholic or did not speak English. The country's political center of gravity also shifted to the South and West, which sowed the seeds for the rise of a new coalition or historic bloc in the late 1820s, the Jacksonian Democrats. Andrew Jackson, war hero and Indian fighter, appealed to commercial farmers in the new states when he advocated the removal of all native peoples east of the Mississippi from their traditional homelands. He appealed to the emerging industrialists of New England and the mid-Atlantic region when he stressed the need for tariffs to protect domestic manufactures. He appealed to the recently enfranchised white male workers, artisans, and small farmers when he spoke of the importance of democratically elected officials (Pessen 1985; Sellers 1991).

These changes are chronicled by the shifting identities and fragmenting images of national heroes. Women, Blacks, and Indians played major roles in molding national myths, even though they had been denied citizenship: women because they were legally dependent, Blacks because many were property, and Indians because their existence and ways of life challenged not only progress but the very concept of property itself. For example, Daniel Boone, the Kentucky frontiersman and farmer of the late eighteenth century, was a hero. He was joined by Yankee craftsmen and sailors and Ohio Valley farmers and riverboat pilots in the 1820s. A decade or so later, new heroes captured the imagination and were added to the pantheon; two were Davy Crockett and Kit Carson, mountain men who fought both Indians and Mexicans and both of whom are closely linked with the Mexican War and the rise of Manifest Destiny in the 1840s and 1850s (Slotkin 1973, 1985).

Manifest Destiny was a political ideology that explained the westward expansion of the United States as the realization of a divine mission by a racially superior chosen people—Anglo-Saxon white Christians (Horsman 1981; Perkins 1933; Weinberg 1935). It coincided with the rise of scientific racism in the United States (Gould 1981, 30–72; Stanton 1960). It was accompanied by strikes in the factories and rebellions on the slave plantations, by efforts to reduce the political influence of immigrants and Catholics, and by attacks on immigrants and people of color in Philadelphia and other eastern cities (Anbinder 1992). Contemporary books—*Uncle Tom's Cabin* and *Moby Dick,* for instance—advocated the abolition of slavery and criticized the brutality of capitalist social relations. Others—such as Francis Parkman's *The Oregon Trail* or biographies of Kit Carson—portrayed the barbarism and hardships of life on the frontier. This genre culminated in the descriptions of Custer's last stand at the Little Big Horn in 1876, which stirred anti-Indian sentiments.

Mexico was the major victim of U.S. expansionist policies between 1848 and 1853. In the early 1840s, the independent republic of Texas maintained a running war with

Mexico as it tried to block Mexican ports on the Gulf of Mexico and to annex Santa Fé. The Texans claimed all of the land westward from the Gulf to the Pacific Ocean and the Columbia River (van Alstyne 1960, 104–5). The United States annexed Texas in July 1845 and declared war on Mexico six months later. When the hostilities ended in 1848, the United States annexed New Mexico, Arizona, Utah, Nevada, and Alta California as part of the war settlement; however, President Polk and Secretary of State James Buchanan, wanted to take Baja California, Sonora, Chihuahua, and Nuevo Leon as well (Zoraida Vásquez and Meyer 1985, 38–50). The treaty ending the war did not resolve the complaints and grievances. Nor did it end difficulties along the frontier: filibusters (raids) by U.S. soldiers of fortune, cattle rustling by settlers, and the "problem of the savage Indians" who subtly merged with Mexicans in the borderlands (Pike 1992, 43–85, 93–104).

The discovery of gold in California a year later put Central America in the sphere of U.S. interests. The goal of the United States was to neutralize the Central American republics as well as British influence in them and to secure a route across the isthmus. The U.S. government invoked the Monroe Doctrine and the ideology of Manifest Destiny to assert a more active voice in the internal affairs of the area (Merk 1950, 1966; van Alstyne 1944, 139–54).

THE IMPLICATIONS OF CLASS AND REGIONAL CULTURES FOR THE PRACTICE OF ARCHAEOLOGY

Each social class and class fraction has the capacity to produce its own intellectuals who give voice to the sentiments and sensibilities of its members (Boggs 1992; Feierman 1990). Traditional intellectuals express the views of classes that already exist. Traditional intellectuals dependent on ruling groups often proclaim their independence from these interests and the universality of their views. In subordinated classes, traditional intellectuals struggle to create critical dissenting forms of discourse that simultaneously recognize the historical contingency of position and claims and challenge hegemonic views.

Organic intellectuals appear during episodes of class formation and articulate the worldview of an emerging class. They attempt to ensure its acceptance in cultural, educational, regional, and religious terms—the arenas where class struggle is waged and won or lost (Gramsci 1971). Organic intellectuals provide the cement that consolidates disparate classes and class strata into new, historically constituted power blocs. In this respect, they are different from technicians and specialists, who possess highly developed skills in limited spheres of activity, who staff universities and bureaucracies, and who serve as intermediaries between the subordinated allied strata and the dominant fractions of historic blocs.

The first individuals who made observations that our contemporaries view as "real archaeology" were not archaeologists. For example, Thomas Jefferson ([1785] 1955, 97–100), who conducted the world's first stratigraphic excavation in an Indian mound in Virginia, has become part of the historical lore of the profession. He is immortalized in the introductory chapters of archaeology texts because of the procedure he used to recover objects and information. However, Jefferson and others like him were intellectuals, not technicians. The technicians came later, after the field was professionalized, after anonymous antiquities markets emerged, and after the demand for certain kinds of information about the past was already established and routinized. Jefferson and other intellectuals used information about the past that was filtered through three lenses and shaped by their intersection: Enlightenment social theorists, classical writers, and religious sectarians, who impinged differentially on intellectuals in different classes and regions of the country.

U.S. intellectuals owed an enormous debt to the Enlightenment thinkers of Europe (Goldmann 1968; Nye 1960, 1974; Parrington 1928–1930, vols. 1, 2). Like their contemporaries, American Enlightenment writers viewed history as philosophy—a storehouse of precedents, moral lessons, and antecedent practices and institutions—rather than an attempt to reconstruct the past as it actually was in order to satisfy some curiosity. This led them to study the peoples of classical antiquity, the Orient, the Americas, and even the South Sea islands. "All the particular histories were like tributaries, each one carrying its own sediments of truth, pouring it into the great mainstream of history where historians could always dredge it up.... Its chief use ... [was] to discover the constant and universal principles of human nature" (Commager 1975, 127).

The Americans drew heavily on analytical categories—savagery, barbarism, civilization, progress, and property—that were reworked and given new meanings by Adam Smith and the other Scottish moral philosophers (Meek 1976). They were especially indebted to William Robertson (1778), who deployed these categories in *The History of America,* first published in 1777. This book was the most widely read and influential discussion of Native-American society and history in the early Republic (Gerbi 1973, 157–69; Hoebel 1960; Humphreys 1954; Keen 1971, 275–85; Pearce 1965, 82–91). It was a point of departure for most of the discussions that followed as the United States gradually took form during the nineteenth century.

Robertson argued that once individuals united together, human society developed through successive stages reflecting changes in their mode of subsistence. Savage peoples hunted and fished; they lived in small communities and were characterized by a sense of independence, attachment to community, and satisfaction with their own condition and circumstances. They had little idea of property and possessed no viable form of government, because their sense of subordination was imperfect. They also displayed no evidence of speculative reasoning or the use of abstract ideas (Robertson 1778, vol. 1, 308–14, 324–40, 410–11). Only the barbarian Aztecs and Incas of Mexico and Peru had progressed toward civilization; however, in spite of the fact that they were great empires, neither were as civilized as the peoples of the Old World. Although they farmed, the fact that they acquired domesticated animals and the use of metals quite late retarded their progress toward civilization (Robertson 1778, vol. 2, 268–69, 298–99). Civilized peoples had a number of distinctive features: cities, social classes, state institutions and practices, commerce, writing, and continuous wars. However, the most important feature separating civilized from lower societies was the right to private property (Robertson 1778, vol. 2, 273–98, 323).

Classical authors were also widely read in the United States, both on the Atlantic seaboard and in the territories that were opening in the West (Agard 1957; Reinhold 1984, 128–33; Schmidt 1936). Both agrarian and merchant capitalists, with Jefferson and John Adams as their respective representatives, incorporated classical authors into the political and social debates of the day. They made more frequent references to Roman writers through the War of 1812, because they were more familiar with them and because "... they considered the example of Rome more rewarding for contemplation ... [since] Rome, the ancient Italian republic which sprang from humble beginnings to become the mistress of the world, was a more glorious model" (Miles 1974, 263). They referred to the United States as the "New Rome" or the "Rome of the West." However, they were also familiar with Greek writers. But Federalists such as Adams or Alexander Hamilton were repelled by their descriptions of political process, which filled them with horror. They were "pained and disgusted" with the factions and confusion they saw leading to the destruction of Greek liberty.

Classical antiquity was a source of symbols and lessons that could be appropriated and adapted to the conditions that were emerging in the United States. Studying classical writers showed that (1) human problems were universal; (2) the collapse of states was not a unique occurrence but rather was something that could be repeated if the conditions leading to their destruction were not eliminated; (3) the corruption of the late Roman Republic demonstrated the need for political and economic safeguards; (4) political systems and states were not permanent; and (5) the downfall of states was caused mainly by wars, which should be limited to only the most important occasions (Burns 1954, 144).

The development of classical studies in the early 1800s occurred when the relationships between church and state had been restructured and American Protestantism was being reorganized. In this context, the study of Greek, the language of the New Testament, gained new meaning and significance. At the same time, study of classics was opposed by advocates of Enlightenment deism and utilitarian education and by the Jacksonians who viewed classics as elitist.

Students of classical writers and participants in the religious debates that flourished after the Revolution were concerned with the issue of civic virtue (Appleby 1992). Both were attempting to come to terms with the individualism characteristic of an emerging capitalist society, an individualism that threatened to destroy the very foundations of the traditional civilized order. The sources of this individualism were varied. The quest for luxury and wealth, the separation of individuals from their parishes, immigration to places that were churchless, infidelity, the threat posed to orthodox sects when rationalist and deist thought were joined to the struggle for political independence and human progress, and the clarification of each denomination's relation with England in the wake of the Revolutionary War combined to challenge the traditional order of society (Bercovitch 1993; Slotkin 1973).

By 1800, the Congregationalist (Calvinist) Puritans, who were dominant in New England, had lost ground to their more liberal kin, the Unitarian-Universalists, and to Baptist and Methodist evangelical preachers who gained converts at revival meetings. Itinerant evangelists attracted large crowds in the frontier areas of the West and in the back country of the South, where there were few ministers and parishes. They chose and discarded theological doctrines to suit their needs (Nye 1960, 217). These circumstances, together with federal legislation that severed the traditional linkages between church and state, threatened doctrinal orthodoxy and created conditions for the proliferation of Protestant sects. They also challenged the cultural leadership and control exercised by the conservative Congregationalists since the 1740s. As a result, the religious denominations and movements that appeared in the early nineteenth century resonated with expansion into frontier areas and the class structures that arose in those borderlands.

The impact was also strongly felt in Massachusetts and Connecticut, where the motive force of the Puritans in the seventeenth century had been to found a society guided by biblical principles. They had journeyed into the wilderness of Babylon and endured hardships in desert wastes surrounded by savage heathens, who were the very personification of Satan himself, in order to establish that society. Their Congregationalist and the Unitarian-Universalist descendants were New England townspeople whose incomes came from land, commerce, and service. For the most part, they were Federalists who subsequently became Whigs. They disagreed over the issues of "... revelation, the authority of the Scriptures, and the proper method of Biblical interpretation" (Nye 1960, 222). The Congregationalists were biblical literalists who believed in the authority of the text. The Unitarians not only denied the doctrines of the Trinity, original sin, and eternal damnation but also argued that the Bible was a human document that had to be interpreted rationally for its truth to be revealed. This meant that they had different views about the role of the clergy, the individual parishioner, and the Bible and their interrelations.

While the established elite argued that it was necessary to reaffirm the old ways and to maintain the traditional social order, others confronted and challenged them with increasing regularity. The dispute between the Congregationalists and the Unitarian-Universalists came to a head in 1805, when liberals were appointed to both the Hollis Chair of Divinity and the presidency of Harvard University. In 1808, a group of conservative ministers withdrew from Harvard and founded the Andover Theological Seminary. For the next thirty years, the two factions struggled over control of the Harvard Divinity School and the Congregational Church in New England (Brown 1969; Nye 1960, 223–34).

As a consequence of theological debates, which were later portrayed as having a major shaping effect on everyday life in early nineteenth-century America, the best known discussions of the relationship of classics and the Bible were those of the merchant capitalists in Boston and Salem. They viewed civilization as an achieved condition of social life, a state of refinement, social order, and modernity that contrasted with barbarism. From their view, one important characteristic of civilized people was that they engaged in commerce. They saw civilization as desirable, a form of excellence that should be emulated. Christianity was the vehicle for becoming civilized. Its adoption by heathens, pagans, savages, and barbarians set in motion the civilizing process that led inexorably to new levels of refinement, social order, modernity, and trade. The view that civilization is both a refined state of being and a process of refinement furnished one important connection between the study of classics and the Bible in the United States during the nineteenth century.

This brings us back to the question posed in the opening chapter: How did the regional cultures affect the practice of archaeology in the United States in the eighteenth and nineteenth centuries? Five observations are germane.

First, the hegemony of Puritan thought in Massachusetts and Connecticut during the seventeenth and eighteenth centuries did not create conditions that were particularly conducive to studying American Indian societies or the archaeological remains left by their predecessors. In fact, the Puritans viewed the Indians as cannibals or heathen savages, subhuman wild beings whose cultures had been shaped in the wilderness; their behavior was an ever-present reminder of what the Englishwould become if they fell from grace or left the community (Bercovitch 1975, 1978; Sheehan 1980). As James Bowdoin (1785, 4, 7), the first president of the American Academy of Arts and Sciences in Boston, remarked in his inaugural address in 1780, "A knowledge in the antiquities of a country implies a knowledge of its antient [sic] history.... [Since the Indians are uncivilized] it would be in vain to search among them for antiquities." Bowdoin's sentiments and those of his Puritan neighbors resonated with the arguments of several influential European writers—notably the Comte de Buffon and Cornelius de Pauw—who claimed that natural environments in the Americas were immature, a source of degeneration, or both (Gerbi 1973).

Second, the Puritans and their descendants, who understood their cultural and historical connections with England, assumed a mythic identity with the peoples of the Old and New Testaments who had resided around the eastern end of the Mediterranean in classical antiquity and before. In light of this construction, they found meaningful portions of their heritage in the Holy Land rather than among the indigenous peoples of the New World, who were part of history only to the extent that they could be shown to be descendants of peoples mentioned in the Old Testament.

Third, learned societies concerned with scientific, technological, antiquarian, linguistic, and ethnological inquiry were both numerous and early. They were organized first in the more heterogeneous and cosmopolitan Middle Atlantic region and then a few years later in New England and in the South and West: Charleston, Cincinnati, or St. Louis (Greene 1984; Oleson and Brown 1976; Whitehill 1967). Their journals and meetings familiarized amateur scientists with the knowledge, inquiries, and discoveries of artisans and natural historians who often had different class backgrounds from their own. The American Philosophical Society, founded in Philadelphia in 1743, encouraged and published inquiries of Indian mounds, comparative studies of Native-American languages, and ethnographic accounts from the early 1780s onwards. It was followed by the *Missouri Gazette*, which published Henry Breckenridge's description of the Cahokia mounds near St. Louis in 1811. A year later, the American Antiquarian Society was established in Massachusetts to investigate and collect American antiquities; its first transaction, which appeared in 1820, was Caleb Atwater's *Description of the Antiquities Discovered in the State of Ohio and Other Western States* (Greene 1984, 350–75).

Fourth, under these circumstances, it is not surprising that the earliest ethnographic and archaeological investigations concerned specifically with the American Indians were conducted by non-Puritans, by pietist Moravian or Baptist missionaries, and by individuals who resided outside the Puritan areas of New England. Consequently, as far as the development of Americanist archaeology in the United States was concerned, Massachusetts and Connecticut constituted a cultural and scientific backwater from the seventeenth century until the years immediately following the War of 1812. However, with regards to the development of classical and biblical archaeology, New Englanders may have played a somewhat different role, especially around the beginning of the nineteenth century.

Fifth, as historian of science Robert V. Bruce (1987, 1–29, 65) has shown, the cultivators and practitioners of science in the United States collectively suffered from an inferiority complex until the 1830s and 1840s. They viewed their inquiries as less sophisticated than those conducted in Europe; they also chafed at the degree to which they were forced to rely on data produced by scientists on the Continent and brought to the United States by pilgrims. This was transformed in the 1840s. The war with Mexico added more than a million square miles to the national territory of the United States and simultaneously provided geologists and naturalists with a vast new domain to explore. The federal government sponsored a series of scientific expeditions—such as the U.S. Navy's South Seas Exploring Expedition led by Captain Charles Wilkes; these provided data and collections for U.S. scientists and museums (Goetzmann 1959, 1966; Stanton 1975, 1991). Some of these were deposited at the newly founded Smithsonian Institution in Washington (Hinsley 1981, 17–20). From 1847 onwards, Joseph Henry, the Smithsonian's first secretary, regularly published translations of papers written by European archaeologists with the aim of improving the quality of archaeological research carried out in the United States (Boehmer 1880). This practice introduced American scholars to investigations of Danish shellmounds, Swiss lake dwellings, and Paleolithic cultures in Europe; it also had immediate effects on the quality of excavations in the United States—for example, William Dall's 1877 observations about stratigraphy in an Alaskan shellmound.

THE BEGINNINGS OF U.S. ARCHAEOLOGY IN THE EASTERN MEDITERRANEAN

One of the founders of U.S. archaeology in the eastern Mediterranean was Edward Everett, a Unitarian minister who was appointed Eliot Professor of Greek Literature at Harvard in 1815. In order to prepare himself for the duties of the position, he studied classics and philology in Germany from 1815 to 1819 (Diehl 1978). Everett and George Tichnor, who later became Smith Professor of Romance Languages and Literature at Harvard and founded the Boston Public Library, traveled together on the continent, visiting collections, collectors, and the heads of states as representatives of the U.S. government. They have been described as the first actual students of classical archaeology in the United States (Dinsmoor 1943, 72–73; Larrabee 1957, 40, 69). After assuming his professorship at Harvard, Everett subsequently became editor of the influential *North American Review,* congressman, governor of Massachusetts, ambassador to England from 1840 to 1845, U.S. senator, and Lincoln's secretary of state (Reinhold 1984, 204–13).

Another was Edward Robinson, who organized biblical archaeology as a field of inquiry. Robinson, a conservative Congregationalist, studied at Hamilton College and married a woman of the New England Kirkland family whose members were merchants, land speculators, clergy, lawyers, and educators during the early years of the Republic. His father-in-law was the president and founder of Hamilton College, and his brother-in-law, John Thornton Kirkland, eventually became president of Harvard University, when Everett and Tichnor were members of the faculty. In 1821, after his wife died, Robinson moved to Andover to oversee the publication of his edition of a Greek text of the *Iliad*. Shortly afterwards, he entered the seminary and became interested in biblical interpretation. From 1826 to 1830, he continued his studies in Germany where, like Everett and Tichnor a few years before, he went to Göttingen; however, he worked mostly with individual scholars at the universities in Halle and Berlin, where he studied the methods of German biblical criticism, Hebrew grammar, church history, and geography. When he returned to Andover, he established *The Biblical Repository,* a journal that was to become a clearinghouse for recent, important biblical scholarship in Germany and the United States. In 1837, he traveled to the Near East to explore and study in Palestine; the results of his travels were published four years later. His *Biblical Researches in Palestine* was dedicated to two of his teachers—the German geographer, Carl Ritter, and the American biblical scholar at Andover, Moses Stuart. In 1842, it won the gold medal of the Royal Geographical Society of London (Brown 1969, 112–18). This influential book and the award it received provided an impetus for creating an American organization to promote overseas research.

Robinson used geographical information derived from historical sources and his own observations to locate places mentioned in the Bible. By situating them more precisely, he sought to illuminate and enhance both the meaning of various scriptural passages and the understanding of them. He challenged the identification of modern sites with biblical places. Several of these were shrines operated by the Roman Catholic and Eastern Orthodox churches. His research potentially jeopardized the revenues of the shrines.

In 1842, Everett and Robinson organized the American Oriental Society in order to cultivate the learning of Asian, African, and Polynesian languages and to encourage various kinds of research to promote knowledge of the East. A classical section was established in 1849. The early corporate and corresponding members of the society were teachers, diplomats, and missionaries (American Oriental Society 1851, xxi, xxiv–xxvii). Many of the early members had lived and worked in one or another of these regions, where they either represented or knew American merchants. For the most part, the missionaries were affiliated with the American Board of Commissioners for Foreign Missions, which was centered in New England (Field 1969; Finnie 1967; Grabill 1971; Handy 1981; Phillips 1969).

The voyages of exploration in the late eighteenth century—such as James Cook's visits to Hawaii—and westward expansion in the nineteenth century called attention to distant lands and to the sad condition of their pagan inhabitants. The American Board of Commissioners of Foreign Missions was founded in 1810 by New England Congregationalists, and, for a while, it represented Presbyterian and Dutch Reform as well as Congregational constituencies (Phillips 1969, vii). Its purpose was to propagate the faith in heathen lands; however, by interpreting "heathen" to mean unevangelized communities wherever they were found, the board rejected any geographical restriction on its activities. It established missions among the Indian tribes and settlers of the frontier areas of the West and the back country of the South, as well as in Hawaii and the Pacific islands, the lands of the eastern Mediterranean, the Middle East, East Asia, Africa, India, Burma, Ceylon, and certain parts of South America.

The first American Board missionaries went to India to work among pagans; however, in 1818, the board resolved to undertake a mission to purify Near Eastern Christianity. Two years later, two graduates of the Andover Theological Seminary reached Smyrna, where they were welcomed by an international trading community. During the next decade, while patriotic Greek merchants attempted to overthrow their Ottoman rulers and establish a sovereign Greek state, U.S. trade with the Levant grew steadily during the 1820s, even though it remained relatively small in terms of the total number of ships that were involved. This traffic was increasingly dominated by Boston merchants who exported rum and, by 1828, were purchasing the entire opium crop of Turkey, which they then smuggled into China and sold illegally to the ruling classes of that country (Field 1969, 93, 113, 119).

While the U.S. government maintained an official policy of neutrality toward the Greek War of Independence, prominent philhellenes—such as Everett and Albert Gallatin, Jefferson's secretary of the treasury and later a highly influential New York banker as well as a founder of the American Ethnological Society—openly supported the Greek cause. Everett argued that the Greco-Turkish conflict was a war of the "Crescent against the Cross" and that liberty was the lesson the United States could teach in the regeneration of the world (Field 1969, 122–23; Phillips 1969, 140; Walters 1957). In 1852, Samuel Cox, a U.S. congressman from Ohio, argued that "... the U.S. had a unique role to play in helping the Greeks to obtain their full independence.... The existence of a Platonic Hesparia in America should possess the power of an ideal made real, which would prove capable of regenerating the East, where the ideal had been conceived" (Larrabee 1957, 260–61). The statements of Everett and Cox resonated with the sentiments of Manifest Destiny that crystallized in the United States during the 1830s and 1840s (Weinberg 1935, 111–12, 144–45).

By the 1830s, American Board missionaries had established themselves from Greece to Persia and from Constantinople to Syria and Palestine. However, there were relatively few missionaries, and, when one of them died or moved, activities were usually suspended until the post was filled. This meant there were two American Board missionaries in Palestine from 1820 to 1825. The mission was discontinued until 1834, when it reopened. It was closed again in 1843. The episodic existence of the mission in Palestine did not reflect a lack of interest by the United States in the "cradle of Christianity" or in the history of the Jews, because organizations for promoting Christianity among the Jews already existed in Boston and New York. It is probably related indirectly to the fact that Palestine was a poor provincial region, whose inhabitants had few goods to export and little cash to purchase imports (Silberman 1982).

One of the more influential missionary-orientalists operating in the eastern Mediterranean from the 1820s to the 1850s was Jonas King. King was a conservative Congregationalist and a professor of oriental languages and literature at Amherst College. He first arrived in the eastern Mediterranean in 1822 and made a tour up the Nile River, visiting ancient temples and the recent excavations made by European archaeologists before returning to Smyrna via Jerusalem and Beirut (Larrabee 1957, 178; Phillips 1969, 137–38). In the 1830s, with the financial support of Gallatin and others in New York, he purchased some land with ruins for $258 in order to open an American school in Athens; at the same time, he was appointed American consul in

Athens (Larrabee 1957, 197). During the 1830s, antiforeign sentiments began to rise in Greece because of the influence of outsiders. In 1854, King was tried by the Greek government for reviling the Eastern Orthodox Church; he was convicted, jailed briefly, fined, and banished. Edward Everett and Daniel Webster sent a U.S. man-of-war to Athens to secure King's release. After his release, he was forced to sell the lands owned by the school; their sale brought $25,000 (Larrabee 1957, 195–97, 203).

The activities of U.S. citizens in the eastern Mediterranean waned during the early 1860s because of the Civil War. However, they were revived almost as soon as the war ended. Various U.S. groups provided financial supported for the Palestine Exploration Fund, which was established in London in 1865. This organization, inspired by Robinson's research, was characterized as "a society for the accurate and systematic investigation of the archaeology, topography, geology and physical geography, natural history, manners and customs of the Holy Land, for biblical illustration" (King 1983, 7). Although it was not a religious organization, one of its purposes was to clarify the Bible.

In 1870, J. Henry Thayer of Harvard University and William H. Ward of the American Oriental Society organized the American Palestine Exploration Society. Its goal was the "... illustration and defense of the Bible. Modern skepticism assails the Bible at the point of reality, the question of fact. Hence, whatever goes to verify the Bible history as real, in time, place, and circumstances, is a refutation of unbelief" (King 1983, 8). The Society expired after fourteen years; it sponsored one expedition under the direction of Selah Merrill, a Congregationalist minister who had studied in Germany and taught Hebrew at the Andover Seminary, before he led the 1875–77 survey party to the Transjordan. He published the results in 1881 in *East of Jordan*. Merrill remained in Palestine, where he served as U.S. consul at Jerusalem on three separate occasions between 1882 and 1907 (Finnie 1967, 147).

In 1875, Charles Eliot Norton was appointed to the chair of art history at Harvard. Norton was the grandson of Samuel Eliot, the wealthy Boston merchant, who established the chair of Greek literature first occupied by Edward Everett; he was the nephew of George Tichnor and the son of Andrew Norton, the Dexter Professor of Sacred Literature at Harvard from 1819 to 1847. Norton was appointed by his cousin, Charles W. Eliot, who was Harvard's president at the time. He was also Charles Darwin's brother-in-law after his marriage to Susan Sedgwick in 1862. Before his tenure at Harvard, Norton had worked in India for the East India Merchants and studied in Europe. He edited the *North American Review* during the Civil War and was one of the founders of *The Nation* in 1865. (Brown 1969, 75–94; Green 1966, 122–42). Norton's biographers indicate that he knew virtually every important literary and political figure of his day. He is described as Harvard's most powerful and influential professor; his courses were large and popular, because they were reputedly easy to pass. Norton was also the driving force behind the organization of the Archaeological Institute of America in 1879.

The creation of the institute marked a turning point in how archaeology was construed. Up to this time, in the cultural context of nineteenth-century New England, it appears that the Congregationalists were drawn toward biblical studies while their Unitarian kin focused their attention on the classical world. While this distinction is somewhat overdrawn, it is true that the traditions of biblical scholarship established in New England by the conservatives at Andover and the Unitarians at Harvard all but vanished during the Civil War. Biblical criticism had been introduced by rationalists to challenge the hegemony of the Calvinists who, in turn, deployed biblical studies, including the study of archaeological remains and historical geography, to defend the literal interpretation of the Bible. By 1890, a new tradition of biblical scholarship, based once more on developments in German criticism, was introduced into the United States (Brown 1969, 180–182).

SAVAGES, MOUND BUILDERS, AND MERCHANT PRINCES: U.S. IMPERIALISM AND THE CONSTITUTION OF AMERICANIST ARCHAEOLOGIES

The theories of wealth and property held by Enlightenment writers such as Robertson and the Scottish historians of society derived from John Locke's ([1690] 1980, 18–30) *Second Treatise of Government*. This tradition vested the origins of property in labor. Any land cultivated by persons for their subsistence was part of their property, as were the fruits they harvested from it for their own consumption. Inequalities in property ownership arose after money was introduced and land could be purchased. In this view, a close connection existed between changes in the mode of subsistence and the acquisition of landed property, the accumulation of wealth, the growth of industry, and the division of labor. The acquisition and ownership of property was essential for the progress of human society.

Two different perspectives on the relationship of wealth and property prevailed in the 1820s. The first was represented by Jefferson, the commercial farmers of the Middle Atlantic and southern states, and the small independent producers who adopted the views of the physiocrats. It was that private landed property and agricultural production were the sources of wealth (Parrington 1928–30, vol. 1, 347–62, vol. 2, 9–19). Because progress was both necessary and inevitable, new lands must be made available for settlers to farm, especially in the territories along the frontier. The second opinion expressed the sentiments of the Federalists and their Whig descendants who saw progress as the expansion of commerce, the maintenance of political stability, the creation of a sound fiscal policy, the establishment and protection of a central bank, the expansion of commerce, and enactment of tariffs favorable to U.S. shipping. In their view, commerce, not land, was the source of wealth and the mainspring of progress, and civilized peoples engaged in trade, which was the hallmark of civilization itself. This, of course, was the conviction of the merchant capitalist.

For the commercial farmers who saw land as the source of wealth, new land had to be acquired in the territories along the frontier for progress to occur. Between the 1780s and 1830s, the federal government granted land to former soldiers and settlers in the Ohio Valley, Tennessee, and Michigan. This ultimately brought them into contact with various American Indian groups, many of whom had already been forced from their traditional homelands. The settlers typically viewed the Indians as savages with no or only poorly developed notions of property. The settlers' desire to transform land into a means of agricultural production and later to develop mineral resources laid the foundations for federal policies that removed the Native Americans from their lands and resettled them west of the Mississippi River. These policies were implemented by every U.S. president in the nineteenth century (Drinnon 1980; Harmon 1941; Satz 1975; Sheehan 1973).

As settlers and land speculators poured into the valleys of the Ohio River and its tributaries, towns were established, and local antiquarians recorded the presence of ancient mounds and earthworks, the existence of which had been mentioned earlier by naturalists, travelers, and Moravian missionaries, most of whom were from the Middle Atlantic states, the South, or the Western territories (Greene 1984, 343–75; Silverberg 1968, 25–58). Their descriptions marked the beginning of the Mound Builder controversy (Silverberg 1968; Tax 1973, 63–122). The importance attached to the debate is reflected by the fact that the Smithsonian Institution, created by the federal government in 1846 to promote original research and disseminate knowledge, published Ephraim G. Squier and Edwin H. Davis's (1848) lavishly illustrated *Ancient Monuments of the Mississippi Valley* as the first volume in the series of *Smithsonian Contributions to Knowledge* (Hinsley 1981, 35–37).

For most of the nineteenth century, the controversy hinged on the question: Who built the mounds? The participants attributed their construction to various groups: a lost non-Indian race from Asia, one of the Ten Lost Tribes, and even the Vikings. Some, like William Henry Harrison who later became the first western Whig president, argued that the Mound Builders had achieved a higher level of civilization than the contemporary Indians, who subsequently drove them from the homelands in the Old Northwest Territory. Others—including Albert Gallatin—argued that the mounds were built by the predecessors of the contemporary native inhabitants, farmers who had been influenced by the civilization of central Mexico (Beider 1986, 16–54). Such theories separated the ancient agricultural populations of the area from the contemporary tribes with their supposedly hunting and foraging subsistence economies. They were used to support arguments that the contemporary Indians could make no claims to prior ownership of the land in the area; they also served to legitimate the federal policies of removing Native Americans from their lands and of resettling them west of the Mississippi River, practices that were implemented by every president of the United States during the nineteenth century (Drinnon 1980).

For the merchant capitalists, commerce was the motor of development and the source of wealth. William H. Prescott was perhaps the most eloquent spokesman of the Boston merchants in the mid-nineteenth century. His father was a Salem lawyer who acquired a fortune by marrying the daughter of a wealthy Boston merchant who subsequently became the American consul in the Azores. Prescott followed his father's example, marrying "... the daughter of a leading Boston merchant," and pursued his grandfather's interest in Spain and its colonial empire (Peck 1970, 15, 43). As a result, Prescott possessed the financial resources to devote his life to scholarship; he published two influential works in the 1840s: *The History of the Conquest of Mexico* and *The History of the Conquest of Peru* (Gardiner 1969).

Prescott had read the Enlightenment historians and appreciated their antiauthoritarian, anticlerical, and anti-Catholic attacks on superstition and coercive religious beliefs. He believed in progress that operated in accordance with both natural and moral laws, an evolutionary universe that was driven by divine providence. He was pro-British and believed that the Anglo-Saxons possessed a superior capacity for government and an innate libertarian impulse. He was also suspicious of the masses, whom he saw as too easily swayed by political oratory. He viewed Native Americans, along with Jews and Moors, as antiprogressive forces because of their links with tradition and the past and the indolence these practices engendered (Darnell 1975, 40–44). In the 1830s, Prescott's attitude toward the revolutions and political instability of Mexico was a combination of mild ridicule and humorous indifference; he reassessed his views during the 1840s as the threat of the war between Mexico and the United States loomed on the horizon. His attitudes now coincided with those of the Mexican ruling class; he opposed the annexation of Texas and detested even more the way in which it was accomplished (Gardiner 1969, 229).

Prescott's book, *The Conquest of Mexico*, appeared in 1843. It was an immediate best-seller. Lucas Alamán, the Mexican scholar-statesman, annotated a Spanish translation that was published a year later in Mexico. Prescott described the sophistication and refinement of the Tezcocan court and ruling class, which had fallen under the sway of the Aztecs—a group too committed to war and sacrifice to be more than partially civilized. He commented on the enormous markets with regular fairs and stressed the importance of merchants, who carried valuable commodities beyond the frontiers of the state, who raised levies and spied for the state, and who consulted with the monarch, advising him on financial and other matters (Prescott 1936, 85–86, 93–117).

The writings of John Lloyd Stephens—the highly successful author of travel accounts and President Martin van Buren's representative to the crumbling Central American Federation in 1839—also exhibit the combination of romanticism and rationalism found in Prescott's works. His perspective on Native-American societies resonated with Prescott's, even though they did not share the same sentiments about merchants and politics. During an 1835 journey through Greece, which had only recently won independence from the Ottoman Empire, Stephens's attention was frequently drawn to ancient ruins—the kind of record studied by antiquarians (Hinsley 1985a; von Hagen 1978). He also alluded to the wealth, social position, and power of merchants and complained about their relationship with the state: As ambassadors and consuls in foreign countries, they frequently made their offices subservient to their commercial interests (Stephens 1839, vol. 1, 195–96, 242–43). He published two widely read accounts of incidents that occurred during his travels: *Incidents of Travel in Central America, Chiapas, and Yucatán* appeared in 1841 and *Incidents of Travel in Yucatán* two years later. The success of his books depended partly on his account of the political and social conditions in the area and partly on his descriptions of ruined cities that lay hidden in the jungle and Frederick Catherwood's illustrations of them. Stephens ([1843] 1963, vol. 2, 307–10) argued that they were the remains of a civilization built by the ancestors of the modern inhabitants of the area; they were contemporary with the Aztecs but independent from them.

Stephens's interest in the archaeology of Central America and the Yucatán waned in the late 1840s as he renewed an old interest in steam-powered transportation. He became president and director of the first ocean steam navigation company in 1847, and, after the discovery of gold in California in 1849, he organized and became president of the Panama Railroad Company, which built a railroad across the isthmus.

MEXICANS AND INDIANS IN THE 1840S AND 1850S

In 1849, the administration of President Zachary Taylor, who had gained fame in the war with Mexico, sent E. George Squier to Central America as chargé d'affaires. Squier was a newspaperman, belligerent nationalist, and archaeologist, whose collaborative study with Edwin H. Davis, a physician from Chillicothe, on the mounds of the Mississippi Valley had been the Smithsonian Institution's first publication, a fact that subsequently cemented his reputation as one of the profession's pioneer Americanist archaeologists. However, during the twelve and a half months he was in Central America, he spent only four days examining ancient monuments; the rest of the time he devoted to intervening in the internal affairs of the various countries and pursuing policies that would probably have provoked a war between Great Britain and the United States, if the two governments had not found it convenient to maintain peaceful relations at the time (Olien 1985; Perkins 1933, 196–200; Stansifer 1959; van Alstyne 1960, 159–62).

In the works he published to defend his actions in Central America, Squier constructed an argument that linked property claims and history with race. He emphasized that the Moskito of the Caribbean coast, who were supported by the British, were of African rather than Indian descent and, hence, had no legitimate claim to territory in Nicaragua. In a letter to the secretary of state, he wrote that they were hunters and foragers without fixed places of habitation, who were "... inferior to the Indians of the United States" (quoted in Olien 1985, 118). Squier (1855, 54–55) was a racist who claimed permanent physical, intellectual, and moral differences between the various families of man and that any admixture would have only disastrous consequences. Squier was certainly not the only racist to write during this period; Louis Agassiz, George Gliddon, and Samuel Morton also argued that cultural differences were rooted on biology (Stanton 1960).

Although not all of Squier's contemporaries accepted his racism, a number of them continued to promote policies that were based on arguments that linked property, history, social milieu, environment, and education. They were asking questions about whether the Native Americans were capable of being educated and, hence, civilized, or whether they were merely resistant to assimilation (Keen 1971, 351–54). Some, like Albert Gallatin (1845, 179–81), continued to argue for the importance of education as a means of promoting assimilation; others, like Lewis Cass (1840, 398, 410)—the leading architect of U.S. policies toward Indians during the first half of the nineteenth century, governor and Indian superintendent of Michigan, Jackson's secretary of war, ambassador to France, president of the American Historical Society, Buchanan's secretary of state, and recipient of an honorary degree from Harvard—were more skeptical about the possibility of change. He found the Native Americans unchangeable in their physical and moral habits, unable to appreciate their own condition, resistant to education and attempts to ameliorate their own circumstances even after several centuries of contact with civil society; they were still nomads, warlike by nature, who seemed incapable of achieving civilization.

The reintensification of efforts to determine or define the character of Native-American groups was a product of the new conditions that developed as a result of westward expansion and settlement along the Pacific coast, increased emigration across the Indian Country, the push for a transcontinental railroad, and the opening of Kansas and Nebraska for settlement. This marked the beginning of the reservation system and dramatically transformed the lives of the Indians living in the territory, as they were deprived of more than 95 percent of the lands they had been granted twenty years earlier and the buffalo herds they subsisted on were systematically slaughtered (Hoopes 1932; Malin 1921; Trennert 1975; Utley 1984, 1–64).

Because landed property was wealth, the appearance of new landholding patterns coincided with the beginning of systematic exploration and survey in the old Indian territories and areas seized during the Mexican War (Goetzmann 1966). A few travelers and army surveyors made cursory observations about archaeological sites in the Old Southwest (Morgan 1869; Schroeder 1979). These observations had no impact in the 1850s. In 1855, Samuel Haven, librarian of the American Antiquarian Society, which was founded in 1812 to discover the antiquities of North America, cited with approval Schoolcraft's earlier remarks in his influential *Archaeology of the United States*. He wrote:

> ... Texas is entirely without aboriginal monuments of any kind; and that neither tumuli, nor remains of ancient ditches, nor attempts at catrametation [i.e., earthwork enclosure], occur, from the plains of that State and New Mexico, east of the foot of the Rocky Mountains, till the prairie country embraces both banks of the Missouri, and reaches to the plains of the Red River, and Sascatawhine, west of the sources of the Mississippi.... [There is an] absence of antiquities in Oregon, Washington, and California....   •
>
> (HAVEN 1855, 153)

When rights to landed property were defined in terms of a history of occupation in the area, Schoolcraft and Haven were denying that Indian groups in the newly acquired territories had any historically legitimate claims to property outside the reservation lands granted them by the federal government (Carlson 1981, 1–25).

Wealth was still produced from land, but agriculture was no longer the only means by which it could be procured. Land had come to be valued for its mineral wealth and as a right-of-way in railroad and canal construction. Mining was particularly important in the Upper Peninsula of Michigan and in California. The lands claimed by the federal government as a result of imperial expansion in the 1840s were especially valued. Land prices remained relatively high until new lands were seized and opened for settlement or purchase. Thus, the public lands in the territories were coveted by settlers, miners, speculators, and individuals and companies seeking grants of free land as rights-of-way for the construction of railroad trunk lines.

The worldviews of the merchant and the farmer, prevalent in the United States after the turn of the century, were reconstituted after the 1840s to incorporate this new vision of how land could be used to create wealth. The sentiments of the commercial sector, articulated by Prescott, were taken up by Hubert Howe Bancroft, who went from upstate New York to California in 1852 with a consignment of books from his brother-in-law's store and established what eventually became the largest bookstore and publishing house west of Chicago (Caughey 1946, 16–43). In the 1870s and 1880s, Bancroft produced thirty-three thick volumes that described the Indian tribes and antiquities of Latin America and the West as well as the history of Mexico, Central America, and the western states. In his introduction to the five volumes dealing with native peoples, he wrote:

> The terms Savage and Civilized as applied to races of men, are relative and not absolute terms. At best these words mark only broad shifting stages in human progress; the one near the point of departure, the other farther toward the unattainable end.... There are degrees in savagism, and there are degrees in civilization; indeed, though placed in opposition, the one is but a degree of the other. The Haidah, whom we call savage, are as much superior to the Shoshone, the lowest of Americans, as the Aztec is superior to the Haidah, or the European to the Aztec.

(BANCROFT 1886, VOL. 2, 1–4)

In reality, Bancroft viewed the lives of the indigenous peoples of the Pacific states "... as mere prelude to the more interesting White civilizations that were to come" (Berkhofer 1978, 108).

Like Prescott, Bancroft was suspicious of the masses, whom he described as "scum and dregs" drained from "the cesspools of Europe." In addition, he held derogatory views about unassimilated Native Americans, Catholics, Japanese, and the decadent rich. During his early days in California, he had supported vigilante justice as a means of making San Francisco safer for business. He opposed education for the working classes because it ruined prospective mechanics and housewives; he hated trade unions because they shackled the development of San Francisco's industry and commerce. He also despised monopolies, which he identified with the construction and operation of railroads. However, as a major land speculator in the San Diego area, he was acutely aware of the value of land and of the dangers to land values posed by marauding Indians from Mexico (Caughey 1946, 246–47, 275, 310, 372).

Bancroft (1886, vol. 2, 1–80) also wrote about civilization and progress. He argued that war and despotism were essential for progress to occur. Cooperation, he believed, was poorly developed among primitive peoples, but it developed as an inseparable consequence arising from aggression and war and escaping from evil, which he identified with the state of savagery itself. Once despotism, government in its various forms, was established and order was brought out of social chaos by the rule of law, progress toward civilization could occur. The path toward civilization was an intellectual one that involved increasing skills to increase comfort. Whereas war was the stimulus, labor was the civilizing agent. Mental and manual labor were gradually differentiated in the process, and intellectual activity slowly asserted its dominance over manual work.

The most articulate spokesman for the view that land, rather than commerce, was the source of value and wealth was Lewis Henry Morgan, a conservative lawyer from Rochester. In 1844, he met Ely Parker, a Tonawanda Seneca, who had been sent by the Seneca to study law in order to defend them from a group of land speculators that, through a combination of legislation and bribery, were attempting to seize Tonawanda lands and resettle them in Kansas. Morgan supported Parker's efforts; however, he did not believe that endless disputes over land titles were ultimately the way to resolve the issue. This could best be accomplished, he thought, by the education of individuals and their integration or assimilation into the politically dominant society (Resnick 1960, 27–31; Stern 1931, 16–18). This experience had a number of effects on Morgan. His friendship with Parker and his Seneca kin stimulated Morgan's interest in Native American societies and eventually in comparative ethnology. His concern about their plight led him to seek public office, to become chairman of the state committee on Indian affairs and to introduce legislation on behalf of the Iroquois. He also tried, unsuccessfully, to become the commissioner of Indian affairs in 1861 during Abraham Lincoln's administration.

The experience heightened his awareness of the role played by the development of property—land and its resources—in the advent of civilization, and of the relation between property relations and the state that protects them (Leacock 1979). In Morgan's view, the early forms of human society were based on personal relationships rather than territory; they were social rather than political.

> Society was first organized on the basis of sex, with "classes" of intermarrying males and females. Later, through the progressive restriction of possible marriage partners, the gens [clan] developed. Subsequent steps toward formal political organization were: (1) the chief and tribal council of chiefs; (2) the confederacy of tribes; (3) the nation with a division between the council of chiefs and the assembly of the people; and, finally, (4) "out of military necessities of the united tribes came the general military commander," a third power, but subordinate to the other two (Morgan [1877] 1963, 330; see also 61, 121–23). Full political organization could not develop, however, until the personal ties of the gens were rendered functionless, and relationships [were] founded instead upon territory and upon property. Preliminary to the disappearance of the gens, descent shifted from matrilineal to patrilineal (Ibid.: 63–64, 67, 315–16, 363, 366).
>
> (LEACOCK 1979, 315)

For Morgan, the Australian aborigines represented the earliest stage of human society; the Iroquois marked the shift to the gens and the subsequent appearance of the tribe and the confederacy; and the Aztecs represented a "military democracy" similar to those of early Greece and Rome. He believed "... that the transformation from social to political organization became necessary when agriculture and the domestication of animals grew to be sufficiently productive to enable city living and the development of private property" (Leacock 1979, 322; Morgan [1877] 1963, 263–64). The political organization of this new social condition dealt "... with persons through their territorial relations" rather than their social relations as individuals (Morgan [1877] 1963, 272). Morgan also emphasized that "... egalitarian traditions are ancient and universal in human history, and this theme recurs throughout *Ancient Society*" (Leacock 1979, 324).

In Morgan's view, social progress depended on increased conscious control over nature—that is, the process of increasing control over subsistence resulting from the development of the "subsistence arts" or productive forces along different lines in different environmental circumstances (Morgan [1877] 1963, 9–14, 23, 110, 470–72). This was the product of rational thought, the capacity for which was universally available to humanity. In some passages of *Ancient Society,* "Morgan's notion that the progressive changes in social organization became inborn capacities led him into a seeming support of racial inequalities" (Leacock 1979, 314). In other passages in the same book, he argued that the differences among the social groups of the various ethnical periods were historically contingent (Morgan [1877] 1963, 513–14). In Morgan's ([1877] 1963, 562) own words, "With one principle of intelligence and one physical form in virtue of a common origin, the results of human experiences have been substantially the same in all times and areas in the same ethnical status." Late in his life, he also believed that "... the outgrowth of property has been so immense, its forms so diversified, its uses so expanding and its management so intelligent in the use of its owners, that it has become, on the part of the people, an unmanageable experience" (Morgan [1877] 1963, 562). Given his experiences after the Civil War, these words reflect his sentiments about how capitalist property relations were developing in the United States during the 1870s.

Early in his legal career, Morgan represented the business interests of Rochester capitalists who were investing in mining and railroad ventures in the Lake Superior region; he subsequently became an investor, partner, and officer in several of the companies they formed (Benison 1953). During the 1850s, he testified before the U.S. Congress about the need for public land grants to companies that were going to build railroads. Morgan profited considerably from his mining and railroad ventures and amassed a modest fortune during the 1850s and the Civil War (Benison 1953, 116–22, 216–17). His business allies were the pioneer capitalists of upstate New York and the merchants and manufacturers of the Great Lakes states. After the war, he found himself and the companies in which he was an officer or stockholder increasingly opposed by the emergence of labor unions; the dominance of the companies and his associates were also challenged and eventually supplanted by a power bloc composed of Eastern capitalists, investment banks, and railroad entrepreneurs including John Jacob Astor, the Farmers Loan and Trust Company, and Jay Gould, which was consolidating in Boston and New York City (Benison 1953, 238, 251–305).

Bancroft and Morgan both wrote about the ancient societies of Central Mexico and the Southwest. In a review called "Montezuma's Dinner," Morgan ([1876], 1963, 191–220) described in detail the differences between his views about Aztec society and civilization and those of Bancroft (1886, vol. 2), who had portrayed the Aztecs as a class-stratified, absolutist monarchy with elaborate court rituals, an intelligentsia that performed mental labor, and an economic foundation based on war, trade, and agriculture. Employing the results of his comparative ethnological studies, Morgan characterized the Aztecs as a tribe and Montezuma, their monarch, as one of a number of equally powerful leaders who jointly administered tribal affairs. He proceeded to portray Montezuma's palace as a communal longhouse, the Aztec capital as a village, and lavish feasts at the palace as a routine meal with relatives. In a word, he had little confidence in the validity of the Spanish chronicles or in either Prescott's or Bancroft's acceptance of them (Keen 1971, 380–410).

In *Ancient America,* John D. Baldwin (1871, 151–57) was critical of Morgan's rewriting of the history of Montezuma's empire. In arguing that the Aztecs had achieved civilization, he recognized chronological differences in the antiquity of the various Maya cities and laid the foundations for what later were called the old and new empires of the Maya. Some Maya settlements were contemporary with the Aztec empire, and other centers of Maya civilization clearly preceded Montezuma's state.

> Those who have sought to discredit what is told of the Aztec civilization and the empire of Montezuma have never failed to admit fully the significance of Copan, Palenque, and Mitla.... Copan and Palenque, and even Kabah, in Yucatan, may have been very old cities, if not already old ruins, when Uxmal was built. Accepting the reports of explorers as correct, there is evidence in the ruins that Quirigua is older than Copan, and that Copan is older than Palenque. The old monuments in Yucatan represent several distinct epochs in the history of that peninsula. Some of them are kindred to those hidden in the great forest, and remind us more of Palenque than Uxmal. Among those described, the most modern, or most of these are in Yucatan; they belong to the time when the kingdom of the Mayas flourished. Many of the others belong to ages previous to the rise of this kingdom.
>
> (BALDWIN 1871, 153–55).

The importance of Baldwin's argument and its implications began to be recognized and utilized in the 1880s and 1890s.

Although their analyses of Aztec society differed significantly, there were remarkable convergences in the way Bancroft and Morgan viewed the societies of Arizona, New Mexico, and northern Chihuahua during the 1870s (Bancroft 1886, vol. 1, 526–47, vol. 4, 681–85; Morgan 1869, 465, 473–74, 495). Both denied the assertions of early travelers, who claimed there were connections between the archaeological monuments in the Southwest and Aztec society. Both viewed the remains as the ancient settlements of nonnomadic, semicivilized farmers, Village Indians as Morgan called them; they distinguished them from the nomadic or Roving Indians of the area. Morgan (1869, 474) also argued that the architecture, and hence the level of progress toward civilization, of the Chaco Canyon ruins was similar to that of the ancient Village Indians of Chiapas and the Yucatán and that both were superior to the ancient structures found in Central Mexico. This was one of the bases for his belief that the Aztecs were not civilized.

Their views about the Southwest and its relations with central Mexico were published during a period when Mexican scholars were actively engaged in research that extolled the sophistication and progressive features of Aztec civilization; these inquiries were supported by every Mexican government from the 1850s onwards, and their results were incorporated into the Mexican state's public representations of itself (Keen 1971, 411–62). Thus, Morgan's work on the Aztecs was not looked upon with favor in Mexico. The 1870s was also a period when the United States was threatening to invade Mexico as a result of incidents and unsettled conditions along the border (Rippy 1926, 282–310). The incidents, which had been the source of friction since the late 1840s, reached crisis proportions in

1877. John Foster, Ulysses S. Grant's minister to Mexico, wrote that officials of the newly elected Hayes administration thought that their position would be consolidated and attention would be diverted from various domestic issues, "... if a war could be brought on with Mexico and another slice of its territory added to the union" (Rippy 1926, 296).

By claiming no close connections between the American Southwest and Central Mexico, that northern Mexico was inhabited by seminomadic tribes without fixed settlements and landed property, and that Chihuahua was linked historically with the semicivilized aboriginal cultures of the U.S. Southwest, Bancroft and Morgan provided arguments that supported rather than reduced the threat of war with Mexico. Their arguments implied that the legitimacy of the Mexican government's claims to lands in northern Mexico were no more, and perhaps even less, valid than those of the United States, because the aboriginal inhabitants of Casas Grandes in Chihuahua constituted an outpost population of the ancient cultures of the U.S. Southwest. The boundaries implied by their characterization of Casas Grandes were reminiscent of those advocated earlier by Buchanan.

War was averted, however, when the United States reached certain agreements with the government of Porfirio Diaz that promoted U.S. investment and protected U.S. citizens and their interests in Mexico. These concessions permitted U.S. railroad builders—Jay Gould, Russell Sage, and others but more importantly the Santa Fé, Southern Pacific, and Denver and Rio Grande companies backed by the Pennsylvania system—to build highly profitable rail systems in Mexico. They were followed by U.S. mining companies: the Hearst Estate, the Guggenheims, Batopilas of New York, the Anaconda group, and the United States Steel Corporation. At the same time came the U.S. ranchers, planters, and land speculators who purchased or leased large estates: agents of the McCormick Harvester Company in Yucatán, the Sonora Land and Cattle Company, the Hearsts in Chihuahua, and the Sinaloa and Sonora Irrigation Company, to name only a few. In the first decade of the twentieth century, oil prospectors such as Edward L. Doheny and his California associates, as well as Standard Oil, Texaco, Gulf, and the other major petroleum producers, also staked out large claims. The lands held by individuals and companies from the United States were not only extensive but also exceedingly valuable (Rippy 1926, 310–19).

The late 1860s and 1870s witnessed a resurgence in the negative stereotypes of both Mexicans and Indians (Pike 1992; Powell 1971; Robinson 1963). The Indian Wars were at their height during this period, as the federal government once again attempted to remove bands from their traditional lands—this time from the trans-Missouri region to large reservations where they would be civilized through education, conversion to Protestantism, and the acquisition of private property (Fritz 1963, 60, 71, 168; Mardock 1971, 3–4, 95, 168, 203, 211). It also marked the beginning of the movement to assimilate Native Americans into the wider society. The question of assimilation was couched in regional terms. By the 1870s, white settlers in the West generally opposed assimilation because of the contempt and hatred they had cultivated during the westward expansion. Easterners, on the other hand, removed from frontier conditions for more than fifty years, had few accurate impressions of the West and often held romantic notions about Indian life.

DISCUSSION

The constitution of archaeology in the United States, both as a means for understanding past societies and a set of practices for acquiring information about them, was intimately linked with territorial and commercial expansion. Americanist archaeology was an integral part of westward expansion across the North American continent and the seizure of more than a million square miles of the national territory of Mexico in the 1840s. The archaeology of the eastern Mediterranean was pursued in large part by individuals representing the commercial interests of U.S. merchants in that part of the world. During the early nineteenth century, this interest subsumed both biblical and classical archaeology, practices that began to separate and become autonomous after the 1860s. Commercial ventures in the Far East during the middle and late nineteenth century laid the foundations for the subsequent development of the study of the archaeology and fine arts of the ancient civilizations of that vast region.

The practice of archaeology was shaped increasingly by the ideology of Manifest Destiny, which crystallized during the mid-nineteenth century. Manifest Destiny, viewed American expansion "... as evidence of the innate superiority of the American Anglo-Saxon branch of the Caucasian race.... [It viewed] the American Anglo-Saxons as a separate, innately superior people who were destined to bring good government, commercial prosperity, and Christianity to the American continents and the rest of the world" (Horsman 1981, 1–2). The advocates of Manifest Destiny and the peoples influenced by their rhetoric viewed this group as a superior race and saw individuals assigned to other races—usually defined as African, Oriental, and American Indian—as having darker complexions and smaller cranial capacities. These were seen as signs of their inferiority, subordinate status in the great chain of being, and separate origins. Thus, Manifest Destiny overlapped with the emergence of scientific racism. Archaeology provided the material evidence—usually crania and other skeletal remains from the Americas, Asia, Europe, and Egypt—used to support such claims and to legitimate the exploitative and genocidal activities they underwrote.

The 1870s witnessed the creation of the Archaeological Institute of America and marked a turning point in how archaeology was conceptualized. Up to that time, the view that it was the study of ancient societies was the dominant one. Afterwards, archaeology was increasingly seen as the study of ancient remains, and this soon became the dominant view. This perception resonated with professionalization: the appearance of new technical specializations; the growth of fine arts, anthropology, and natural history museums; development of technically specialized languages and discourses; and the gradual exclusion of amateurs from participation. It also marked the beginning of a much narrower discourse dominated by technicians whose goal was to use archaeological remains to reconstruct the past as it actually was instead of using archaeological evidence from ancient societies to provide lessons for the present.

In the next chapter, we will explore how the changes in archaeology are related to the transformation of U.S. society that was also set in motion in the 1870s, as new forms of capitalist production and production relations took hold. Native Americans, Latinos, African Americans, and working-class immigrants from Europe and Asia were incorporated into a permanent underclass that was, and still is, largely defined in racialist terms. At various times, all of them were portrayed as rude, childlike, and uneducable, as savages and barbarians whose separate identities were constructed as meaningful images only when it was necessary to foment divisions and prevent collective action. The 1870s was the period of the great reform movement in the United States, which marked the rise of the technician; the constitution of professional organizations, institutions, and museums; the organization of periodic world's fairs whose dominant ideology was based on white supremacy and cultural hegemony; and the assertion of a conservative cultural, social, and political agenda by business leaders.

CHAPTER 3

The Professionalization of Archaeology,

1877 to 1932

The Civil War, which was fought between 1860 and 1865 to prevent the secession of the South, signaled both class struggle and class formation. Although it abolished slavery and granted citizenship to all native-born residents, except Indians, neither the war itself nor the decade of Reconstruction that followed clarified what abolition and citizenship actually meant. While the war devastated the plantation economy of the South and temporarily challenged the hegemony of its planter ruling class, it completely transformed the political economy of the North.

The expenditures and policies of the northern Union turned it into a gigantic consumer of goods and services. They created a new class of finance capitalists who forged linkages between money markets and the state, which established the foundations for expansion. They provided enormous economic opportunities to northern speculators and venture capitalists—especially those who built railroads to move soldiers and supplies, opened meat packing plants in Chicago, patented machines to increase agricultural productivity, or manufactured goods such as woolens and furniture in the Northeast and Great Lakes states. Many of this group used wartime profits to pay off debts and to concentrate their control over the production, financing, and marketing of steel, petroleum, and other commodities. This shifted power from the merchants who dominated the prewar economy to the new class fraction dominated by finance and industrial capitalists, whose fortunes were closely linked with those of the state and the Republican Party in power (Foner 1980, 1988).

Whereas the federal bureaucracy grew during the Civil War and Reconstruction, the rapid expansion of the state apparatus occurred during the post-Reconstruction period after 1877. The policies carried out by a civil service—whose numbers were swelled by tax collectors, local postmasters, and land agents, especially in the South—penetrated further into the fabric of civil society than ever before (Bensel 1990; Skowronek 1982). The U.S. Post Office facilitated the development of a national market, and the tax collectors provided the revenues required to underwrite its realization and also to promote the development of the West. The new state was also committed to protecting American industry from foreign competition and to servicing the national debt (Bensel 1990, 401–2).

The struggles and tensions of the 1860s and 1870s were resolved or at least papered over by the Compromise of 1877, and the significance of the new structures that had been or were being established became clearer (Woodward 1966).

Ostensibly, the compromise guaranteed the election of Rutherford B. Hayes, the Republican candidate for the presidency, in spite of widespread election irregularities in several southern states and the fact that his Democratic rival received more votes. More importantly, it removed federal troops from South Carolina and Louisiana and returned political power to the separatist planter ruling class, whose members instituted debt peonage among freedmen and poor whites and rebuilt their power base on racist "Jim Crow" legislation and practices. While the compromise suppressed the separatist tendencies of the planter ruling class, it ensured that the South would subsidize industry in the North and economic development in the agrarian West, and that New York, rather than southern cities like Charleston or New Orleans, would mediate cotton production for the world market. It also gave northern finance capitalists control over the railroads and industrial development in both the South and the West.

The compromise established the foundations for political parties that crossed class lines. The Republicans consisted of industrialists, merchants, and yeoman farmers in the North, wealthy agrarian capitalists in the West, and impoverished freedmen and poor upland whites in the South. The Democrats were composed of workers and marginal farmers in the North and West and the planter elite in the South. This meant that the ruling class fractions of both parties could simultaneously wage class warfare against marginalized workers and farmers in the regions where they were dominant—promoting nativist, anti-immigration policies in the North and racist policies in the South—and forge alliances with the oppressed classes of other regions. It also meant that the political structure of the time institutionalized racism and nativism in ways that prevented either party from confronting their consequences or from dealing with the fundamental contradiction of the time: the increasing levels of exploitation resulting from the redistribution of wealth both within and between regions (Bensel 1990, 366–415).

Protective tariffs, pensions for Union but not Confederate veterans, and imperialism were major points of contention that were increasingly linked during the depression of the late 1880s and 1890s. Protective tariffs, which benefited industrialists and large export farmers, were the major source of revenue for the federal state. They were supported by the industrial and financial elites of the North, pensioners, commercial farmers, elements of organized labor, and some small producers. After 1887, they were opposed by Democrats who saw them as "the mothers of trusts" and by southerners who viewed them as an indirect form of taxation that increased the price of consumer goods. Military pensions were opposed from their inception in the South, where they were viewed as an intrusion by the federal government, and, by the early 1900s, in the Midwest and Great Plains, where they were seen increasingly as unwarranted expenditures that sustained imperialist expansion (Bensel 1984).

Calls for imperialist expansion reappeared after the Indian wars of the late 1870s and early 1880s were quelled and various tribes were resettled on reservations. Their lands were divided into 160-acre plots allotted to Indian men by the Dawes Act of 1887. The imperialist lobby—supported by industrial, financial, and commercial interests in the Northeast and by agrarian capitalists in the West—called for the penetration and control of foreign markets. This would be accomplished by building a navy and acquiring fueling stations and deep-water ports in the Caribbean and Pacific. Their rationale for imperial expansion combined arguments rooted in Manifest Destiny, Social Darwinism, and scientific racism—distinctive discourses that converged and effectively coalesced in the 1890s. The annexation of Western Samoa in 1890 and the abortive attempt to acquire Hawaii in 1893 once again put imperialism on the agenda. The acquisition of the Philippines and Puerto Rico and the conquest of Cuba as a result of the Spanish-American War of 1898 were responses to demands for further territorial expansion. The ruling planter class in the South opposed imperialism because it expanded the size of the federal government, especially the military, and the government's ability to intervene. Poor upcountry whites in that region, however, saw the army as a potential source of social mobility and supported imperialism. Also opposed to imperialism were non-ruling-class groups in the Midwest and Great Plains states—the most economically self-sufficient regions in the country—whose members disliked the English as well as the bankers, industrialists, and munitions manufacturers of the East and did not particularly benefit from protective tariffs (Bensel 1984; Tompkins 1970).

More than ten million immigrants poured into the United States from Europe during the 1880s and 1890s. At the time, they constituted more than a tenth of the country's population. Most were from southern and eastern Europe—Italians, Jews, Russians, Greeks, and Slavs who seemed more alien to the native-born Americans than the Irish and German immigrants who arrived a generation or two earlier. Many settled in the industrial cities of the Northeast and Great Lakes states, where they were joined by native immigrants from rural areas, creating a labor surplus that kept wages low. While the members of these emerging urban communities increasingly saw themselves as exploited wage workers, the ruling class saw them as parts of a hierarchy of buffer races that separated white Protestants, whose ancestors were northern Europeans, from Indians, African Americans, and Chinese immigrants (Foner 1978; Goldfield 1991; Higham 1957; Roediger 1991, 133–67; Saxon 1990, 293–319; Spoehr 1973; Takaki 1990).

The new arrivals were viewed with suspicion—their craniometry suggested mental inferiority or potential criminality to scientists from Cambridge, Philadelphia, and New York who wrote about race and laid the foundations for a new scientific racism that resonated with movements advocating eugenics, conservation, restricted immigration, and imperialism (Allen 1976, 1986, 1987; Darnovsky 1992; Haller 1971; Pick 1989; Weston 1972). William Z. Ripley described a number of races in *The Races of Europe,* published in 1899; these formed a series of buffer races separating the white Anglo-Saxons of northern Europe and the United States from the darker-skinned Oriental, Indian, and African races. The armories, built amid urban working-class neighborhoods in the 1870s and 1880s, bear silent testimony to how the state and ruling class saw them: savages and barbarians, potentially unruly mobs, whose members had a penchant for violence, immorality, and illegal acts and whose ancestors lacked the refinements of civilization and perhaps even the capacity to acquire them (Beckwith 1989; Higham 1981; Trumpbour 1989).

Class struggle and surveillance extended far beyond the confines of the urban neighborhoods where the workers lived. They are reflected in the strikes and massacres after 1877 and the rise of trade unions to protect workers' rights (Brecher

1979). They are also represented by management reforms initiated by employers to control the work habits, attitudes, and life-styles of their employees; the profession-alization of management and the creation of white-collar technicians; and the devel-opment of scientific management techniques, called Taylorism, concerned with standardization and the systematic organization of production (Montgomery 1979). The white-collar managers emerging in industry found their interests converged with those of the trained professionals in the civil service and the universities (Bledstein 1976; Wiebe 1967, 111–32). In Max Weber's view, they were the "iron cage" that simultaneously shaped and was trapped by the bureaucratic organization and ratio-nalization of capitalist culture (Beetham 1985; Scaff 1989). In the wake of univer-sity reform, their members professionalized the social sciences in the United States (Furner 1975; Gedicks 1975; Haskell 1977; Ross 1991).

Class struggle took other forms besides trade union movements, whose centers of gravity were situated in urban and rural industrial areas. The most potent forms of opposition to ruling-class interests have historically been located outside the Northeast and Middle Atlantic states. However, these challenges to ruling-class hege-mony and the power of the state were largely disconnected from one another. They included diverse manifestations of the civil rights movement centered originally in the South; the women's movement; the various populist movements that continue to erupt periodically in the agrarian areas of the South, Midwest, and West and see polit-ical causes underlying their economic problems; and diverse religious and commu-nitarian movements that find the values of capitalist culture both alienating and antithetical to realizing the full potential of human beings (Furniss 1954; Goodwyn 1976; Gusfield 1966; Hahn 1983, 269–89; McNall 1988; Moldow 1987; Pollock 1962; Rossiter 1982; Solomon 1985).

POLITICAL HEGEMONY AND THE RECASTING OF CULTURE

Class struggle is waged on terrains shaped by culture, education, region, and religion. It is alternately a war of maneuvering and a war of position, where the battle of ideas and the struggle for power are waged in every theater of civil society. The var-ious fractions battle to establish intellectual and moral leadership within their bloc. Once that is achieved, they attempt to extend their influence in the wider society and to gain and advance their share in state power. They strive to assert dominance not simply through the organization of force but rather through the creation of a sys-tem of cross-class alliances, based on agreement or consent, that support a particu-lar social order. The fabric of the society, under the hegemonic leadership of the dominant ruling-class fractions, "... is created and re-created in a web of institu-tions, social relations, and ideas" (Sassoon 1983, 201).

Paul DiMaggio's (1982a, 1982b) explanation of how a particular class fraction gained hegemony in Boston between 1850 and 1900 provides a model for describing similar processes with different details that were occurring in other cities and towns in the United States at the same time (for example, Horowitz 1976; Jaher 1972; Kusmer 1979). Before 1850, the most important arbiters of culture in Boston were

Congregationalist or Unitarian ministers who used their pulpits to comment on matters of importance and to differentiate those objects and practices that elevated the spirit from those that debased it. However, at the time, there was little distinction between art and entertainment or agreement regarding what constituted culture; objects subsequently called fine arts were often displayed in cabinets or circuses with other curiosities, such as stuffed animals or bearded women, and actors reciting Shakespearean sonnets performed next to jugglers and clowns.

By the 1860s, the political and cultural leadership was in jeopardy. Immigrants—many Irish Catholic—and their descendants, who composed nearly 70 percent of Boston's population, and the Know-Nothings, who had gained control of the state government in the 1850s,

> ... attacked the social exclusivity of Harvard College, frontally, amending its charter and threatening state control over its governance, hiring and admissions policies (Story 1980). Scalded by these attacks, Boston's leadership retreated from the public sector to found a system of non-profit organizations that permitted them to maintain some control over the community even as they lost their command of its political institutions.
>
> (DiMaggio 1982a, 40)

The organizations created, controlled, and governed by the Boston Brahmins included the Boston Museum of Fine Arts and the Boston Symphony Orchestra. These established sharp boundaries between art and entertainment and between high and popular culture. High culture—certain forms of art, music, theater, and literature—was appropriated by the ruling class, which claimed to be the custodian of culture. This classification was acknowledged and legitimated by members of the emerging white-collar professional and managerial middle class, whose members visited the museum galleries and attended the concerts; at the same time they were differentiating themselves from their immigrant neighbors and kin, who toiled in the city. In spite of interventions by the ruling class, popular culture continued to thrive in Boston. More people read dime novels about factory girls and mechanics than high-culture literature written by Longfellow or Hawthorne, and music halls, sporting events, and circuses regularly drew larger crowds than the symphony or the museums (Denning 1987).

The Boston ruling class extended its control over education and popular culture in the early twentieth century. It established the evening educational programs through the Young Men's Christian Association (YMCA) for men who worked during the day. One of them, the Evening Institute for Young Men, which initially offered law courses staffed by Harvard faculty, expanded its offerings to include engineering and business courses as well as cooperative projects with local firms; it eventually changed its name to Northeastern University. Northeastern and the other schools created in this manner, including Suffolk Law School, ensured a continued flow of low-level managers and technicians from the immigrant communities to the region's economy and state bureaucracy. They were also buffer schools that served to maintain the purity of the student body at the elite educational institutions. Moreover, as the popularity of increasingly diverse forms of music grew, the ruling class also established and funded the summer concerts of the Boston Pops Orchestra, once again attempting to domesticate popular culture and to appropriate for itself the roles of proprietor and sole arbiter of good taste.

The Boston ruling class was not alone in its cultural entrepreneurship in the closing decades of the nineteenth century. In New York City, J. Pierpont Morgan and other Wall Street "architects of their own fortunes," not the old aristocracy, established the American Museum of Natural History in 1868 and the Metropolitan Museum of Art a year later to possess, exhibit, and lock up scientific facts and fine art that caught their fancy. Besides their own bequests, they requested and received gifts of land and financial support from the Tammany Hall politicians of the city to erect buildings and purchase collections, which they controlled (Kennedy 1968). Custodians of culture in other cities also opened fine arts or natural history museums that collected antiquities: Washington, Philadelphia, Chicago, Detroit, Brooklyn, St. Louis, Cincinnati, Pittsburgh, San Francisco, Newark, and Davenport, Iowa (Meyer 1979). Other museums established during this period were linked with universities or world fairs: the Peabody Museum of American Archaeology and Ethnology at Harvard (1865), the U.S. National Museum (1879), the University Museum of Archaeology and Paleontology affiliated with the University of Pennsylvania (1887), the Field Museum in Chicago (1893), and the Museum of Archaeology at the University of California (1899). All of them acquired or purchased art objects and archaeological collections, especially from colonies or countries that were economically dependent; this promoted the rapid expansion of both art and antiquities markets and the looting of archaeological sites for profit (Wade 1985).

Two historic blocs crystallized in the 1880s and 1890s. Both involved cross-class alliances and were dominated by fractions of the ruling class. Elsewhere, I have called them the Eastern Establishment and the Core Culture (Patterson 1986a). The appearance of the Eastern Establishment was recognized and acknowledged at the time, judging by Lewis Henry Morgan's (1963, 537) observation in 1877 that modern civilization brought "... into full vitality that 'greed of gain' (*studium licri*), which is now such a commanding force in the human mind" and by numerous condemnations of investment bankers and industrialists from the East Coast.

The Eastern Establishment was dominated by the leaders of large corporations and the investment banks of Boston and New York, who came to exert a preponderant influence in the decision-making processes of the government in Washington. They promoted expansion, both domestic and overseas, to ensure the continued prosperity of their firms (Kolko 1963; Weinstein 1968; Williams 1961, 343–89). They oversaw the formation of technical agencies in the government and the emergence of specialists. They shaped American educational policy and created a national science policy "more responsive to the needs of society" through the activities of various philanthropic foundations like the Carnegie Institution of Washington (Dupree 1957, 271–301; Reingold 1979; Slaughter and Silva 1980; Weischadle 1980). The leading intellectual of the Eastern Establishment, who promulgated and shaped many of the policies of the Progressive Era, was Elihu Root from the Hudson River Valley. Root served variously as a corporate lawyer for the House of Morgan and other monopolies, secretary of war, secretary of state, U.S. senator, and chairman of the boards of trustees of the Carnegie Institution of Washington and the Carnegie Corporation (Jessup 1938; Leopold 1954).

Although the national capitalists, who constituted the ruling fraction of the Core Culture, shared the Eastern Establishment's views about the sanctity of private property and apprehension of the largely immigrant urban working class, they opposed the intrusion of East Coast investment banks and the formation of industrial monopolies. Many were also anti-imperialists who saw overseas business ventures as a threat to jobs at home. The Core Culture dominated in the new cities and towns and rural areas outside the Boston-Washington axis. Its centers of gravity were located in the South, the Midwest, and the West—those parts of the country that had only recently been incorporated or brought back into the national state and where resistance to the state and the ruling class was most intense and diverse. This opposition included organizations that promoted the traditional values of the laissez-faire entrepreneur and opposed the ideas, interests, and intrusion of the East Coast industrial monopolies and Wall Street investment banks; it also included democratic movements that advocated civil rights, women's suffrage, trade unionism, populism, prohibition, and new religions.

As a result, the organic intellectuals who were fully immersed in the social relations of the Core Culture and gave voice to its sentiments regularly had to confront and tame more varied and potentially volatile groups and circumstances than their counterparts in the Eastern Establishment. Those intellectuals included Edgar Lee Hewett, founder of the Santa Fe renaissance; Charles Fletcher Lummis, city editor of the *Los Angeles Times;* Basil L. Gildersleeve, Confederate officer, classics professor, and spokesman for southern culture; Joseph LeConte, the Carolina-born, Harvard-educated geologist and educator at the University of California; John Wesley Powell, explorer and naturalist of the West, advocate of arid land democracy, and government bureaucrat; and Dwight L. Moody, Chicago-based evangelist and founder of the Moody Bible Institute (Briggs and Benario 1986; Chauvenet 1983; Darrah 1951; Davis 1990, 20–30; Marsden 1980; Stegner 1953). For the most part, they could not remake history and tradition in the same way Eastern Establishment intellectuals did when they succeeded in casting the New England Puritans and their Yankee descendants as the symbolic founders and true representatives of the American nation itself. The effect is that the Core Culture has had, from its inception, a much more complex and richly textured fabric than the historic bloc dominated by international monopoly and finance capital (Cronon, Miles, and Gitlin 1992; Nash 1991; Nash and Etulain 1989; Woodward 1960).

American society changed slowly but perceptibly after the Spanish-American War and more rapidly during and after World War I. The government accumulated capital through taxes and became a consumer of goods and services. It acquired land in the West. The population began to shift westward as immigrants from the East, the Midwest, and the South poured into the western states. The Great Lakes industrial states gained new importance because of the steel, tire, and automobile factories in the Detroit-Chicago-Pittsburgh triangle; their cities attracted immigrants, especially ones from the rural areas of the South who came northward to work in the factories. As consumption and the demand for new commodities grew, new firms appeared to meet them; for example, the number of automobiles in the United States quadrupled in the 1920s. At the same time, some firms began to build refineries, factories, and assembly plants in low-wage areas outside the northern industrial states.

The dominant class fractions of Eastern Establishment and the Core Culture temporarily set aside their differences after World War I. The Eastern Establishment retained control of foreign policy, while the emerging national capitalists of the Core Culture—for example, Henry Ford and the independent oil producers from the Gulf states or California—gained a larger voice in domestic affairs. Nationalism, emphasizing a perceived WASP heritage and a crusade for "100 percent Americanization," cemented the alliance (Higham 1981, 194–299). The dominant classes moved against the urban working class: The radical unions were suppressed; the socialist movement was crushed through legislation, raids, and deportations; restrictive immigration laws were imposed; and Jim Crow laws denied African Americans their rights in both the North and South.

The chief architect of the alliance was Herbert Hoover, secretary of commerce under Harding and Coolidge and president from 1928 to 1932. Hoover perceived the corporate political economy of the United States as being composed of three functional elements: capital, which included industrialists, financiers, and agricultural operators; labor; and the public, which government represented. He believed no element should be dominant and argued that the role of government was to balance, coordinate, and regulate the relationships of the other two (Williams 1961, 425–38). His functionalist interpretation of U.S. society had considerable support from corporations, conservative labor leaders, and the inhabitants of small towns. Opposition to his views was strongest in the industrial cities and in the poor, rural states of the Deep South.

NEW NEEDS, NEW EDUCATION, NEW PROFESSIONS

The expansion and reorganization of old businesses and the creation of new ones in the wake of the Civil War and Reconstruction provided a new medium for regional conflicts manifested in the divergent interests of the national and international capitalists and expressed in the emerging cultural concerns of the Core Culture and the Eastern Establishment. They also opened new employment and educational opportunities for both men and women, as the work force became increasingly segmented and hierarchically organized. These changes were mirrored by the reorganization of college curricula, a dramatic expansion in the number of institutions of higher learning, and the professionalization of science. Up to that time, science had largely been the domain of independent amateurs and a scattering of scientists employed by the government to perform specific activities in the Coast Survey, the Geological Survey, the Department of the Navy, and perhaps the Smithsonian Institution (Bruce 1987; Shils 1979, 22–23).

Several factors combined to change the structure of college curricula during and after the Civil War. First, the Morrill Land Grant College Act of 1862 required colleges receiving these awards to teach agriculture and mechanical arts without excluding scientific and classical studies. By the 1880s, more than forty institutions had received land grants; whereas some of them, such as Yale or the Agricultural College of Pennsylvania (Penn State), existed before 1862, others—the University of California, for instance— came into existence with the aid of the grants (Solomon 1985, 44–45).

Second, the dissolution of the old curricula was also fueled by gifts from wealthy philanthropists who stipulated that certain courses or lines of inquiry be pursued. For example, Joseph Sheffield, who made his fortune in cotton and railroads, established the Scientific School, which taught engineering at Yale; George Peabody's gift to Harvard in 1866 required the college to use the income from his bequest to purchase collections and books about American archaeology and ethnology, to establish a professorship in those subjects, and to build a fireproof museum; Jacob H. Schiff's gift to Harvard in 1889 required the college to show what the Semites had done for civilization; and the endowment of Phoebe Apperson Hearst—widow of the mine owner, land speculator, and U.S. senator—to the University of California in 1899 established and sustained the Museum of Archaeology, several monograph series, and the Department of Anthropology (Bruce 1987; Parker 1971, 155; Thoresen 1975).

Third, the adaptation of the German university system converted the Ph.D. degree at Johns Hopkins University in 1877–78, and a few years later at other institutions, into an advanced degree for students who intended to pursue research in a single field. In the decade that followed, university scientists and their students pushed to make scientific research an integral part of college programs, and, in the 1890s, graduate students formed an association to press various universities to establish uniform requirements for the doctoral degree (Hawkins 1979; Higham 1979; Reingold 1987). However, in spite of both legislative and philanthropic support for science, college students apparently did not flock to science courses. Figures from the University of Michigan for 1894 indicate 784 students enrolled in French, 736 in German, 679 in English, 662 in Latin and Greek, 648 in history, and 447 in physics or chemistry (Guralnick 1979, 119).

Thus, higher education was a minor growth industry in the United States between 1870 and 1900. It provided employment opportunities for a few and witnessed significant changes in who attended college. During this period, the number of institutions increased from 582 to 1,082, and the number of students rose from 52,000 to 230,000. In 1897, the chair of the managing committee of the American School of Classical Studies at Athens wrote that fifty-one of sixty-two men and eleven women who had attended the school between 1882 and 1896 were teachers or professors (Seymour 1897, 103). Nevertheless, it is essential to keep the changes in these numbers in perspective. The population of the United States was about one hundred million in 1900 and, as the figures indicate, only a small fraction of men and women attended college.

Land-grant universities in the Midwest and West began to accept women as students after the Civil War, whereas the elite private institutions in the Northeast and colleges in the South continued to exclude them. While a few private women's colleges had existed earlier, schools that opened in the North after the Civil War—Vassar (1865), Wellesley (1875), Smith (1875), and Bryn Mawr (1884)—were quickly emulated elsewhere. Both the number and percentage of women enrolled in U.S. colleges and universities rose steadily during this period: 11,000 and 21 percent in 1870 to 85,000 and 37 percent in 1900. In 1902, 52 percent of the students at the University of Chicago were women, and they received 56 percent of the degrees awarded that year. The women attending college in the United States during this period came

largely from the emerging middle classes rather than the wealthy, which "... pre-
ferred to educate daughters privately at home, in boarding schools, and through travel
abroad" (Solomon 1985, 44, 62–64). About a quarter of the students auditing classics
lectures in Germany during this period were Americans, and a majority of those were
women (Gildersleeve 1896, 728–30). A number of women pursued archaeology as
a profession or serious avocation between 1890 and the 1920s; for example, they
delivered eight of the thirty-eight papers presented at the general meeting of the
Archaeological Institute of America in 1923.

Between 1875 and 1900, most of the individuals who conducted archaeological
research in the United States worked for the government. They were employed by
four agencies with intertwined histories: the Smithsonian Institution, the Geological
Survey, the National Museum, and the Bureau of American Ethnology. Their archaeological observations and reports were often incidental to their primary employment
as surveyors, artists, naturalists, or geologists. This group included John Wesley
Powell, William H. Holmes, William H. Dall, James Stevenson, Cosmo Mindaleff,
Cyrus Thomas, and Otis Mason, all of whom were educated in the Midwest or
Washington. For the most part, their work was centered in the territories of the
Southwest or on Indian mounds in the East and Midwest, although Holmes became
increasingly involved in a dispute over the antiquity of people in the Americas during
the 1890s. Jesse W. Fewkes, a naturalist who had been director of Harvard's Museum
of Zoology, joined the Bureau of American Ethnology in 1897 to continue research in
the Southwest and later to continue work in the Caribbean possessions (Hart 1976;
Hinsley 1979, 1981; Lacey 1979; Meltzer and Dunnell 1992, xii–xiv; Noelke 1974).

During the 1880s and 1890s, some archaeologists supported their research with
income derived from other sources; for example, Frederick Ober, who spent one
semester at Massachusetts Agricultural College, used commissions from the
Smithsonian Institution for ornithological specimens and royalties from his travel books
and adventure novels to sustain inquiries in the Yucatán and Mexico and to lay the
foundations for Caribbean archaeology. Others were paid to conduct archaeological
research by institutional sponsors and private patrons. One was Adolph Bandelier, the
Illinois shopkeeper, whose research in the Southwest was subsidized by the
Archaeological Institute of America and whose excavations in Peru were paid for by the
American Museum of Natural History. Another was Frank Hamilton Cushing, whose
archaeological research in the Southwest in the late 1880s was underwritten by Mary
Hemenway, a wealthy Boston capitalist, and whose excavations at Key Marco, Florida,
in 1895–96 were supported by Phoebe Hearst and William Pepper, a Philadelphia
physician and the provost of the University of Pennsylvania (Mark 1980, 26, 96–130).
Hearst's subsequent gift to the University of California in 1899 underwrote the inves-
tigations and collections made by two German-trained, professional archaeologists,
Max Uhle in Peru and George Reisner in Egypt. With later gifts, she transferred
Reisner's work to Harvard and the Boston Museum of Fine Arts, which allowed him
to pursue his research in a new institutional setting and to provide U.S. students—A. V.
Kidder, among others—with training in field research and recording methods in Egypt.

Museums became major loci of employment for archaeologists between 1890
and 1932. The earliest with explicit commitments to archaeology were the Peabody
Museum of American Archaeology and Ethnology at Harvard established in 1866

and the University Museum of Archaeology and Paleontology at the University of Pennsylvania founded in 1889. Philanthropist George Peabody's donation to Harvard was brokered by his nephew, dinosaur paleontologist Othniel Marsh, who had close personal and professional relations with Louis Agassiz, the immigrant Swiss naturalist who founded the Museum of Comparative Zoology at Harvard (Lurie 1988; Parker 1971, 154–55). Two of Agassiz's students were the first appointments. Jeffries Wyman, a comparative anatomist, was named curator. After Wyman's death in 1874, the next curator was Frederic Ward Putnam, who had organized the museum established by Peabody in Salem. By 1868, the museum had already received gifts of Indian antiquities from residents of the Merrimac Valley in eastern Massachusetts, purchased collections of stone implements and pre-Roman objects from northern Europe, and sponsored archaeological excavations in the eastern United States and Nicaragua. An 1888 bequest from Charles Bowditch permitted the museum to initiate long-term archaeological activities in Honduras and the Yucatán and to begin sporadic explorations in the Andean countries (Brew 1968; Hinsley 1984, 1985b).

The driving force behind the creation of the University Museum of Archaeology and Paleontology was William Pepper, the provost of the University of Pennsylvania in the 1880s and 1890s. Pepper understood archaeology as "the past history of human civilization from an evolutionary perspective ... [and included] the study of living peoples ... [as] part of 'Archaeology'" (Darnell 1970, 81). He made several faculty appointments to cement the ties he envisioned between the new museum and the university: anthropologist Daniel Brinton, the German-trained Babylonian archaeologist Herman V. Hilprecht, and Morris Jastrow, a German-trained Near Eastern philologist. The linkages quickly disintegrated after his death in 1898, as local amateurs, museum patrons, and board members led by Curator Sarah Stevenson pushed for the collection of objects rather than the construction of a historical social science. Stevenson's seven-year reign over museum affairs was apparently marred by almost continuous conflict between the professional archaeologists and museum administrators (Darnell 1970, 1988; Winegrad 1993).

Frederic W. Putnam—after a successful career as director of the Peabody Museum in Salem, owner-publisher of *The American Naturalist,* permanent secretary of the American Association for the Advancement of Science, and research archaeologist—became Curator of the Peabody Museum at Harvard in 1874. He was subsequently named Director and Peabody Professor. Putnam was recognized as a museum administrator skilled in the construction of anthropology programs. During the 1890s, he was consulted by the American Museum of Natural History, the Field Museum, and Phoebe Hearst when she established the Museum of Archaeology at the University of California. This does not mean that everyone followed his advice. William Rainey Harper, the orientalist who became president of the Rockefeller-financed University of Chicago in 1892, and the Core Culture capitalists who bankrolled the Field Museum and the Chicago World's Fair did not (Cole 1985; Miller 1975; Rydell 1978, 1984). However, it does mean that many associates of Putnam—Franz Boas, for example—and most of the men trained in Americanist archaeology at Harvard between 1894 and 1914 were either affiliated with or employed by museums actively acquiring collections; others—such as Marshall Saville or Samuel Lothrop—purchased collections for wealthy patrons, notably the

Duc de Loubat and George Heye, and published papers about the materials to increase their monetary value.

With respect to professionalization and the increasing specialization that inevitably accompanies it, two features combined to make Harvard somewhat unique between the late 1880s and the 1920s. The first consisted of the immensely popular fine arts courses, emphasizing classical antiquity and the Renaissance, taught each semester by Charles E. Norton and his successors at the Fogg Museum of Fine Arts; Julius Sachs' course on museums, which introduced its students to the dealers, curators, and collectors of the art world; the courses on American archaeology and ethnology, Paleolithic archaeology, and physical anthropology taught at the Peabody Museum; and the research program in Middle American archaeology underwritten by Bowditch. The various museums built at Harvard—the Peabody, Fogg, Semitic, and Yenching Institute—and the map of world history they create celebrated the increasing specialization of archaeology after the 1880s, whereas the University Museum hid the fragmentation behind the facade of a single building. The second feature was the Archaeological Institute of America, established by Norton, Putnam, and others in 1879, whose center of gravity was firmly controlled by Harvard and the Boston ruling class with their Eastern Establishment cultural outlook. Many of its founders were also involved in creating the Boston Museum of Fine Arts and the Boston Symphony.

The primary focus of the Archaeological Institute of America was ancient civilization, the study of which had to be pursued in the lands bordering the eastern Mediterranean, especially Greece. However, it did provide financial support for Bandelier's research in the Southwest territories and Mexico in the early 1880s. The institute was also concerned with increasing the collections of various museums and with establishing scholarships for the study of archaeology at Harvard, Yale, Columbia, and other colleges (Norton et al. 1880, 13–26; Sheftel 1979). In 1881, it established the American School of Classical Studies at Athens to promote the study of classical literature, art, and antiquities; in 1895, the institute founded the School of Classical Studies in Rome. To a certain extent, this both acknowledged and institutionalized the separation of classical studies into Greek and Roman specializations. In 1900, the institute collaborated with the American Oriental Society, the Society of Biblical Literature, and a number of universities and theological seminaries to launch the American Schools of Oriental Research in Palestine to pursue various kinds of biblical studies, including archaeology, in the Holy Land (King 1983, 27).

While its interest in American archaeology did not waver, the institute cut back its support for research in the Americas in the late 1880s, precisely at the time the Peabody Museum of American Archaeology and Ethnology and the federal government were expanding their support for archaeological investigations in the United States and Middle America. Like William Pepper of the University Museum, the executive committee of the institute believed that Native Americans had never attained a high degree of civilization and, consequently, had little direct bearing on its progress. The importance of American archaeology, in their view, was to complete the picture of the early history of the human race, of its primitive condition, and of its first steps out of savagery. It afforded analogies with the prehistoric archaeology of the Old World (Hinsley 1985b; Norton et al. 1880, 18–21). However, the institute renewed its interest in Americanist archaeology in 1905, largely as a result of intense lobbying by the residents of New Mexico; this led to the formation of the School of American Research under the direction of Edgar L. Hewett, who maintained an ambivalent relation, at best, with the Eastern Establishment (Hewett 1910; Hinsley 1986). For instance, in the 1920s, Hewett resisted the efforts of John D. Rockefeller, Jr., to transform Santa Fe into a "Williamsburg West." Rockefeller responded by creating and generously funding the Laboratory of Anthropology, which competed with the school for financial support for the next thirty years (Douglas Schwartz, personal communication, 1992; Stocking 1982b).

The shifting emphases and increasing specialization of archaeology, its fragmentation, are revealed in the titles and contents of the journals it published. Eleven volumes of the *American Journal of Archaeology and History of Fine Arts* were published in Boston between 1885 and 1896; their pages regularly contained news about excavations and discoveries in Europe, Africa, Asia, and America. The title was abbreviated in 1897, and a new series, the *American Journal of Archaeology,* which continues to the present day, was initiated (Donohue 1985). However, the topography of the news department and annual bibliography were modified; the new categories were Classical, Egyptian, Oriental, Christian, Byzantine and Medieval Art, Renaissance Art, and America. The classification became even more fine grained in 1932 to include Classical, Oriental and Egyptian, Far Eastern, Prehistoric, Early Christian and Byzantine, Medieval, Renaissance, United States, Mexico, and Central and South America. In the new classificatory scheme, the archaeology of civilization—that is, Mediterranean Europe, especially Greece and, to a lesser extent, Rome—remained hegemonic, both in terms of the financial support it received from members and patrons and the number of pages devoted to materials from that part of the world.

The creation of the Archaeological Institute of America marked a turning point in how archaeology was conceptualized. Up to that time, the view that archaeology was the study of ancient societies was the dominant one. Afterwards, it was increasingly seen as the study of ancient remains. This perception resonated with professionalization: the appearance of new technical specializations; the growth of fine arts, anthropology, and natural history museums; technically specialized languages and discourses; the gradual exclusion of amateurs from participation; and the growth of state bureaucracies and university faculties. The backdrop was the emerging "war between science and religion"—the rapid rise of the neopositivist worldview of pragmatism and the related decline of transcendentalism, which underpinned, among other things, the controversies surrounding the acceptance of Darwinist thought in the United States (Cashdollar 1989; Kuklick 1977; Russett 1976).

The professionalization of archaeology transformed archaeological discourse. The arena in which it occurred gradually shifted from one that was open to the amateur cultivator of the field to another that was increasingly restricted to the academically certified and employed scholar. As amateurs were gradually squeezed out of the arena and their place usurped by the employed technician, their word no longer carried the same weight as that of the professional archaeologist. As the views of the professional became increasingly privileged in the discourse, the content of the discourse was also transformed. Besides more detailed descriptions of objects and sites, they introduced an elaborated technical language involving new concepts—stratigraphy, associations, and gravelots—new procedures for acquiring and recording information.

The new language eliminated any claims and assertions that were justified by reference to the speaker's social position rather than social competence. Arguments grounded in this new linguistic code became increasingly important in buttressing arguments that sustained or refuted positions related to wider social issues. In the early 1890s, W. H. Holmes (1893, 135), the archaeologist at the Bureau of American Ethnology, summarized views he was already clarifying a decade earlier:

> In a recent number of *Science* I ventured to express the hope that a new era was dawning in American archaeologic science.... I laid particular stress upon the deceptive and meagre nature of the evidence already on record and ventured to point out the demands of the future with respect to certain lines of research.... I strongly deprecate personalities in scientific discussion....

The rapid development of the new methods is perhaps most easily recognized by comparing Squier and Davis's 1848 detailed descriptions of mounds in the Mississippi and speculations about their origins with later writings. In a set of instructions for archaeological research that he prepared fourteen years later, George Gibbs wrote:

> The Smithsonian Institution, being desirous of adding to its collections in archaeology all such materials as bears upon the physical type, the arts and manufactures of the original inhabitants of America, solicits the cooperation of officers of the army and navy, missionaries, superintendents, and agents of the Indian department, residents in the Indian country, and travellers to that end.
>
> Among the first of the desiderata is a full series of the skulls of American Indians.... It is requisite for the purpose of arriving at particular results, that the most positive determination be made of the nation or tribe to which the skull belongs.... Unless, therefore, information of a direct nature is obtained, the collector should be guarded in assigning absolute nationality to his specimens. It would be better to state accurately the locality whence they are derived.

> (GIBBS 1962, 392–94)

He continued, indicating that specimens of art, especially the period from the arrival of the Europeans, were also desired. He wrote that "[t]he utmost care should be taken to ascertain with utmost certainty the true relations of these objects" (Gibbs 1862, 394). While stressing the importance of provenance and the depth at which objects were found, he did not point out the fact that objects recovered from the same stratum were contemporary with one another. This contrasts markedly with William Dall's (1877, 47) observation that the ditch "... gave us a clear idea of the formation and constitution of the shell-heaps; enabled me to distinguish between the different strata and their contents; to make the observations repeatedly; to fully confirm them by experience in many localities; and thus to lay the foundations for the generalizations [about cultural development] suggested in this paper."

By the time archaeological discourse was being professionalized in the 1880s and dominated increasingly by technicians, the emergent professional archaeologists already possessed a well-established set of analytical categories to describe people. Depending on their character, the objects of their attention might be savages, barbarians, or civilized peoples; Christians, Semites, or pagans; members of different races or tribes. Furthermore, none of the categories had unproblematic single or fixed meanings. Barbarians, for instance, might be farmers, nomadic Celtic shepherds, German tribes menacing the Roman Empire, Aegean populations that neither spoke Greek nor recognized the polis as a form of society, or pagans threatening Christendom. All were possible referents (Jones 1971; Shaw 1983; Stepan 1986; Stocking 1982a, 42–68; Tisdall 1894).

Thus, when a people was described as savage, barbarian, or civilized, the term had multiple layers of meaning. Each category was a construction, a combination of interrelated unit ideas that could be assembled and dismantled at will in order to meet the needs of a particular situation. These unit ideas resonated with what authors think about the essence of the human condition, the role of history, the meaning of progress, the implications of ideas about superiority and inferiority, the effects of environment, the existence of race and the importance of heredity, the degree to which different groups were educable, laissez-faire economic policies, social reform, imperial expansion, colonial rule and the relation of subject population to the state, as well as their sentiments about assimilation and segregation or the different forms such practices and institutions might take. The categories used to organize news and bibliographies in the *American Journal of Archaeology* were also codes: *Christian* was equated with the New Testament, Greece, Europe, and Eastern Establishment culture rooted in Unitarian or liberal Congregationalist thought and missionaries from New England. *Semitic* resonated with the Old Testament, Egypt and the Orient, the Core Culture, and actual or potential missionaries of a more fundamentalist or evangelical persuasion, such as William Albright or James Breasted, who came from the Midwest, South, or Far West.

It is clear that the categories were not always applied consistently, even by the same individual. For instance, the ruling class generally believed around the turn of the century that hierarchies of races and cultures existed; however, they were either inconsistent or disagreed with each other about the placement of particular groups in this hierarchy. Henry Cabot Lodge, a U.S. imperialist of the late nineteenth century, was generally sympathetic to African Americans but quite antagonistic toward Indians, whom he thought deserved to be crushed because they were cruel and stood in the way of expansion and the spread of civilization (Williams 1980, 815). Thus, individuals overlapped and interlocked old categories—savage, civilization, racial hierarchy, and progress, in Lodge's case—to create new images and metaphors. Meanings were added and erased in process, and the inconsistencies and discrepancies they generated often passed unnoticed or were at least not mentioned in the circles where they were deployed.

THE DEVELOPMENT OF AMERICANIST ARCHAEOLOGY

From the 1880s onward, archaeologists were concerned with acquiring collections for museums. For instance, in 1881, James Stevenson, the geologist employed by the Geological Survey, sent ten thousand pounds of archaeological objects from Moki Pueblo and twenty thousand pounds from Zuñi Pueblo, both in New Mexico, to the U.S. National Museum. A decade later, Jesse Fewkes sent forty thousand pounds of artifacts in a single year. However, they had other goals as well. Those conducting research in the United States sought to resolve three questions: Who built the mounds, how long had people lived in the Americas, and why were the American Indians of the Southwest apparently so different from their neighbors or native peoples in the eastern United States? Archaeologists working in Central America, the Yucatán, and the Caribbean surveyed regions that were increasingly dominated by U.S. political and economic interests and provided potentially important background information about the history of humanity and the degree to which civilization had or had not developed in those regions.

In *Ancient Mounds of the Mississippi Valley*, Squier and Davis (1848) concluded that the Mound Builders were a separate race from the contemporary Indian populations of the eastern United States. During the last half of the nineteenth century, writers, who ignored the fact that historic Indians built mounds, used their conclusion to embellish what was already an elaborate image: The mounds "... were the vestiges of a dense and extinct population whose advance in civilization was much superior to that of the known American Indians" (Henshaw 1883, xxxi). For some, especially the German immigrants who belonged to the Davenport (Iowa) Academy of Sciences, animal figurines attributed to the Mound Builders clearly showed that they had immigrated and brought civilization to the Plains (Silverberg 1968, 166–221). This view echoed the sentiments of the new immigrants, most of whom came from the agricultural region of southern Germany, where the practice of agriculture, not industry or commerce, was the sign of civilization and refinement. Another claimed that effigies—apparently fakes carved to cater to the whims of the burgeoning antiquities markets—showed that the Mound Builders were contemporary with mastodons, which implied they arrived in the distant past when herds of shaggy elephants still browsed in the Mississippi Valley.

During the nineteenth century, the federal government built its Indian policy on John Locke's argument that any land cultivated by persons for their subsistence was part of their property. In its view, because most of the indigenous populations in the eastern United States did not farm, they had no legal claims on the land and could be dispossessed of their homelands and removed to Indian territories or reservations, where they would be granted lands and taught agriculture and civilization. The federal government was still actively dispossessing Indians from surplus lands in 1887, and it had no interest in promoting questions about their property rights. Consequently, in 1883, the U.S. Congress directed the Bureau of American Ethnology to investigate the mounds; Cyrus Thomas was placed in charge of the Division of Mound Explorations, which was organized to examine the mounds and other works east of the Rocky Mountains. In order to determine who built the mounds, Thomas spent seven years traveling and gathering information about hundreds of mounds. Although Thomas's (1894) final report did not appear until 1894, his conclusions were already evident a decade earlier: (1) The mounds were either built by Indian tribes that resided in those regions when the Europeans arrived or by their ancestors; (2) there was no evidence that the Mound Builders came from the tropics or migrated from the Old World; and (3) the level of cultural development of the Mound Builders was similar to that of contemporary Indians with subsistence economies based on hunting and foraging. Because Manifest Destiny reigned, Thomas never really came to grips with the implications of the fact that some of these tribes farmed; agricultural practices and their origins were transformed from legal questions to technical matters that could be resolved with further investigation.

The second issue that weighed on the minds of U.S. archaeologists concerned the origins of American Indians and their antiquity in the New World, questions that had been asked since the sixteenth century (Huddleston 1967). Although the early writers believed they had not been in the Americas for very long, perhaps only a few centuries, the later ones inquired whether they lived there during the Ice Age when now extinct animals roamed across the landscape. In the 1870s and 1880s, Frederick W. Putnam, C. C. Abbott of Philadelphia, and others argued for great antiquity (Meltzer 1983). They pointed to stone tools from the Trenton Gravels that were morphologically similar to those associated with extinct animals in Europe. They claimed the tools, found in geological deposits believed to date to glacial times, were ancient and indicated that a Paleolithic race had entered the Americas during or before the last Ice Age. In the 1880s, the term Paleolithic implied Ice Age, old, and European.

The existence of Old and New World branches of a Paleolithic race provided an explanation for the formation of buffer races, which built on established intellectual debates of the Gilded Age: geographical separation and subsequent degeneration in the inferior environments of the Americas (Gerbi 1973). This perception, which remained implicit in their work, was eventually brought to life in a series of murals at the American Museum of Natural History (Rainger 1991, 147–81). These portrayed prehistoric life in Europe; they emphasized that (1) race was a real biological category that determined physical features and culture, (2) the European race was pure and fixed over a long period of time, and (3) the Cro-Magnon race was superior over both Neanderthals and nature.

W. H. Holmes (1897) of the Bureau of American Ethnology disputed the claims of Putnam and Abbott in the 1890s. He argued that it was wrong to assume that simple tools have great antiquity, because American Indians still used such implements. He also argued that the glacial age of the Trenton Gravels was not proven and that the objects Putnam and Abbott claimed were ancient were actually quarry refuse left by modern Indians. The physical anthropologist Aleš Hrdlička entered the fray in 1902, and, after examining the anatomical features of the purportedly early skeletal remains in the United States, he concluded that all of the skeletons were morphologically modern and that none of them exhibited the amalgam of neanderthaloid and modern features he expected to observe among the earliest immigrants to the Americas (Hrdlička 1907).

Whereas Holmes argued that the American Indians were recent immigrants because their skeletal and artifactual remains had not been recovered from demonstrably old geological contexts, Hrdlička asserted that the skeletal remains from archaeological sites and the modern Native Americans he had measured were quite similar anatomically and exhibited no significant changes over time. In their view, the American Indians had neither evolved in the New World nor lived there very long. Their arguments resonated with the views of the capitalists who built museums, sponsored world's fairs, and understood "anatomically similar" to mean a homogeneous American Indian race producing a homogeneous culture that was part of nature. Those businesspeople saw American Indians as a baseline against which to measure the extent of the material progress that they themselves had created in such a short time (Rydell 1984). Thus, Hrdlička, like Franz Boas, challenged the ideas of biologically fixed races and racial hierarchies, which underwrote restrictive immigration and Jim Crow laws of the day.

The third area that attracted the attention of archaeologists in the 1880s was the American Southwest. White settlement was expanding in the territories, and U.S. investments in northern Mexico, as well as the Yucatán and Central America, were growing explosively. The territories also had spectacular ruins, which were the hallmark of people who were almost civilized and surely farmed as their descendants who still lived in the pueblos of the region did. Bandelier (1892, 579–90) believed that Casas Grandes, a site in northern Mexico, was an outlier of Southwest culture connected to the Pueblos by commerce and that similarities in architecture ultimately linked the Southwest and the Yucatán. His views echoed those of U.S. landowners in the border states of northern Mexico, who saw the area as an extension of the New Mexican and Arizona territories that the United States should annex.

Cushing and Fewkes, who worked in the Southwest between the late 1880s and 1910, used archaeology to inform their studies of myths and to suggest further connections between the Pueblos and Mexico and Central America. Their investigations strengthened the view that there were ancient connections between the U.S. Southwest and the civilizations to the south. However, after 1910, Fewkes's work was challenged by A. V. Kidder and others who complained about the way he used archaeology to verify migration myths. He had not dealt adequately with the chronology or spatial variation of Pueblo culture. By 1915, they had constructed chronologies based on changes in ancient pottery and architecture showing that aboriginal cultural development was autochthonous in the American Southwest and its outliers in northern Mexico. Consequently, the ancient civilizations of central Mexico, which were then being appropriated as symbols by parties struggling to control the revolutionary state, were no longer regarded as closely connected with what had happened in the Southwest. This isolationist perspective that separated the Southwest from neighboring peoples was pervasive throughout the twentieth century.

Around the turn of the century, archaeologists began to work more intensively in Latin America. Archaeological investigations in Peru, Mexico, and Central America, already the scene of significant U.S. and foreign investment, were sponsored by patrons or museums; those in the Caribbean involved both museums and the federal government. Institutions staked claims on different regions. Max Uhle worked in Peru for the University of California. The Caribbean was explored by Stewart Culin and William Farabee for the University Museum and by Fewkes for the U.S. National Museum. Middle America—effectively the Maya area of the Yucatán and Central America—was appropriated by Harvard and the Carnegie Institution of Washington. Frederick Starr from the University of Chicago and Hewett's School of American Research claimed northern Mexico. U.S. involvement in the archaeology of central Mexico was episodic until 1929, when George Vaillant and the American Museum of Natural History launched a research program in Mexico City. These investigations had the political support of Robert Morrow, the U.S. ambassador to Mexico; Theodore Roosevelt; and Clarence Hay, whose father had reformulated U.S. foreign policy when he was McKinley's secretary of state (Brunhouse 1971; Godoy 1977; Hinsley 1984; McVicker 1989; Rowe 1954; Sullivan 1989).

With the financial support of Charles Bowditch—descendant of Salem merchants and shipmasters, Boston investor, president of the Massachusetts Hospital Life Insurance Company and Pepperell Manufacturing Company, and a director of the Boston and Providence Railroad and American Bell Telephone companies—the Peabody Museum sent a series of archaeological expeditions to Central America and southern Mexico. These yielded information about previously unknown settlements, augmented the museum's collections, and provided training for the first generation of academically certified archaeologists in the United States. Bowditch established fellowships at the Peabody Museum and the Archaeological Institute of America to train students in the linguistics, ethnography, and epigraphy of the Maya region. He also paid for the translation of a series of papers, written in German, that were concerned with the calendrical systems, antiquities, and history of the Maya of southern Mexico and Central America (Holmes 1904, 9–10).

Bowditch's own research focused mainly on the intellectual labors of the Maya: their numeration, calendrical system, hieroglyphics, and astronomical knowledge. He adopted Morgan's assertion that writing or hieroglyphics marked the beginning of civilization; thus, the Maya were transformed from semicivilized barbarians to fully civilized peoples because of their hieroglyphic inscriptions. This also implied that the Maya had an elaborate system of law and government, engaged in commerce, lived in cities, and had achieved significant levels of development in the arts and sciences, including architecture.

Bowditch collaborated with William H. Holmes, head curator of anthropology at the Field Museum in Chicago from 1894 to 1897, and Zelia Nuttall, the European-educated granddaughter of a prominent San Francisco banker, to produce a new image of the historical development of Maya and Mexican society. They viewed ideas rather than work as the engines of social development. While continuing to emphasize the apparent autonomy of the Maya and the central Mexicans, they also pointed to the close connections between them. If the Maya were civilized, like ancient Greece or imperial Rome, then the ancient cultures of central Mexico were analogous to the barbarian kingdoms on the frontiers of those societies. Moreover, these semicivilized cultures in the borderlands of central Mexico were derived from the lost Maya civilization.

In their perspective, civilization was distinguished from barbarism because of the differentiation of intellectual activity from manual labor; they described Maya and Mexican civilizations increasingly in terms of the activities of an intelligentsia that was closely linked with the state and with the ruling class, if they did not themselves constitute that class. This formulation of the concept of civilization permitted divergent views about certain issues that could be investigated. For example, did an intelligentsia from the Old World introduce civilization to the Americas, or did this stratum and the activities associated with it develop autochthonously in the New World? Answers to such questions resonated in different ways with broader political-economic trends in U.S. society, such as the constitution of white-collar managerial and technical strata in offices and factories, as well as with various social and intellectual currents that developed between 1890 and 1914.

Before World War I, patrons supported archaeological investigations with gifts to individuals or donations to museums. The Carnegie Institution of Washington and the International School of American Archaeology and Ethnology in Mexico supported the research of "exceptional men" (Godoy 1977; Reingold 1979, 329; Rowe 1954, 6–7). The geographical focus of these inquiries was either outside the United States or in the newly annexed areas of the American Southwest. While some of the domestic excavations were carried out by individuals affiliated with museums, amateurs did most of the digging (Fagan 1977, 266–78, 293–98, 318).

Three aspects of the social transformation accompanying World War I were particularly significant for the development of Americanist archaeology. One was the extension of the educational franchise to sections of the middle classes; as college enrollments grew during the 1920s, the number of anthropology departments or programs increased. Another was the construction of a national science policy. The third involved new ways of financing archaeological research; these were promoted by Eastern Establishment philanthropies and channeled the kinds of archaeological activities that were important in popular culture.

Foundations supported by the Carnegie and Rockefeller philanthropies promoted educational and scientific policies that would strengthen the position of the United States vis-à-vis the other capitalist countries (Howe 1980; Marks 1980; Reingold 1979). They rationalized the production of knowledge and mobilized and organized scholars on a national scale by providing funds for scientists who had previously worked on uncoordinated research projects (Slaughter and Silva 1980, 76). A new breed of entrepreneur emerged in the 1920s who organized and administered large-scale projects involving teams of scholars and who moved easily within and between the university and business communities (Arnove 1980, 8).

The National Research Council (NRC)—a federation of educational, governmental, philanthropic, and industrial research agencies—was formed to organize scientific research for the war and to advise the government. The NRC was supported by the federal government during the war and then by the private sector. The Carnegie Foundation of New York contributed more than 60 percent of the $8 million it received from private sources between 1919 and 1922.

The Division of Anthropology and Psychology was constituted when the NRC was reorganized in 1919 (Stocking 1976, 1–12). Its purpose was to coordinate research already in progress, to advise those seeking advice, to encourage personnel development, and to foster a small number of projects. During the 1920s, it administered small grants from the Rockefeller Foundation, nineteen of which supported archaeological research in the United States. In 1921, the division created the

Committee on State Archaeological Surveys, the purpose of which was to promote a greater interest in archaeology (Wissler 1922, 233). Interest was first directed toward the Mississippi Valley—especially Indiana, Illinois, Iowa, and Missouri—in the 1920s. The committee became a clearinghouse for archaeological research in the United States and Canada; it published annual reports of the activities of the various local societies. In 1929, the Carnegie Corporation provided financial support to help the committee continue its work.

The committee was quite successful. The number of state archaeological societies increased, especially after the 1929 crisis. This was associated with the growth of archaeological sites as tourist attractions and the increased looting of archaeological sites and sale of antiquities. These activities were probably most prevalent in areas such as Oklahoma and the Southeast where rural peoples were separated from their lands and means of production. Some of the dispossessed supported themselves and their families by looting and selling objects in the rapidly expanding antiquities markets created by museum curators and private collectors. Thus, an alliance of sorts, based on a shared interest in objects from the aboriginal past, formed between the middle and working classes. The middle classes collected objects; the working classes looted them to survive.

During the 1920s, which marked the peak of policies aimed at Indian assimilation, U.S. archaeologists accepted the view that American Indian societies were effectively destroyed or so dramatically transformed by European contact that their arts and crafts were fundamentally different from those recorded by early travelers or ethnographers (Trigger 1980a, 668–70). They incorporated this perspective into their research and concerned themselves mainly with the form of objects rather than how they were used or who used them. They viewed ancient American Indian societies as static and saw diffusion and migration, rather than internal development, as the major motors of change. Implicit in their interpretations was the perception that the communal and tributary societies of the American Indians were weak or inferior, because they were unable to withstand the onslaught of American capitalist development.

During the 1920s, views about the fragility of pre-Columbian Indian societies were seized and quickly deployed by the proponents of nativism who sought to assert or affirm the superiority of WASP culture. The stereotypes of the American Indian formulated before the war remained largely unchallenged. They became part of the resurgence of racism reflected by the passage of segregation and immigration laws and the increased support of eugenics research by the National Research Council and the Carnegie Institution of Washington (Allen 1986; Higham 1981, 264–330; Woodward 1974, 111–48).

The archaeologists' treatment of America's past dovetailed with new attitudes about history held by the Core Culture and the Eastern Establishment (Bodnar 1992; Glassberg 1990). Henry Ford, who underwrote the development of an ultramodern form of capitalism based on assembly-line production, also reflected many of the attitudes of the Core Culture. He financed the restoration of history at Greenfield Village and the Henry Ford Museum, which celebrated life in the rural republic, the harmonious relations between craftspeople and peasants, and the common people rather than the patrician elite. John D. Rockefeller, Jr., who had grown up with corporate capitalism, began the construction of Colonial Williamsburg, which celebrated the planter elite as the progenitors of those timeless values and ideals that constituted what was truly American (Wallace 1981, 68–78). American Indians were part of neither vision.

Americanist archaeology outside the United States served a different purpose. It was pragmatic and relativist: supporting the status quo in some countries, undermining it in others. The political conditions in Latin America had important consequences for archaeologists from the United States. Guided by the ideology of Pan-Americanism and the Monroe Doctrine, U.S. corporations and the state penetrated deeply into the economies of the Latin American nations during the 1920s. This was accomplished by stepped-up economic and military interference in the internal affairs of those countries, especially those in Central America and the Caribbean. The U.S. ruling class also viewed the Mexican Revolution and the changes it wrought as a real threat to the economic and social stability of the countries north of the Panama Canal. Between 1914 and 1916, Mexico seemed as threatening as the German submarines that ultimately brought the United States into World War I. U.S. relations with Mexico were also strained during the 1920s, because some U.S. business and political leaders believed Mexico was exporting Bolshevik propaganda to Central America and shipping arms to Sandino's rebels in Nicaragua, which was occupied at the time by the U.S. Marines who propped up its dictatorship (Katz 1981; Smith 1972).

This was the milieu in which several U.S. archaeologists worked in Latin America—for example, Sylvanus Morley, Herbert Spinden, J. Alden Mason, Samuel Lothrop, and Mark Harrington—and used their profession to obscure their activities as intelligence officers. It was also the milieu of the Carnegie Institution of Washington's Maya Project, which Morley planned and directed from its inception in 1915. For its first decade, the program was carried out exclusively in Guatemala, where it had close ties with the Boston-based United Fruit Company. Morley did not begin working at Chichén Itzá until 1924 because of the strained relations between the United States and Mexico, and Guatemala remained a safe place for the Carnegie personnel into the 1940s. Alfred V. Kidder, who became director of the Carnegie Institution's Division of Historical Research in 1929, reorganized the Middle American program to include ethnographic research in the Yucatán and Chiapas, which were not well-integrated into the Mexican state, and archaeological investigations in the American Southwest.

The Reorganization of Classical and Biblical Studies: Archaeology in the Context of Gilded-Age Racism and Anti-Semitism

The intimate connection that existed between classical and biblical studies before the Civil War was severed in its wake. Both fields fragmented internally. Classics witnessed the appearance of increasingly autonomous philological and archaeological specializations. Biblical studies divided along the linguistic and religious fracture line separating the Semitic texts of the Old Testament from the Greek books of the New Testament (Bernal 1987; Moore 1919; Shorey 1919). In the 1880s, U.S. students of classical and biblical literature traveled to Leipzig and Berlin to learn firsthand the historical-critical methods of the eminently successful "higher criticism" developed and taught in the German universities. Julius Wellhausen, one of the founders of higher criticism, believed that the Old Testament should be subjected to the same methods of analysis as other texts. Needless to say, this had an enormous impact on biblical studies. Consequently, classical philologists and New Testament scholars examined Greek texts, whereas students of the Old Testament examined texts written in Hebrew and other Semitic languages, including those found on the cuneiform tablets that were being unearthed in Mesopotamia (King 1983, 14–16).

The fragmentation of classics began shortly after the war. The American Philological Association, established in 1868, was modeled after the American Association for the Advancement of Science and the American Oriental Society. The "linguists, educators, and literary gentlemen" who founded it professed deep respect for German philological research; foreseeing the need for an increasingly fine-grained division of labor, they organized the society into seven sections. Comparative philology and literature dominated the early discussions, but the center of interest shifted in the 1880s toward classical philology—Greek or Latin— and the interpretation of ancient life along the northern littoral of the Mediterranean (Moore 1919, 13–15). These shifts were fueled by news of the French excavations at the Acropolis, the Germans' work at Olympus, and Schliemann's discoveries at Troy and Mycenae.

Whereas Rawlinson's discovery of cuneiform texts in 1835 and Layard's *Nineveh and Its Remains* published in 1850 had little apparent impact in the United States, they attracted the almost immediate attention of biblical scholars in England and Europe, who recognized their importance for Old Testament studies. As a result, biblical scholars, especially in Germany, began to focus their attention increasingly on the Hebrew texts of the Old Testament. They recontextualized the Bible in terms of its Afro-Asiatic connections rather than its linkages with the Greco-Roman world. But the initial enthusiasm for Assyriology waned rapidly among literalists, once it became apparent that the cuneiform texts challenged rather than supported literal readings of the Scriptures. At the same time, the Assyriologists, that handful of individuals who could read the cuneiform texts, struggled to assert and maintain the autonomy of their field of study rather than allowing it to be subsumed completely by biblical scholars (Kildahl 1959; Meade 1969).

This occurred in an intellectual milieu shaped by the increasing racism and anti-Semitism of the Gilded Age, and by the destabilization and reconstitution of American Protestant thought through its engagement with positivism, scientific naturalism, and Darwinism (Herbst 1965; Hofstadter 1955; Ross 1972, 1984; Russett 1976). The reconfiguration of classics and biblical studies toward the end of the nineteenth century mirrored these intellectual currents. New links were forged to join classics with Europe, civilization, Christianity, and the white race. In this new map, Hebrew and the Semitic languages were linked to Egypt, the Orient, Assyriology, Judaism; races that were not quite white; and oriental societies that did not achieve the same levels of development as those of ancient Greece or Rome. This was the milieu that led Jacob Schiff—New York banker, philanthropist, and a leader in the American Jewish Reform movement—to underwrite the Semitic Museum at Harvard "to show what the Semites had done for civilization." As a result of the reconfiguration of classics and biblical studies, classical archaeology and Assyriology came to occupy different spaces, both metaphorically and literally (Bernal 1987; Silberman 1982, 171–88).

Since its inception in 1842, the American Oriental Society had been one of the most broadly based learned societies in the United States; its members included academics, missionaries, diplomats, and amateurs devoted to promoting knowledge about the East. After the Civil War, most individuals interested in the Orient, including the Assyriologists and Old Testament scholars, belonged to this organization. In the 1880s, almost half of its members were professors, most of whom taught in theological seminaries. By contrast, the Archaeological Institute of America, like other Eastern Establishment professional societies established in the 1870s and 1880s, was almost devoid of clergy and individuals employed by seminaries from its inception. In 1890, when Cyrus Adler of Johns Hopkins and Morris Jastrow of the University of Pennsylvania proposed a series of reforms that would transform the "unprofessional character" of the American Oriental Society, the Core Culture members not only rejected their proposals but also eliminated the Classical Section (McCaughey 1984, 47–49). In other words, from the 1880s onwards, the two organizations appealed to different constituencies, and few individuals belonged to both. Those who did, such as William Albright and James Breasted, arguably the leading biblical and orientalist archaeologists of the first half of the twentieth century, were typically much more involved in Egypt and the Orient than in Europe or the Americas.

The chasm separating the two organizations reflected important geographical and cultural features that began to crystallize in the society during the 1870s. While Johns Hopkins and the University of Pennsylvania rivaled each other for dominance in Oriental Studies in the late 1880s, most of the other institutions providing some form of training at the time were located outside the Boston-Washington corridor; these included Chicago's Baptist Union Theological Seminary, Colgate, Missouri, Illinois, Vanderbilt, Michigan, and the University of Chicago (Meade 1969, 60–97). Classical archaeology and fine arts had two centers of gravity before World War I, judging both by the membership lists of the Archaeological Institute of America and by who published regularly in its journal. Universities in the Boston-Washington corridor—Johns Hopkins, Princeton, Yale, and Harvard—formed the eastern axis, whereas Cincinnati, Chicago, Cleveland, Michigan, and Washington University in St. Louis formed another in the Midwest.

Sociologically, this suggests that classical archaeology and the fine arts have deeper roots in Eastern Establishment culture and that oriental studies are more deeply and complexly embedded in the Core Culture. In contrast, both James Breasted and William Albright had deep roots in the Core Culture. Breasted, born in the Midwest, was influenced by Moody's evangelical Volunteer Student Movement as a young man and briefly flirted with the idea of becoming a missionary (Breasted 1977, 16–17). Albright was a lifelong evangelical Protestant, the Chilean-born son of missionaries, who attended public school and college in Iowa before he went to Johns Hopkins in 1913 as a graduate student and then a faculty member. He once remarked that, while "... very few Methodist students ever studied under him, there was a profusion of other Protestants (in particular Lutherans and Presbyterians) as well as many Catholics ... and Jews" (Freedman 1972, 7). These are religions well represented in the Core Culture.

Archaeological investigations in the Greco-Roman world and the Orient were financed in much the same way from the 1880s to 1932. These included gifts from individual patrons or from local societies that either supported particular expeditions or established funds to support exploration in particular areas. For example, one of the two expeditions sent to the Middle East between 1884 and 1900—an archaeological reconnaissance of Mesopotamia directed by William Ward—was organized by the American Oriental Society and financed entirely by Catherine Lorillard Wolfe, a New York philanthropist, art patroness, and tobacco heiress. The second was the Nippur Expedition, conducted over a series of years by the University of Pennsylvania and financed to a considerable extent by the Oriental Club of Philadelphia, a group of professors, clergy, bankers, and merchants (Bliss 1906; Hilprecht 1903; King 1983, 11–13). The major goal of the excavations at Nippur was to acquire cuneiform tablets for the University Museum.

The major organizational innovation of the Archaeological Institute of America was the creation of semiautonomous overseas schools and research centers based in national, colonial, or provincial capitals around the Mediterranean. These included the American School of Classical Studies at Athens founded in 1881 and the American School of Classical Studies in Rome created in 1895. Five years later, it collaborated with the other learned societies and a few seminaries and universities to launch the American Schools of Oriental Research in Palestine. A second center of the American Schools of Oriental Research was established in Baghdad in 1913 to facilitate U.S. archaeological research in Mesopotamia. These overseas institutes involved significant capital investments in buildings, personnel, and equipment that could sustain long-term investigations in a single region or at a major site of particular historical or cultural importance. They were organized along the lines of a modern corporation: The director, a senior scholar with an established reputation, supervised the largely autonomous activities of a large staff of technical specialists. Beginning scholars were concerned mainly with particular aspects of the investigation—for instance, architecture, epigraphy, coins, pottery, or sculpture. There was also the local staff—maids and cooks at the residence, clerks in the office, and hundreds of workmen who moved dirt during the field seasons or campaigns at the excavations (Stephen Dyson, personal communication, 1987).

The American School in Athens was particularly active before World War I; there was always much less activity at the school in Rome, presumably because of relative labor costs and the depth of nationalist criticism in Italy. In the mid 1890s, when the Archaeological Institute of America underwrote an expedition to Crete, the personnel of the school were engaged in a separate, long-term project in Corinth. Before World War I, the school had also conducted excavations on a smaller scale in Crete and the Agora in Athens. Several individuals who originally came to the school as students eventually joined its staff and established professional reputations before returning to the United States. For example, William Dinsmoor spent twelve years there before joining the Columbia faculty in 1920. Carl Blegen was continuously associated with the school for seventeen years before accepting his first teaching position at the University of Cincinnati in 1927; he completed his doctorate dissertation while serving as its secretary and assistant director. The record for longevity apparently belongs to Oscar Broneer, who was continuously affiliated with the school for twenty-five years before accepting a professorship at Chicago in 1949.

Individuals such as Howard Butler or T. Leslie Shear of Princeton, who had been affiliated with the school in Athens as students, subsequently led or partici- pated in expeditions to the eastern Mediterranean. Like the projects organized by the school, these expeditions frequently lasted several years or even decades. Butler directed a project in Syria from 1899 to 1909 and work for the American Society for the Exploration of Sardis in Asia Minor from 1910 to 1914. George Chase's partic- ipation in the 1914 season at Sardis marked Harvard's appearance in the archaeol- ogy of Asia Minor; Chase and George Hanfmann, one of the two appointments in classical archaeology at Harvard in the mid-1930s, maintained an almost continuous presence at Sardis and in the region until the early 1970s. Shear, who also worked in Asia Minor before World War I, turned his attention to work at Corinth from 1925 to 1931. For the next nine years, he directed the clearing of the Agora in Athens, a project underwritten financially by John D. Rockefeller, Jr.

Rockefeller's interest in archaeology was evident soon after he created the University of Chicago in 1892 and installed William Rainey Harper as its first pres- ident. Rockefeller regularly contributed to the support of the Haskell Oriental Museum established in 1894, which housed not only the museum but also the uni- versity's Departments of Comparative Religion and Semitic Languages and its Baptist Divinity School. In 1903, he gave $50,000 to the university, which Harper used himself to establish the Oriental Exploration Fund and to support excavations directed by his brother, Robert Harper, at Adab in Babylonia. In 1919, Rockefeller donated another $50,000 to establish the Oriental Institute, because of the confi- dence he had in the administrative ability, judgment, and foresight of Egyptologist James Breasted, who had written a best-seller in 1916 aimed at junior high school students: *Ancient Times, A History of the Early World.* As director of the new institute, Breasted used the funds to underwrite research on the ancient civiliza- tions of the Near East that crosscut established disciplines and to begin a monograph series that would publish the results. By 1929, Rockefeller had contributed an addi- tional $2.5 million to the Oriental Institute, which made Breasted one of the major academic entrepreneurs of the era (Breasted 1977; McCaughey 1984, 95–101; Meade 1969, 192–96).

In the decade preceding World War I, James Breasted and Albert T. Olmstead laid the foundations for ancient history in the United States. Both used inscriptions recovered from archaeological sites to write detailed histories. Breasted's *A History of Egypt,* which appeared in 1905, was quickly translated into German, Braille, and Russian. As a student, Olmstead, who was studying Akkadian at Cornell, became interested in Assyrian history. While a Fellow of the American Schools of Oriental Research in Jerusalem, he examined inscriptions and used them as the basis for his dissertation, *Western Asia in the Days of Sargon of Assyria,* which was written in 1906 and published in 1908. He spent 1906–7 at the American School in Athens and directed Cornell's excavations in Asia Minor in 1907–8. A year later, he became instructor of ancient history at the University of Missouri, teaching courses not only on the ancient Near East but also Greece and Rome. His *Assyrian Historiography,* which appeared 1916, was a critical examination of sources and the pitfalls of taking inscriptions at face value. He moved to the University of Illinois in 1917, and his *History of Assyria* appeared six years later (Meade 1969, 196–206). Although Breasted's and Olmstead's efforts were widely read and emulated by others, including the classical archaeologists, ancient history was a discipline whose center of gravity remained largely in the Midwest during this period.

Interest in European archaeology on or beyond the margins of the Greco-Roman world surged in the United States after the First World War. The impetus came from two sources and was a response to issues regarding race and human origins and redrawing national boundaries in Europe after the war. One involved an extension of the traditional interests of classical archaeologists into new domains. These included Christian and medieval archaeology in Spain or France, Roman Britain, Romanesque sculptures in France, Etruscan tombs, and the arrival of the Greeks, the consummate speakers of Indo-European or Indo-Aryan languages, in the Aegean area. The other source was the Smithsonian Institution's translation and publication of articles by European archaeologists—a practice introduced by Joseph Henry in 1847. This introduced U.S. scholars to the Paleolithic cultures of Europe.

The issues of Paleolithic cultures and the origin of human races attracted the attention of Charles Peabody and George G. MacCurdy, two of Putnam's students at Harvard in the early 1890s. By the turn of the century, they were conducting archaeological investigations in Europe and the Americas that incorporated ethnographic and physical anthropological information. They called their inquiries paleoethnology or prehistoric archaeology. For MacCurdy (1913, 1924), who believed both in the great antiquity of the genus Homo and in a hierarchy of relatively fixed racial types, ethnographic details from contemporary peoples were important, because they could shed light on cultural practices that were initially and most elaborately developed by the Paleolithic and Neolithic races of northwestern Europe. In 1921, MacCurdy and Peabody founded the American School of Prehistoric Research in Europe, which was affiliated with the Archaeological Institute of America. Three years later, MacCurdy published *Human Origins,* which surveyed European archaeological discoveries from Eolithic and Paleolithic times through the Bronze and Iron Ages, relating them to the physical and racial types that had produced them.

The formation of the school and the intermittent appearance of its publications from the Peabody Museum at Harvard beginning in 1926 effectively mark the beginning of sustained continuous interest in the preliterate history of Europe outside the confines of the Greco-Roman world and before its formation. At the time, its aim was to show how the civilization had emerged and flowered in the high cultures of the Mediterranean and then passed to the peoples of northern Europe. However, this happened at precisely the moment the existing interpretive framework for Europe was being challenged. On one hand, orientalists were beginning to portray European culture and technology as derivative from those of the Near East; on the other, the German archaeologist Gustav Kossinna and his followers were arguing that Central Europe had been a cultural mosaic since the Upper Paleolithic, that archaeological cultures reflected race and ethnicity, and that archaeological evidence provided a means for locating the ancient homeland of Indo-European (Aryan) speakers and for setting new national boundaries after the war. Kossinna was a migrationist who maintained that there was a hierarchy of passive and culturally creative races topped by blond, long-headed Aryans who spoke Indo-European. He claimed that the culture-creating peoples came from northern Europe, that they enslaved the inferior races of the south, that they used them to build great civilizations, and that they were ruined when they subsequently interbred with them. Only the Indo-Europeans who had remained in their Germanic homeland remained racially pure and therefore creative (Trigger 1989, 163–67).

DISCUSSION

Both classical and biblical studies were reconstituted toward the end of the nineteenth century. Archaeological evidence from different parts of the eastern Mediterranean was still incorporated into this set of loosely articulated discourses. New linkages were forged when archaeology was professionalized. Classical and biblical studies—not to mention Assyriology, New World archaeology, and Old World prehistory—were suddenly connected in ways that acquired new meaning. The activities of individuals who studied archaeological remains in the Old and New Worlds were linked, and a variety of theoretical perspectives—positivist, idealist, and Darwinist—gave rise to historicist explanations of the political-economic and social conditions that were emerging in the United States. Each of them challenged the Enlightenment and theological worldviews that prevailed in the United States. They questioned whether the Bible was a record of the unfolding of God's will or even whether history itself was governed by moral laws that passed eternally from one generation to the next. In place of divine intervention, they substituted naturalism and historicism—the ideas that society was the product of continuous historical change and that the changes could be best explained by reference to prior historical events or the unfolding of natural processes. For them, the past was different from but causally linked to the present; however, the nature and cause of that connection became the focus of debate.

Once archaeology became a profession, its practitioners focused their attention increasingly on narrow technical concerns and consolidated a division of labor based mainly on geography and, to a lesser extent, on whether the objects of their inquiries were civilized, that is, literate. This meant that they never had to deal with human history as a totality or confront the consequences and implications of their own or their colleagues' work. Each technical specialization became increasingly embedded in a distinctive discourse with its own limits and relations to power. However, organic intellectuals from the ruling class who used information about ancient societies and civilizations in earlier discourses continued to deploy archaeological evidence or material culture to make their points and legitimate their views. Politicians and museum directors such as Theodore Roosevelt or Henry Fairfield Osborn, president of the American Museum of Natural History, alluded to archaeological evidence or the absence of it to buttress claims that the colored races had either never produced a civilization or were incapable of sustaining this level of cultural development (for example, Pike 1992, 140–41).

The participation of professional archaeologists in these wider debates diminished after 1900, with a few notable exceptions—for example, William Rainey Harper,

James Breasted, and William Albright. Those who did address the wider issues of the day frequently were drawn largely from the Core Culture, whereas many of their Eastern Establishment colleagues focused their attention on narrow technical matters. As Breasted and Albright wrote about Egyptian and Semitic contributions to the rise of Western civilization, their East Coast contemporaries elaborated techniques or provided detailed descriptions of material remains—for instance, the detailed studies of the Maya calendrical system, which purportedly showed that this ancient people was civilized and, by contrast, that their modern descendants in Guatemala, Chiapas, and the Yucatán were not.

After 1880, professional archaeologists began to reformulate what they meant by civilization and how it developed. They began to shift their attention away from agriculture, resources, and commerce as engines of development toward a distinction drawn increasingly between mental and manual labor. Civilization, they argued, was the product of this emerging division of labor and was achieved when intellectual activities became dominant over physical work. The leaders of these emergent civilized societies were intellectuals, who either constituted the ruling class and the state or were closely linked with them as trusted advisers. The development of this view of civilization coincided with questions about the educability of various subject and client populations that were constituted and defined in terms that incorporated archaeological, historical, and ethnological information. The expertise of professional archaeologists was deployed to explain, mediate, or legitimate various practices that were connected directly or indirectly with U.S. imperial expansion in the late nineteenth and early twentieth centuries: Indian resettlement, the Mexican Revolution, and the resistance the United States encountered in Central America and the Caribbean as it attempted to create more favorable climates for U.S. investment and exploitation.

CHAPTER 4

Archaeology and the Corporatist State, 1933 to 1968

Nineteen thirty-three was not a good year for many people in the United States. Nine hundred thousand farmers had gone bankrupt since the beginning of the Great Depression in 1929; more than seventeen million, nearly a third of the work force, were fully unemployed, and one in three of those who still had jobs worked reduced hours; industrial output was half of what it had been four years earlier; the volume of foreign trade had plummeted by 70 percent; and the international position of the country was weakened, and its capitalists struggled with their British counterparts for investment opportunities and markets in Latin America and Canada.

The economic crisis of the Depression deepened steadily during Herbert Hoover's presidency. When Franklin Roosevelt assumed office in 1933, the paralysis of the banking system only fueled the pervasive sense that the country was in crisis. Because the Democratic Party controlled both the legislative and executive branches of the government, it had a mandate for action. At that moment, Eastern Establishment businesspeople, bankers, and intellectuals wielded hegemony over their Core Culture allies in the Democratic Party—the southern landowners and northern industrial workers. Their model for action was the war economy of World War I, during which the federal government had initiated programs that organized economic life, nationalized transportation and communication, created shipbuilding and other industries, intervened in labor disputes, and established prices for the duration (Higgs 1987, 123–54). These and other programs had marked the unprecedented intervention of the state in the economic affairs of the nation's markets. Many programs lapsed after the war, when overt control was reclaimed by the private sector.

When the state intervened in 1933, it portrayed itself as neutral and independent of particular interest groups. It claimed the aim of its policies—the New Deal—was to resolve the existing crisis by reorganizing business and labor relations in ways that would promote economic growth and foster harmony in the face of conflict (Ekirch 1969; Pels 1973). The regulatory state that emerged after 1877 was transformed in the process. The New Deal established the foundations for a corporatist state structure based on a cross-class alliance, in which political intervention occurred through direct ownership and management. The state created public corporations that were constituted on the basis of their function within the division of labor instead of the geographical organization of the legislative branch. This meant that specific targets of intervention—public corporations such as the Tennessee Valley Authority—were directly and permanently represented in the executive branch and that they were protected with varying degrees of success from a legislature popularly elected on the basis of geography (Jessop 1990, 110–43).

The New Deal consolidated the syndicalist and reformist tendencies of the Progressive Movement by rationalizing the political economy of the large corporations and enlarging the government's regulatory activities and role as a consumer of goods and services. Most of the progressive legislation of the early 1930s served the corporate and finance sectors of the economy, although public relief programs, the minimum wage provision, social security, and the Wagner Act, which supported independent unions, aided some of the working poor and unemployed. The Tennessee Valley Authority, perhaps the most progressive program of the thirties, built a network of dams and canals to protect the area from floods. In conjunction with various hydroelectric projects in the West, it made the federal government one of the country's major producers of electricity for domestic and business use. The New Deal also added significantly to the number of technicians and specialists employed by the federal government (Higgs 1987, 159–95).

The New Deal did not go unchallenged. The Core Culture opposition coalesced around the issue of government intervention, both at home and abroad. Power companies and corporate leaders such as Henry Ford and Wendell Wilkie opposed the TVA, arguing unfair competition. The Supreme Court, whose majority represented the views of the Core Culture, invalidated much of the early legislation of the New Deal. They based their arguments on the right of private property and the unconstitutionality of the power that had been concentrated and centralized in the executive branch of the federal government. Elements of the urban and rural poor whose lives remained unaffected by the New Deal were attracted to populists such as Huey Long. Strikes increased in the mid-1930s, even though more than ten million workers were still unemployed in 1937.

The continuing economic crisis provoked the hegemonic Eastern Establishment to embark on a new course of action: overseas expansion and the internationalization of American business. The strategy was not new, but it was pursued with unprecedented intensity contributing to the spread of war in Europe and the Pacific. The corporations sought to strengthen their share of the overseas markets, especially in Latin America and the Pacific. This meant creating favorable investment climates for the corporations outside the United States, supporting political regimes that were disposed to their presence, and eliminating competition from other capitalist countries. Big business and the investment banks sought the government's support for every phase of their expansion, from aid for exports, the construction of branch factories, or the exploitation of raw materials to loans for developing ports, roads, and other facilities and for promoting public health and other services in the countries where investment would take place (Williams 1961, 451–78; 1972, 162–201).

Thus, in the late 1930s, the Eastern Establishment laid the foundations for a period of sustained economic growth that would last for nearly three decades. The federal regulatory activities initiated at the time promoted continuous economic growth after World War II broke out; however, the extent to which the federal government intervened in the economy after 1940 was massive and without precedent. This took myriad forms. For example, the Selective Service Act of 1940 established conscription on a massive scale: ten million men, 65 percent of those who served in the military during World War II, were drafted. The War Powers Acts of 1941 and 1942 gave the president broad powers: to reassign personnel; to censor communications between the United States and any foreign country; to negotiate cost-plus, no-bid contracts with private suppliers for war-related products; and to use the Treasury as a printing press to finance deficits. The Office of Price Administration, established in the summer of 1941, fixed prices and rents and used indirect sanctions to enforce its regulations. The Labor Disputes Act of 1944 permitted the federal government to seize production facilities and to intrude into labor markets (Higgs 1987, 199–225).

In the process, Congress surrendered constitutional powers to the executive branch, and civil rights were trampled, as in the incarceration of 110,000 Japanese-Americans in concentration camps in the West. These and other actions were quickly upheld by the Supreme Court. Companies that supplied products to the government—especially large ones such as General Electric—made enormous profits, billions of dollars, from the war. The military-industrial mobilization of 1940 to 1945 laid the foundations for the military-industrial complex: the "... institutional arrangement whereby the military procurement authorities, certain large corporations, and certain executive and legislative officials of the federal government cooperate in an enormous ongoing program to develop, produce, and deploy weapons and related products" (Higgs 1987, 212). There were no structural antecedents for the military-industrial complex, which still continues to dominate everyday life in the United States (Diggins 1988; Graebner 1991; Perrett 1974).

The programs that established the foundations of the war economy continued to operate after 1945 in a world situation that was dramatically different from what it had been a few years earlier: The capitalist economies of Western Europe and Japan were in shambles; the prestige of the Union of Soviet Socialist Republics (USSR) was enhanced; and national liberation struggles erupted in various parts of the colonial world. To secure its place in the postwar world, the United States undertook extensive relief programs in Western Europe and Japan and then in parts of what was coming to be recognized as the Third World. It unleashed the Cold War and support for certain Third World regimes, providing continuous fuel for the military-industrial complex for the past forty-five years and steadily strengthening the position of national capitalists concentrated in the defense and aerospace industries and the international capitalists in the petrochemical and mining sectors (Goldman 1960; Hamby 1985; May 1989; Wish 1966, 609–80; Wolfe 1981).

Three other processes interlocked with the Cold War to shape everyday life during the postwar period of sustained economic growth that lasted from 1945 to the late 1960s. One was a renewed attack on the political Left. It began with the Taft-Hartley Act of 1947, which strengthened the prerogatives of management and pressured labor unions, especially those in the Congress of Industrial Organizations, to severe their ties with the Left. This eventually split the labor movement and broke the political alliance that sustained much of the progressive New Deal legislation. During the 1950s, it was fueled by the Cold War ideology; the congressional committee hearings, such as the House Un-American Activities Committee; and the dismissal of several thousand teachers and professors because of their affiliations, real or alleged, with organizations designated as subversive by the federal government

(Heale 1990, 122–90). In this climate, the Left quickly became feared, and the mere mention of Marx was seen as dangerous if not subversive.

The second process involved the expansion and reconstitution of the middle class. This was set in motion by the GI Bill of 1944, which underwrote college educations for returning veterans, and by the Federal Housing Administration, which provided them with low-interest loans to purchase their own homes in new suburbs, such as The Levittown, that mushroomed after the war in Pennsylvania and Long Island. Many of the newly educated, homeowning veterans—especially those in California and the South, where large numbers of defense plants had been built during the war—became managers and workers in businesses that were either part of the military-industrial complex or indirectly related to it. This process spawned new consumption patterns: automobiles, the demand for purchasable art and culture, and college educations to name only few. The bomb shelters, threat of nuclear destruction, and uncertainties about the meaning of family and self in a period of sustained growth and rapidly changing expectations and desires provoked new anxieties. The dialectic they produced was captured by Paul Goodman's (1960) *Growing up Absurd* or when Norman Rockwell's characters are viewed in juxtaposition with those in *Rebel without a Cause,* and *Death of a Salesman.*

The third process was the Civil Rights movement. During the war, the federal government used the rhetoric of freedom, democracy, and equality to mobilize people—including African Americans and members of the various buffer races—to fight Hitler and the Nazis, spokesmen for conservative European capitalists who deflected class struggle along racial and ethnic lines in the late nineteenth century and whose propagandists proclaimed the superiority of the Aryan race. African Americans took this call seriously and, after the war, pressured the federal government to live up to its own rhetoric. As the 1948 election approached, President Harry Truman, responding to black voters in mostly northern cities, issued an executive order that desegregated the military and implemented a policy of racial equality in the armed services. In 1954, the National Association for the Advancement of Colored People (NAACP) brought a series of cases to the Supreme Court challenging segregation in public schools. The Court overturned the "separate but equal" doctrine in education in *Brown* v. *Board of Education;* however, the federal government moved slowly to enforce this decision, and, a decade later, only one in four school districts was integrated. The Montgomery bus boycott, sit-ins, the Freedom Rides, mass demonstrations in southern states and Washington, D.C., and numerous murders provoked legislative and judicial action in the late 1950s and early 1960s, culminating in the Voter Rights Act of 1965. On one hand, these were followed by a wave of urban riots and rebellions that erupted throughout the country between 1965 and 1967 and were provoked, in almost every instance, by police action against a black man, woman, or child; on the other, they were followed by the election of a small but steadily increasing number of African Americans to public office.

Once again, issues involving class and race—and gender to a lesser extent—were placed on the table for discussion in a milieu defined by the intersection of fear, apprehension, the pursuit of happiness, and hopes that the economy would continue to grow indefinitely into the future. However, the era of sustained growth was almost over. The U.S. economy was restructured during the 1960s. Factories closed in the northern and Great Lakes industrial states, and new ones opened in the South and the West—regions increasingly dominated by antilabor and anticommunist sentiments in the postwar years. For the first time, the demographic center of the country shifted west of the Mississippi River. The federal government was also deeply committed to the war in Vietnam, which was the central issue in the Democratic Party defeat in 1968 and the re-emergence of Core Culture hegemony in domestic affairs. Real earnings had declined because of the war, while inflation, taxes, and prices increased; the cities were falling apart; riots in the cities and demonstrations on college campuses across the country saw youths protesting and expressing their dissatisfaction with the war, racism, the dehumanization of education, and the inability of the technological society that was emerging in the United States to provide for the development of the individual or even to ensure work for the younger generation. The center of the political spectrum crumbled, and Richard Nixon was elected to the White House on a platform of "law and order" (Sayres et al. 1984).

ARCHAEOLOGY DURING THE DEPRESSION AND WORLD WAR II

Nineteen thirty-three was a vintage year for archaeology in the United States. It marked the beginning of large-scale federal support for archaeological research in the United States. Up to then, archaeology had largely been the province of amateurs or individuals affiliated with the Smithsonian Institution, various museums, and anthropology departments. Professional archaeologists, those who received wages and those with advanced degrees, were underwritten by the government, universities or museums, or private donations. Before 1933, they probably received lower levels of financial support than archaeologists working in Athens, Jerusalem, Baghdad, Cairo, or Chichén Itzá. When the various New Deal programs were launched, the funds available for research in the United States increased dramatically and initially favored those archaeologists in departments or museums of anthropology rather than classics or fine arts. Problems of management, cooperation, and standards arose almost immediately. Archaeologists working in different parts of the United States plunged headlong into an unknown terrain created by circumstances over which they had almost no control and by rapid professionalization.

By 1930, archaeology was taught in a number of colleges. But it was already fragmented and housed in various academic departments—often anthropology, classics, or fine arts—or it was combined with other disciplines, such as sociology or geography. Seven universities offered doctoral degrees in anthropology: California, Chicago, Columbia, Harvard, Pennsylvania, Southern California, and Yale. Others offered undergraduate courses or awarded master of arts degrees. A few universities had already initiated archaeological research and training programs at local sites; for example, William Webb, Arthur Miller, and William Funkhouser worked out of the University of Kentucky in the early 1920s, and the University of Chicago's program was organized by Fay-Cooper Cole in 1925. Other field programs appeared by the end of the decade.

Several New Deal programs created in 1933 aimed to put the unemployed to work. In the summer of that year, the newly organized Tennessee Valley Authority was encouraged—largely through the lobbying efforts of Major William S. Webb, political adviser, physicist, and head of the University of Kentucky's newly formed Department of Anthropology and Archaeology—to undertake archaeological investigations in the areas that would be flooded (Fagette 1985, 168–69; Haag 1965); by the following spring, more than 1,000 workers from the Civil Works Administration (CWA) were engaged in field projects in various parts of the Tennessee Valley. In the summer of 1933, the city council and the local office of the Federal Emergency Relief Administration (FERA) in Marksville, Louisiana, requested the Smithsonian Institution to send someone to supervise a crew of more than one hundred men who were employed to restore the Marksville Mounds (Lyon 1982, 30; Willey 1988, 51–74). In November, CWA officials called on the Smithsonian Institution to provide archaeologists to direct field projects in states with warm winters and high unemployment. Two months later, in January 1934, eleven field projects employing 1500 workers were initiated in California, Georgia, Florida, North Carolina, and Tennessee (Fagette 1985, 112–90; Lyon 1982, 29–99; Stirling 1934). Archaeological research was appealing, because it was labor intensive; consequently, most of the money allocated by relief agencies was spent on labor. However, the sudden demand for competently trained archaeologists to supervise workers supported by the TVA and the CWA far outstripped the supply and stretched the ability of universities to provide them on short notice.

When the Works Progress Administration (WPA) was established in August 1934, archaeology became even more deeply embedded in the federally funded relief programs. The great advantage of relief archaeology was that it did not produce a product that competed with the private sector. Various state agencies—museums and universities, for instance—would submit proposals through state-level WPA offices that would be approved by personnel from the Smithsonian Institution and the National Park Service. In return for grants permitting them to hire unemployed white-collar workers, the state agencies agreed to pay the salaries of trained supervisors and to prepare quarterly progress reports and final publications, many of which were never completed because of World War II. By the end of the decade, this program underwrote archaeological and paleontological investigations across the country, including the cataloging and analysis of materials excavated outside the United States at the University Museum at the University of Pennsylvania (Fagette 1985, 225–51; Lyon 1982, 66–99; Quimby 1979).

As archaeology became part of federally funded relief programs, the government-employed archaeologists found themselves in the forefront of the field. By the end of 1934, they formed an alliance with academic and museum anthropologists to create the Society for American Archaeology. In December, they came together in Pittsburgh, where six women and twenty-five men signed the constitution of the new organization (Guthe 1967). Its purpose was

> ... to stimulate scientific research in the archaeology of the New World by: creating closer professional relations among archaeologists and between them and others interested in American archaeology; guiding, on request, the research work of amateurs;

advocating the conservation of archaeological data and furthering the control or elimination of commercialization of archaeological objects; and promoting a more rational appreciation of the aims and limitations of archaeological research.

(SOCIETY FOR AMERICAN ARCHAEOLOGY 1935, 146)

The professional archaeologists formed the society to develop a voice in creating policy, to curb the increased looting of archaeological sites, and to limit or channel the activities of amateurs, especially in the midcontinent, who collected, sold, and forged Indian relics (Brain 1988; Harrington 1991, 26). The professionals succeeded to a certain degree in curtailing their activities after the passage of the Historic Sites Act of 1935. This law authorized the secretary of the interior to take a leadership role in protecting archaeological sites and marked the beginning of federal involvement in specific archaeological research projects (Kelly 1940; Wallace 1981, 79). These projects, which often involved amateurs, were directed by professionals.

The two-tiered membership of the Society for American Archaeology represented a second line of attack on the activities of the amateurs. "Persons willing to coöperate in furthering the objects of the Society may be elected Affiliates. Affiliates who have engaged in scientific research in American archaeology, and who have published their research in recognized media may be elected Fellows" (Society for American Archaeology 1935, 146). Article II of the By-Laws of the Society spelled out in more detail the difference between the affiliates of the lower class and the fellows of the upper class:

> Section 2. An application for affiliation must state the business or professional connections of the applicant, and the nature of his interest in American archaeology. It must be endorsed by at least one Fellow and one Affiliate in good standing, one of whom must know the applicant personally.
> Section 3. An application for election as a Fellow must include a brief biography of the applicant; the nature of his interest or training in American archaeology; the extent of his experience in field and laboratory research; and a list of his publications. It must be endorsed by at least two Fellows in good standing, one of whom must know the applicant personally [and be approved by the Council or its Executive Committee, whose members are Fellows].

(SOCIETY FOR AMERICAN ARCHAEOLOGY 1935, 148–49)

The organizational structure of the Society minimized the role of the amateurs in decision and policymaking. The professionals continued to consolidate their power in the prewar years. By 1940, the Society had more than doubled in size; however, only 72 of its 823 members in that year were fellows (Guthe 1940, 98). Two years later, the Society revised its constitution, replacing the dual membership categories with a single type of affiliation and initiating procedures for denying membership to "... persons who habitually misuse archaeological objects or sites for commercial purposes" and for removing "... from the membership roles any member who does so, or who otherwise makes improper use of his membership" (Society for American Archaeology 1942, 206).

Between 1933 and 1941, various federal relief agencies provided funds that indirectly supported archaeological research in the United States. Relief programs—such as the WPA, which eventually dispensed more than $7 billion—were multitiered bureaucracies that operated simultaneously at the federal and state levels. The WPA was accountable initially to the executive branch and then to Congress, which began annual audits of their budgets and performance in 1938. In this context, the archaeologists had to confront the issue of standardized criteria for evaluating performance. The federal archaeologists and some archaeologists working through state-level WPA offices supported standardization; others, notably in New Mexico and Tennessee, vigorously opposed uniform criteria, arguing that control of archaeological research should be vested at the level of individual states and that such efforts represented too much federal interference or insufficient appreciation of local circumstances and relations.

These issues were discussed at the annual meetings of the Society for American Archaeology, organized in 1934, and at conferences sponsored by the Anthropology and Psychology Division of the National Research Council. They were also aired at various regional archaeological organizations launched in the late 1920s and the 1930s: the Pecos Conference (1927), the Plains Archaeological Conference (1931), and the Southeastern Archaeological Conference (1931), for example (Fagette 1985, 81–82; Woodbury 1993). The need to organize data and to establish procedures for comparing data from different sites and regions underwrote W. C. McKern's (1939) Midwestern Taxonomic System in the mid-1930s. It also laid the foundations for related debates over typology, classification, and the meaning of various concepts—types, horizons, and traditions—that persisted for more than three decades (Gladwin and Gladwin 1928; Ford 1938; Rouse 1939; Krieger 1944; Taylor 1948; Spaulding 1953; Ford 1954; Willey and Phillips 1958, 11–56).

In 1939, the National Research Council was asked by the assistant director of the WPA to establish the Committee for Basic Needs on American Archaeology. The committee—composed of professional archaeologists and anthropologists employed by state and private universities and museums—was charged with developing standardized criteria for evaluating research. It was chaired by W. Duncan Strong and included William C. McKern, William S. Webb, J. O. Brew, A. V. Kidder, Fay-Cooper Cole, Clark Wissler, and Carl Guthe. The first meetings, held in May and June, were productive, and the group published its recommendations in *Science* (Guthe 1940). What it proposed was "a universally accepted and methodologically sound management paradigm" to deal with the vast amount of empirical information that had been gathered by the various relief archaeology programs (Fagette 1985, 370).

Government anthropologists at the Smithsonian Institution—William Duncan Strong (1936), Julian H. Steward (1937), and Frank M. Seltzer (Steward and Seltzer 1938)—had already absorbed the tenets of logical positivism and were introducing them into anthropology. They adopted the perspective that (1) only statements whose contents were accessible to all had cognitive value; (2) there was a single, unified scientific method, which began with a logical analysis of analytical categories and statements; (3) only individual things existed; and (4) that the anthropologists opposed metaphysical statements on the grounds that they could not be tested experimentally and disproved by any method.

The government anthropologists argued for the unity of the discipline, which undermined the dichotomy between archaeology and ethnology that existed at the turn of the century and was resurfacing in the 1930s; they used the term cultural anthropology to include both archaeology and ethnology. They were also critical of contemporary archaeological praxis, which was dominated on the one hand by amateurs without significant professional training and on the other by those professional archaeologists who paid little or no attention to the theoretical foundations of their work.

Academic anthropologists, especially from Harvard and the University of Chicago, supported the thrust of their attack (Kluckhohn 1940). These institutions were also centers of concentration for the refugee logical positivists who had fled from Germany and Austria after 1936 (Feigl 1969, 643–51). Logical positivism acclimatized easily in the United States, because its assumptions were compatible with those of pragmatism, perhaps the dominant strain of positivist thought on the East Coast at that time (Kolakowski 1969, 149–200; Heyl 1968; Rucker 1969, 132–57). Both stressed the need for a rigorous scientific methodology in order to eliminate from intellectual life pseudoknowledge based on irrational prejudice and ideological fanaticism. Both also downplayed the significance of factual knowledge because of its potential accessibility. Politically, the European logical positivists were middle-class academics who favored parliamentary democracy; like their American counterparts, they were reformists, hostile to both fascism and communism (Kolakowski 1969, 197).

Logical positivism became the unacknowledged theoretical and ideological perspective of this emerging group of professional archaeologists. It accompanied their continuing attempts to create standards that distinguished professional experts from amateurs and to develop uniform terminologies, procedures, and standards for measuring performance. It allowed scholars to focus their attention on methodology rather than content. How their colleagues did something became more important than what they did or why they did it. In other words, logical positivism provided the expanding technical bureaucracy with tools for assessing the performance of their peers. Writing in 1942, John W. Bennett (1943, 217) observed that "Joseph Caldwell, a [Chicago-trained] southeastern archaeologist, has recently suggested that a feasible method for criticising archaeological reports lies in the study and analysis of the concepts a given worker uses in interpreting his data." Bennett, who was the most astute observer of trends in the field during this period, reaffirmed his suggestion. So did Walter W. Taylor (1948) in his *A Study of Archeology*, completed in 1943 as a doctoral dissertation written under Clyde Kluckhohn's supervision at Harvard.

Federal support for archaeological investigations outside the United States began in 1940, though the groundwork was laid a few years earlier. In 1936, Congress created the Division of Cultural Relations to implement Pan-Americanism at a time when private U.S. investments in Latin America had declined and investments from other capitalists countries were increasing in the area. Federal funds were to be used in place of private money to promote the Good Neighbor Policy. Two years later, Nelson Rockefeller was appointed Co-Ordinator of Inter-American Affairs. He had traveled extensively in Latin America during the mid-1930s and had an excellent grasp of the needs of the Eastern Establishment. The archaeological research program funded by the Office of the Co-Ordinator of Inter-American Affairs was organized and administered by the Institute of Andean Research centered at the American Museum of Natural History (Erb 1982).

The Institute of Andean Research was founded in 1936 after Rockefeller intervened to secure the support of Peru's president for Julio C. Tello's plan to build a new archaeology museum in Lima (Patterson 1989a). Tello, who subsequently came to the United States to obtain technical assistance and cooperation for the museum, and Alfred L. Kroeber organized the institute with the financial backing of Mrs. Truxton Beale and Robert Woods Bliss of Dumbarton Oaks (Lothrop 1948, 52). In 1940, the institute received a grant of about $140,000 from the Office of the Co-Ordinator of Inter-American Affairs to support ten relatively autonomous archaeological projects in Latin America; these projects, coordinated by George Vaillant and Wendell Bennett of the American Museum of Natural History, were carried out in 1941 and 1942, just before and immediately after the United States entered World War II.

Archaeological research was disrupted in the United States as archaeologists became involved in the war effort. Classical and Old World archaeologists, such as Sterling Dow and Carleton Coon, were recruited into the Office of Strategic Services, the forerunner of the Central Intelligence Agency. Some served as cultural or military officers attached to U.S. embassies in various Latin American countries; George Vaillant and Ledyard Smith were among their number. Others, enlisted by the war bureaucracy in Washington, had a considerable shaping influence on the discipline. They included W. Duncan Strong, who directed the Smithsonian's Ethnogeographic Board; Julian Steward, who edited the *Handbook of South American Indians* for the Bureau of American Ethnology; Wendell Bennett, a member of the Ethnogeographic Board and executive secretary of the Joint Committee on Latin American Studies at the Social Science Research Council; and Froelich Rainey, who directed the Board of Economic Warfare and the Defense Supply Corporation's Quinine Mission in Ecuador before joining the Foreign Service (Kidder.1954; Rainey 1992, 101–33; Willey 1988, 62, 91, 119–20).

ARCHAEOLOGY DURING THE POSTWAR ERA OF SUSTAINED CORPORATIST ECONOMIC GROWTH

In 1946, archaeology in the United States entered a period of sustained growth and prosperity; it adopted new forms of organization to take advantage of developments that were unfolding in U.S. society. The growth of archaeology was shaped by (1) the extension of the educational franchise to new layers of the working class; (2) the sustained growth of the economy throughout the period; (3) the construction of a new infrastructure; and (4) the restructuring of scientific research in the years after the war. As George Stocking (1976, 42) observed, "The war had opened up broad new vistas, and the problem ... was how to capitalize on them."

The concerns of archaeologists working in the Americas were partly reflected by those that led to the reorganization of the American Anthropological Association in 1946. The year before, Julian Steward broached the idea of founding a new organization composed of professional anthropologists. It would provide a forum for professional rather than purely scientific problems. During that summer, a number of anthropologists met in Washington to discuss his proposal. A committee was established at the annual meeting of the association to canvass opinion. It mailed a questionnaire to five hundred anthropologists, some of whom were not members of the association. Of the 115 who responded, all but ten favored reorganization rather than forming a new group (Stocking 1976, 37–42).

The committee returned to the association the following year with its recommendations, which were adopted. The most significant aspects of the reorganization

> ... involved such matters as supporting the proposed national research foundation and seeing to anthropology's place in it; developing a "comprehensive plan of research that is likely to meet the requirements for participation in the benefits" of such a foundation; expanding areal studies; seeking representation in consulting groups planning research in the Pacific; making contact with the United Nations Organization to "explore the possibility of applying anthropological viewpoints" in their research and policy-making units; surveying anthropological personnel and university curricula; developing the "public relations" of the discipline; and investigating the possibility of establishing a "permanent secretariat" to serve the professional interests of anthropologists....
>
> (STOCKING 1976, 41)

To maximize its position and whatever benefits might accrue at that time, the association elected to present the field as an integrated scientific discipline, despite the strong humanistic orientation of some members and the divisive, separatist tendencies of others. This was strategic at a time when science was held in awe by the public.

Many archaeologists continued to participate in the united front initially established in the 1930s and reaffirmed after the war with the reorganization of the American Anthropological Association. It was to their benefit to do so. At the same time, however, they continued to pursue and build independent relations with the federal government through the Committee for the Recovery of Archaeological Remains, which formed in 1944 (Johnson, Haury, and Griffin 1945). With WPA archaeology still fresh in their minds, the committee members were concerned with (1) ensuring that adequate archaeological investigations would be carried out in areas that would be inundated by future flood control projects; (2) developing an organization with proper administrative control so that the scientific work could be carried out in a manner that was consistent with the ideas of modern archaeology; and (3) lobbying, writing clauses in pending legislation, and developing relations between existing government bureaus.

The committee's achievements were substantial during the period from the late 1940s to the 1960s when building industries and developers were tearing up the cultural and historical fabric of the country (Brew 1959; Johnson 1955). It promoted and lobbied for legislation that increased the federal funds available for archaeological research within the United States. It collaborated with archaeologists from the Smithsonian Institution and the National Park Service to promote the formation of the Interagency Archaeological Salvage Program. By 1961, the program had grown to include the Corps of Engineers, the Bureau of Reclamation, and sections of the Federal Power Commission and the Bureau of Public Roads (Johnson 1961, 3–4). This involved the cooperation of a number of state agencies and universities, many of which shared the financial burden of the emergency archaeological salvage program by expending their own funds. The collaborative efforts of archaeologists on the committee and those in the various federal and state agencies eventually spread the costs of some of the research carried out in the country to the private sector.

The activities of the Committee for Recovery of Archaeological Remains and the Interagency Archaeological Salvage Program were important for other reasons as well. First, many future archaeologists enrolled in universities in the late 1940s and 1950s received their initial field experience and employment as archaeologists in the field projects sponsored by the program. A significant number continued to pursue interests developed during this formative stage of their careers. Second, it legitimized the scientific value of archaeological investigations begun during the 1930s as an important element of federal relief. Third, it shifted some of the costs of archaeological research in the United States from the federal government to various state agencies and eventually to the private sector. Fourth, it promoted the creation of state archaeological surveys in states where they had not existed before. Fifth, it provided employment for professional archaeologists trained in the postwar era.

The other major source of funding for archaeological research that developed rapidly after 1954 was the National Science Foundation. World War II had witnessed the restructuring of U.S. society and its relations with the rest of the world. Scientists, including anthropologists, had enlisted in the war effort and participated in committees and organizations created to meet needs produced by the war (Compton and Bush 1942; Dupree 1957, 1972; Kevles 1977). After the war, scientists led by Vannevar Bush, Franklin Roosevelt's science adviser and former head of the Carnegie Institution of Washington, sought to create a permanent, government-financed "National Research Foundation"; their ideas did not meet with unanimous acceptance. After a prolonged debate in Congress, Bush's proposals were accepted with significant modifications, and the National Science Foundation came into existence in December 1951. The social sciences were not provided for in the initial legislation, but, partly through the efforts of Senator William Fulbright, a Social Sciences Division was created in 1954 (McCune 1971).

The National Science Foundation awarded $30,000 to sponsor two archaeological projects in 1954. Five years later, it granted $219,000 to support a dozen projects. By 1962, it funded forty-eight projects with budgets totaling more than $900,000. By 1967, the foundation was spending slightly more than $2 million annually on archaeology. Perhaps 60 percent of the NSF-supported archaeological research occurred outside the United States. The foundation had replaced the Carnegie Institution of Washington and museum patrons as the major benefactor of U.S. archaeologists working overseas. The data also suggest that archaeologists working overseas were better supported by the foundation, given the relatively small number of them, than their colleagues who conducted nonsalvage investigations in the United States.

The GI Bill of Rights passed in 1944 provided the war veterans with certain social and economic benefits. It guaranteed four years of free education, including study at technical schools and universities. It extended the educational franchise to the working class, and hundreds of thousands of veterans arrived on college campuses throughout the United States. In 1949, 49 percent of the college students were veterans, and, by 1956, 2.2 million veterans, including nearly 65,000 women, had used their educational benefits.

Nourished by growing enrollments, departments employing archaeologists grew slowly but steadily in both size and number following the war; the pace quickened after the Baby Boom generation began to arrive on college campuses in the mid-1960s. The expansion of existing departments, as well as the creation of new colleges and academic programs, provided an increasingly important source of employment for archaeologists with Ph.D. degrees. By the mid-1960s, colleges and universities were probably the major source of employment for archaeologists with Ph.D. degrees (Murphy 1976, 4–6). The two professional organizations also grew during this period. The Society of American Archaeology, which had 661 members in 1946, grew at an annual rate of about 3 percent until 1956, when 976 individuals belonged. The growth rate almost doubled during the next decade as its membership swelled to 1,707 individuals in 1966. The Archaeological Institute of America, whose membership had plummeted from 3,692 in 1931 to 955 in 1944, grew to 2,271 individuals by 1950; the numbers remained stationary until 1952, then expanded to 3,245 in 1957, and fell rapidly to 2,746 in 1960, after which they expanded steadily to 6,753 in 1970. These data are summarized in Tables 1 and 2.

The GI Bill, however, disproportionately extended the educational franchise to men. This is reflected in the fact that the percentage of women enrolled in colleges declined steadily from an all-time high of 47.1 percent in 1920 to 40.1 percent in 1940 to 35.2 percent in 1958 (Solomon 1985, 142, 189–91). Also, the number of

TABLE 1
INDIVIDUAL MEMBERSHIP OF THE SOCIETY FOR AMERICAN ARCHAEOLOGY, 1935-1988

Year	Total	Men	Women	
1935	332			
1936	573	517	56	(9.7%)
1941	721			
1946	661	586	75	(11.3%)
1951	710			
1956	976	843	133	(13.6%)
1960	1,176	1,029	147	(12.5%)
1966	1,707			
1969	1,794	1,531	263	(14.7%)
1973	3,916	2,722	923	(23.6%)
1976	5,094	3,654	1,440	(28.3%)
1981	5,179			
1985	4,453			
1988	4,955*			(35.0%)
1991	c. 4,200			

*May include both individuals and institutions
Source: The numerical information is derived from annual reports and irregularly published membership lists in *American Antiquity*. The 1988 percentage of women in the association comes from a count of the SAA mailing list made by Alison Wylie.

TABLE 2
INDIVIDUAL MEMBERSHIP OF THE ARCHAEOLOGICAL INSTITUTE OF AMERICA, 1931-1990

Year	Total	Men	Women
1931	3,692		
1935	2,188	1,370	818 (37.4%)
1944	955		
1946	1,371	835	536 (38.4%)
1950	2,271	1,414	857 (37.8%)
1957	3,245	1,960	1,285 (40.0%)
1960	2,747		
1964	3,747	2,242	1,505 (40.2%)
1970	6,753		
1976	6,063		
1981	9,680		
1986	7,755		
1988	7,230		
1990	8,484		

Source: The numerical information is derived from the annual membership data and irregularly published membership lists in the *Bulletin of the Archaeological Institute of America*. The counts of membership lists do not always correspond to the membership numbers appearing in the annual reports.

women in the Society for American Archaeology increased more slowly than the number of men in the postwar years. For instance, 75 women and 586 men belonged to the organization in 1946; a decade later, there were 133 women and 843 men; by 1960, there were 147 women and 1,029 men. In other words, between 1946 and 1956, 58 women and 257 men were added to the membership roles, roughly 4.4 men to every woman. Between 1956 and 1960, 14 women and 186 men were inscribed on the membership roles—13.3 men to each woman. The percentage of women in the organization also declined during this four-year period from 13.6 to 12.5 percent, reversing a slow but steady increase that had begun in 1936 when women constituted 9.7 percent of the 573 fellows and affiliates.

By comparison, 532 women and 839 men belonged to the Archaeological Institute of America in 1946; there were 857 women and 1,414 men in 1950; by 1957, there were 1,285 women and 1,960 men; and, in 1964, there were 1,505 women and 2,242 men. The percentage of women in the organization increased steadily from 37.8 percent in 1950 to 40.2 percent in 1964. In the four years immediately following the war, 1.8 men joined the organization to every woman; during the next fourteen years, the ratio was roughly 1.3 men to each woman. The Archaeological Institute of America did not experience the same explosive increase in the ratio of men joining the organization during the postwar years, and most particularly during the late 1950s, that occurred in the Society for American Archaeology. In other words, the pattern of growth for the two organizations is the same, given the fact that they started with very different sex ratios. The GI Bill sustained a skewed sex ratio in both after the war.

The participation of women relative to men in the two professional organizations also shifted in the postwar years. Three-year running averages indicate that women typically presented about 20 percent of the papers at the annual meetings of the Archaeological Institute of America during the 1930s and 1940s; their participation peaked at about 26.5 percent in 1953-54, declined precipitously to about 15 percent in 1959–62, and rose again to about 22 percent in 1963–68. The numbers are slightly different for their participation in the Society for American Archaeology; women presented 13.8 percent of the papers in 1935–41, 3.9 percent in 1946–55, 10.2 percent in 1956–60, and 7.5 percent in 1961–68.

The boundaries that separated different kinds of archaeological practice before World War II—reflected by the various schools of Classical Studies, Oriental Research, American Research, and Prehistoric Research—gradually evaporated in its wake. As the old coalitions fragmented, archaeologists had to forge new alliances, redefine their mission, create new images, and seize new opportunities in postwar America. The expansion of higher education, the creation of area studies programs, and the formation of a federally funded science establishment were three potential motors for growth. The Americanist archaeologists who worked in Washington during the war were particularly attuned to the possibilities that might be afforded by each engine. Archaeologists began to redefine their identities and professional relations in the postwar years. The reconfiguration of archaeology was effectively completed by 1954, when the National Science Foundation (NSF) began to support social scientists in a milieu marked by declining private financial support for their research.

Archaeologists had to forge new alliances and redefine the discipline after the war. The postwar reconstruction of the field is mirrored in changes in the *American Journal of Archaeology*. Immediately after the war, the journal published an "Archaeological News" column that provided information about activities in more than twenty countries or regions. By 1952, archaeological news came almost exclusively from Greece, Asia Minor, Rome, and infrequently the Near East, Cyprus, or Israel. About the same time, *American Antiquity*, the organ of the Society for American Archaeology, expanded its regular coverage of ongoing research in different parts of the Americas. Thus, both the classical and American archaeologists reaffirmed their traditional geographical interests. The prehistorians quickly confirmed their ongoing interests in what happened in Europe before or outside the crystallization of Greco-Roman society and virtually disappeared from the pages of the *American Journal of Archaeology* (Hencken 1946). Many Near Eastern archaeologists, housed mainly in museums and the Oriental Institute, continued to define their interests in terms of Assyriology and the American Oriental Society; however, some saw common interests with their Americanist and prehistoric colleagues, a view reinforced by the writings of V. Gordon Childe (Trigger 1980b).

The classical archaeologists also reaffirmed their historic linkages with art history, fine arts, and the humanities. The pages of the *American Journal of Archaeology* were filled increasingly with articles that discuss inscriptions or describe classes of objects—pottery, sculpture, coins, portraits, or architecture and such—in great detail. Their descriptions frequently incorporated such technical information as the arsenical composition of particular bronze implements, obtained with the aid of technical procedures developed in chemistry, metallurgy, or one of the other sciences. In their view, the hard sciences merely provided information that enhanced their understanding of the objects; the significance of this information must still be interpreted by archaeologists in light of particularistic historical knowledge about the civilized or nearly civilized societies of the classical world.

Anthropologists strengthened their position vis-à-vis access to federal funding after the war by proclaiming themselves social and behavioral scientists. Americanist and prehistoric archaeologists reasserted their historic relations with ethnologists and claimed their rightful place in a discipline that made increasing use of the language and rhetoric of science. This was accomplished mainly in colleges and universities. For the most part, the curricula of anthropology departments in the postwar era reflected the ideological stance adopted by the American Anthropological Association. In this perspective, anthropology was a unified scientific discipline com-posed of four subfields. Students, both undergraduate and graduate, were obliged to acquire familiarity with the methods and theory of each before focusing their inter-ests. In practice, it meant enrolling in required introductory or survey courses. This experience frequently did little to promote the idea of a unified science, because each of the subfields continued to develop its own theoretical agenda and funding sources.

The centrifugal pulls on individuals in the different fragments of archaeology and in the reconstituted subfields of anthropology were not insignificant. For some, not understanding what their colleagues were doing created a genuine sense of curiosity. For others, it provoked insecurities that stifled curiosity at the same time it heightened disinterest, fed contempt, and fueled antagonisms. Fragmentation and the centrifugal tendencies it promotes were quite pronounced in some universities—the University of Chicago and Harvard, for example—especially when they could be linked or attributed to the personalities of particular individuals, such as Clyde Kluckhohn or some of Radcliffe-Brown's students at Chicago. Their effects on graduate students during the mid-1950s have been depicted in novels, such as those written by Elizabeth Peters (1989), who received a Ph.D. in Egyptology from the Oriental Institute about that time. They are also mentioned in memoirs written by archaeologists who were active in the postwar era (Binford 1972, 8–12; Griffin 1985, 21; Willey 1984, 10).

In anthropology departments, two kinds of courses were central to graduate training in archaeology. One consisted of seminars, usually organized around par-ticular geographical areas such as the American Southwest or Peru. Students famil-iarized themselves with the primary and secondary literature on the area and with the major problems of interpreting the archaeological record. In the other, called something like "Archaeological Method and Theory" or "The Fundamentals of Archaeology," they read and discussed current debates over typology, analogy, evo-lutionism, seriation, the use of statistics, or settlement patterns; this course often provided them with some idea about the history of the field as well.

During the era of Eastern Establishment predominance following the war, archaeologists believed that knowledge was cumulative and that the business of archaeology was to acquire data—objects and associations from sites—in order to extend and refine our understanding of past cultures and long-term processes of change. In their discussions, they separated theory and practice and gave priority to the latter. They were overwhelmingly concerned with methodological issues and the clarification of concepts, while theoretical concerns were shoved into the back-ground. Their discussions were shaped by logical positivism and its concern with precise language, uniform terminologies, and standardized procedures. Their debates did not occur in an intellectual vacuum; they occurred in the context of and were ultimately shaped by a broader discourse that was taking place in U.S. society.

One of the central contradictions that emerged after the war involved the problem of maintaining order in a society while simultaneously promoting certain kinds of social change. This was shaped by broad discussions in U.S. society concerning social order and the meaning of race. Intellectuals who discussed these questions tended to separate the study of society from the study of history. They distorted what historians did, portraying them as chroniclers of unique events who were unconcerned with the processes underlying the growth of society. In some senses, their portrayal of history during this period was accurate. Historians were also under attack for treating certain periods of the past as "golden ages." Their romantic tendencies implied that the contemporary society of the West was in some way inferior or less humane. Such romantic tendencies, however, continued to be tolerated or even promoted in foreign area studies programs, because they implied that the modern Third World societies were inferior to that of the West or that they were deformed or distorted versions of their historic or prehistoric predecessors.

The problem of social order had been a central concern of Emile Durkheim, whose ideas were incorporated into the structural-functionalism developed by Radcliffe-Brown and Talcott Parsons at Chicago and Harvard in the late 1930s. In Durkheim's perspective, social order was maintained by moral incentives. After the war, Parsons and others emphasized the utility of certain cultural or social arrangements for integrating and maintaining equilibrium in a society. The major limitations of this kind of functionalism were that it was ahistorical and it could not adequately deal with the growth and change.

Julian Steward was an Eastern Establishment intellectual who attempted to resolve the problem posed by the ahistorical character of functionalism. He accepted the distinction between the study of society and the study of history, reaffirming the scientific character of the former and the essentially narrative quality of the latter. Between 1947 and 1951, he formulated what was essentially a historical functionalism that appeared to overcome the limitations of the earlier versions. He argued for a method of cultural ecology, including the concept of levels of sociocultural integration; outlined a methodology for area studies; and promoted the adoption of cultural evolutionism, a scientific materialist view of historical development (Steward 1955, 11–63; Gregory 1977). His methodology and programmatic statements about area studies afforded anthropologists with a way of applying their traditional research techniques to the study of developing nation-states. His appropriation of the materialist conception of history, accomplished by distinguishing his methodology from those of the Marxist archaeologist V. Gordon Childe and the radical anthropologist Leslie White, removed some of the limitations imposed on materialist thought by the Cold War. Steward formulated an approach to the problem and provided scholars, including archaeologists, with a means for combining them with area studies and a methdology for undertaking comparative studies of long-term processes of economic or cultural growth (Steward 1950; Patterson 1986b, 1987; Peace 1993; Rostow 1960; Willey and Phillips 1958).

The issues of race and racism also came to the fore in the wake of World War II. Those archaeologists who addressed the issues of race and racism in the postwar era did so in a framework shaped by anthropologists; however, they were explicit concerns only in Paleolithic archaeology and paleoanthropology. Otherwise, assumptions about race remained implicit in discussions of other topics, such as the universal or natural standards of beauty supposedly reflected in classical Greek sculpture.

Archaeologists generally dealt with race rather than racism. For instance, they did not deem it important to acknowledge that several of the WPA field crews were African-American or that one in Georgia was racially integrated and included both men and women. When they dealt with the issue of race, they implicitly accepted prevailing views or relied on physical anthropologists for their interpretations. Unfortunately, the Eastern Establishment physical anthropologists who discussed the race concept after World War II and the formulation of the United Nations' notions of race and universality held very different views about its significance. Some— Earnest Hooton (1946) or Carleton Coon (1939, 1962, 1965), for instance—argued that races constituted real biological units. Others, such as Sherwood F. Washburn (1963), who were influenced by developments in the "new evolutionary synthesis biology," which crystallized between the late 1930s and 1950s, argued that race was not an especially useful biological concept. Other anthropologists, notably Ruth Benedict (1945), pointed to the highly politicized nature of the race concept and the way it was deployed in U.S. society.

Linkages that connected physical anthropology, paleolithic archaeology, and the eugenics movement in the 1920s and 1930s were severed and reconstituted after the Second World War. The eugenics movement, but not the notion of racial hierarchy associated with it, was discredited during the middle and late 1930s (Allen 1986, 1987). The connections between physical anthropology and paleolithic archaeology, which had underwritten the formation of the American School of Prehistoric Research in the 1920s, were strengthened. These were gradually combined with ideas drawn from "modern evolutionary synthesis" biology, which established the foundations for the consolidation and growth of paleoanthropology in the 1950s and 1960s (Haraway 1988).

ARCHAEOLOGY AND ANTHROPOLOGY

During the interwar years, many U.S. archaeologists believed that historians were primarily concerned with the temporal succession of events, the actions of human beings, whose unique and distinctive characteristics rendered systematic and extensive classification impossible. In their view, historians illustrated the particularities of culture change, the vast array of choices available to individuals or societies, and the operation of free will or some principle of national or cultural autonomy culminating in the nation-state, which they regarded as the perfect vehicle for progress. Those historians who claimed their goal was to narrate political, diplomatic, or military events supported this view. They eschewed theoretical statements and implied that the facts would speak for themselves. In doing so, they adopted the perspective of classical empiricists who believed that knowledge was based exclusively on information derived from the senses. However, most of the archaeologists writing at this time also accepted the tenets of classical empiricism.

Whereas historians generally came down on the side of the state, archaeologists usually stressed the importance of the community or culture—concepts they used almost interchangeably. In their view, each community, whether in ancient Greece or Illinois, had its own distinctive culture, which consisted of a particular configuration of elements that were socially learned and transmitted from one generation to the next. These cultural elements were interrelated so that a change in one affected or modified others. Some archaeologists argued that each element was as important as any other, and that it was not possible to distinguish core elements that had a greater shaping effect than others.

Both the historians and the archaeologists separated their discussions of culture and history. It was not always clear how the actions of the great, the characters of narrative history, were played out in the ancient cultures reconstructed from the archaeological record. Whereas historians frequently saw the acts of the great as the motor of change, archaeologists tended to view either diffusion or independent invention as the engine of culture growth. The image they most often used to describe the development of ancient societies was that of a bush with complexly intertwined branches; just such a shrub appeared as the frontispiece in Alfred L. Kroeber's (1948) *Anthropology,* which was a summary of what anthropology had been before the war and a blueprint of what it should become in the future.

The interwar-period archaeologists, who believed cultures were unique, often discussed them in comparative terms, although they usually refrained from examining the assumptions underlying their reconstructions and comparisons. Instead, they chose to let the metaphors and images speak for themselves. Thus, A. V. Kidder's (1932, 89) remarks that the Maya were "the most brilliant culture of the pre-Columbian world" or that the Carnegie Institution of Washington conducted research "... in two regions whose people were preeminent as builders of aboriginal culture, the Maya area of Middle America and the Pueblo country of the United States" were not value-neutral observations. Their intent was to convey both meaning and a particular image. By virtue of being civilized, the Maya were more like the Greeks and the modern West than their neighbors in Mexico or the contemporary hunter-gatherers of Tierra del Fuego.

As a result of investigations carried out both before and immediately after the war, archaeologists produced a steady stream of publications that depicted everyday life in the communities whose remains they had excavated (DiPeso 1951, 1956; Lewis and Kneberg 1946; Martin 1936, 1938, 1940; Strong 1935; Willey 1953). Architecture, pottery, tools, adornments, subsistence activities, burial customs, settlement patterns, and occasionally even the physical appearance of the residents themselves were described. Many of these accounts built on the idea of trait lists in which each of the various elements are treated conceptually as equivalent and of equal importance in shaping the cultural patterns of the different communities.

As archaeologists confronted the issues raised in the late 1930s by the debates over classification, concepts, and standardized criteria, the tenets of classicial empiricism that underpinned much of the interwar research were increasingly called into question. The challengers, who came from inside and outside the archaeological community, included Clyde Kluckhohn (1939, 1940). John Bennett (1943, 1946), and Walter W. Taylor (1948). They criticized traditional archaeological practice, which assumed that facts derived from sensory experience were the sole basis of knowledge and denied the role theoretical concepts played in the construction of knowledge. They argued that archaeological research should be organized around particular problems. The Depression and World War II provided the problem: how to promote and sustain economic growth.

Most archaeologists who grappled with this problem after the war advocated a cultural evolutionist perspective. They adopted a new set of images and metaphors. Instead of growing like branches on a bush, culture evolved through a ladder-like succession of stages or types culminating in civilization (Steward 1955, 43–63, 178–209). Cultural evolutionism rapidly became the dominant theoretical position in archaeology in the postwar era. In this view, culture resembled a layer cake built on a cultural core composed of functionally interconnected elements related to subsistence activities and economic arrangements (Steward and Seltzer 1938). This economic core had potent shaping effects on sociopolitical organization, which in turn conditioned the belief systems of a society. This contrasted with the views of Kidder and others, who believed that every part of a culture had the same potential to structure change. In other words, for the cultural evolutionists, culture progressed or developed as the economy shifted from hunting and foraging through simple farming to irrigation agriculture. Successive changes in the productive forces underwrote an increasing division of labor and the spread of exchange.

The cultural evolutionist perspective adopted by U.S. archaeologists in the late 1940s had its origins in the work of the Australian archaeologist V. Gordon Childe; however, U.S. archaeologists working in the Old and New Worlds apparently came to adopt his work by different routes. Many of the Old World specialists knew Childe personally and were familiar with his publications. For example, Theodore D. McCown of Berkeley, who excavated Skhul and el-Tabun caves in Palestine, recalled the impact that Childe's (1929) *The Danube in Prehistory* had on his own thinking while he was a graduate student in the 1930s (Theodore D. McCown, personal communication, 1964). Robert Braidwood, the Near Eastern archaeologist at the Oriental Institute in Chicago, engaged in a dialogue with the ideas Childe (1934, 1936, 1942, 1951) developed in *Man Makes Himself, What Happened in History* or *New Light on the Most Ancient East,* and *Social Evolution,* which was published after the war (Braidwood 1952; Braidwood and Braidwood 1953).

For the Americanists, including Julian Steward, the shift was initiated by Rafael Larco Hoyle, a major Peruvian sugar planter and knowledgeable *aficionado* of north coast archaeology. In 1946, Larco organized a conference on Peruvian archaeology at his hacienda for the U.S. archaeologists who were participating in the Virú Valley Project (Willey 1946). At the conference, Larco described the time-space framework he was using to organize the materials he excavated or purchased from professional looters on the north coast (Larco Hoyle 1948); it was inspired by Childe's *What Happened in History.* This framework, with minor modifications, was codified two years later with the publication of *A Reappraisal of Peruvian Archaeology* (Bennett 1948; Willey 1946). By the early 1950s, it had already become the dominant viewpoint in U.S. archaeology.

The archaeologists who adopted and promoted this view were concerned with explaining the similarities of development in different cultural traditions rather than their unique or divergent features. They sought cross-cultural, cause and effect regularities. They saw the state as the end-product of history and history as a continuum or development that culminated in the formation of the centralized state. Their methodology was, in the words of Julian Steward (1955, 88) "... avowedly scientific and generalizing rather than historical and particularizing." They proposed to use science to replace or update historical knowledge formulated in terms of the empiricist perspective that had dominated anthropological thought in the interwar years. The scientific methodology they advocated was derived ultimately from the logical positivists, who stressed the importance of clear concepts, procedures, and standards for measuring performance. The rationality of their approach resonated with the growing professionalism of the field and with the demand for scientific knowledge about the development of civilization. The scientism of their claims must be viewed in the context of the nationwide debates surrounding the formation and development of the National Science Foundation and the levels of support it would grant to the social sciences in general and archaeology in particular. Their claims also provided a historical backdrop for the economic growth and modernization theories that underpinned the political and economic policies of the U.S. government in the postwar era.

They were functionalists who accepted the distinction between synchronic and diachronic forms of analysis. Their goal was diachronic: to study how cultures changed. Their perspective was regional and comparative rather than particular or universal. To accomplish their aims, they separated the study of culture change or growth from the study of history. They were concerned with *evolutionary* rather than *historical* changes. The former were cumulative, reflecting the natural growth or unfolding of the potential inherent in the culture type itself, the gradual and continuous accumulation of small incremental shifts. When the potential of the stage was finally exhausted, a new, qualitatively different culture type with its own distinctive economic, political, and social arrangements developed rapidly. Historical changes, on the other hand, were conceptualized in terms of unique events, accidents that impinged on the normal growth and development of culture.

During the 1950s, these archaeologists produced detailed accounts of the succession of culture types in Peru, Mexico, and the Near East. Their studies supported an elaborate conception of world history: In these areas, identical developmental processes and succession of stages led to the formation of archaic civilizations and culminated, ultimately, in their domination by the West. Few archaeologists would have dissented with this view, which was most clearly expressed by Julian Steward (1950, 102–5), who wrote:

> The rise and decline of the kingdoms in the ancient centers of civilization in Egypt, Mesopotamia, India, China, Meso-America, and the Andes is often described as the rise and fall of civilization. It is true that the particular kinds of societies found in these centers did not survive, but most of the basic cultural achievements, the essential features of civilization, were passed on to other nations. In each of these centers both culture and society changed rather considerably during the early periods, and

everywhere the developmental processes were about the same.... At first there were small communities of incipient farmers. Later the communities cooperated in the construction of irrigation works and the populations became larger and more settled. Villages amalgamated into states under theocratic rulers.... Finally culture ceased to develop, and the states of each area entered into competition with one another.

... [A]n era of cyclical conquest followed. The conquests conformed to a fairly stable pattern.... Each state began to compete with others for tribute and advantages. One or another state succeeded in dominating the others, that is, in building an empire, but such empires ran their course and collapsed after some ... years only to be succeeded by another empire not very different from the first.

For the historian this era of cyclical conquests is filled with great men, wars and battle strategy, shifting power centers, and other social events. For the culture historian the changes are much less significant than those of the previous eras when the basic civilizations developed or, in the Near East, those of the subsequent Iron Age when the cultural patterns changed again and the centers of civilization shifted to new areas.... The industrial revolution brought profound cultural change to Western Europe and caused competition for colonies and for areas of exploitation. Japan entered the competition as soon as she acquired the general pattern. The realignments of power caused by Germany's losses in the first world war and by Italy's and Japan's in the second are of a social order. What new cultural patterns will result from these remains to be seen.

The general assumption today seems to be that we are in danger of basic cultural changes caused by the spread of communism. Russia acquired drastically new cultural patterns as a result of her revolution. Whether communism has the same meaning in other nations has still to be determined.

Steward recognized that this conception of world history was still too general and that certain areas did not fit neatly into it. The Puerto Rico Project, which he conceived in the late 1940s and which the Rockefeller Foundation funded, was intended to overcome its limitations. The project was designed to study the social anthropology of one of those areas "... with modern civilizations of different kinds or with folk cultures and societies that have come under some form of Euro-American or Russian dominance;" it would broadly concern itself with finding out "... how the influences emanating from a highly industrialized society [such as the United States] affected the local and regional varieties of culture found in one of its agrarian dependencies" (Steward 1950, 154, 129). In Steward's view, anthropology was a historical social science, and archaeologists were the technical specialists in the discipline who provided information about that portion of historical record that predated the appearance of written accounts.

Archaeologists advocating a cultural evolutionist viewpoint produced different kinds of accounts in the 1950s. These included reports describing cultural development in particular regions—the Virú Valley on the north coast of Peru or the Tehuacán Valley in central Mexico, for example (MacNeish 1964; Willey 1953). There were efforts to use information gleaned from a particular region or from various localities to construct a picture of cultural development in entire culture areas, such as the central Andes or Mesoamerica (Bennett and Bird 1949; Coe 1962). There were innovative attempts to provide accounts of continental or even hemispherical scale (Willey 1960a, 1960b; Willey and Phillips 1958). Comparative studies on a global scale dealt with the rise of irrigation civilizations in semiarid areas and the development of cities (Steward et al. 1960; Braidwood and Willey 1962).

By the mid-1950s, the steady flow of site reports and surveys significantly increased the amount of empirical information available about the aboriginal cultures of the New World. Seminars sponsored by the Society for American Archaeology in 1955 examined these data in order to clarify and elaborate theoretical concepts and to gain an increased appreciation of the archaeological record. The participants discussed a range of topics including an archaeological classification of culture contact situations, an archaeological approach to the study of cultural stability, and the functional and evolutionary implications of community patterning (Wauchope 1956).

Criticisms of the cultural evolutionary perspective began to appear in the mid-1950s. They were mounted by Robert Adams at the Oriental Institute in Chicago and John Rowe at the University of California, both of whom worked in areas—the Near East and Peru, respectively—where existed ancient civilizations and written accounts. Adams worked in a milieu where archaeological applications of cultural-evolutionary thought and efforts to reconstruct ancient Mesopotamian social patterns from textual materials coexisted productively in the same building. Rowe (1963), who earlier had combined textual and archaeological information to describe Inca society at the time of the European invasion, was increasingly critical of attempts to describe cultural development in the central Andes on the basis of what happened in the Virú Valley, especially when archaeological data from the south exhibited different patterns of change. Whereas Adams was generally sympathetic to the cultural evolutionary theory, Rowe was not; in spite of their different sentiments regarding cultural evolutionism, their criticisms were, in fact, remarkably similar.

They focused on three features of cultural evolutionist theory. First, they questioned the functionalist assumptions related to the integrity of economic core and the presumed association of given technologies with particular forms of social organization and ideas (Adams 1960; Rowe 1962). Second, they demanded greater specification of the relation between the economic and political spheres of particular cultural types (Adams 1956). Third, they challenged the way cultural evolutionists separated the study of cultural processes from history and advocated, instead, studies that synthesized and explained in a convincing fashion the historical specificity of particular archaeological sequences (Adams 1960; Rowe 1962, 1963).

Their criticisms coincided with other critiques of economic growth and development studies, which also stress the importance of historical specificity. By the late 1950s, the crucial wider question was how to promote capitalist development in the face of intense and increasingly frequent social and political reactions against it. Studies of particular culture types or their succession did not provide a satisfactory answer to this policy question. What was needed was specific historical information that would permit the identification and secure the political dominance of those groups in the Third World that would promote capitalist development. Neither the cultural evolutionists nor the early economic growth studies came to grips with the real events and transformations of the historical record. They were unable to deal with the mechanisms that produced the conditions and balance of forces specific to particular societies (Bock 1963; Smith 1973).

A second body of criticism appeared in the early 1960s and crystallized rapidly after 1965 (Wylie 1981, 76–140). Its proponents—notably Lewis Binford (1962, 1964, 1965)—criticized the traditional aims and practices of archaeologists, arguing that they failed to serve either scientific or historical objectives. Binford argued instead for a New Archaeology that would go beyond the classical empiricism that underwrote both the conceptual frameworks and practices of the older generation. He adopted the logical positivism advocated by Steward, Seltzer, and Kluckhohn in the 1940s and the procedures for hypothesis testing propounded by Carl Hempel (1965) in the 1950s. He embraced the perspective that culture was a complex, highly textured, multidimensional system that could not be reduced to a single plane; that the artifacts excavated by archaeologists functioned in different cultural contexts; and that changes in one part of the cultural system led to changes in other parts. Binford chose Old Copper Culture artifacts from the Great Lakes region to illustrate his claims. He maintained that the increased production of copper tools in the Late Archaic Period was related to population increase following the shift to more permanent fishing villages along the shores of the lakes during the Nipissing highwater stand. The inhabitants of these villages made items out of copper that functioned as status markers rather than tools, as most archaeologists had argued. In Binford's view, they functioned in different cultural contexts or subsystems. This line of criticism rapidly became dominant after the 1968 publication of *New Perspectives in Archeology* (Binford and Binford 1968). I will examine this development in more detail in the next chapter.

ARCHAEOLOGISTS AND THE EASTERN MEDITERRANEAN

While the Americanist and prehistoric archaeologists sought evidence that shed light on the evolution of human society from the state of nature through savagery and barbarism to civilization, archaeologists investigating the classical world knew the objects of their inquiries were already civilized. The orientalists who worked in the Ancient East knew their subjects were either civilized or at least well on the way to civilization; they sought to prove the temporal priority of these societies and to demonstrate their relations with the ancient peoples of Asia Minor, Greece, and, more distantly, Rome. The biblical archaeologists who toiled by their side in Syria and Palestine—or more broadly "from Gibraltar to the Indus valley" in the lands touched by the Bible—knew the objects of their investigations had discovered both the road to civilization and the means of salvation: the Judeo-Christian religious tradition.

Because of their subject matter, the classical archaeologists, the orientalists, and their biblical colleagues already had well-formed ideas about what they would find among the "older civilizations" as Sterling Dow (1946, 14) called them. Their excavations and surveys, as well as the close studies they made of inscriptions and objects in museums or private collections, merely added detail to the outlines and images that were fixed in their minds. In light of Thomas Kuhn's (1970, 35–42) views about the structure of science practice, they were engaged in the puzzle solving of normal science—using all of the available pieces and finding new facts to fill the existing holes in the final picture. The activities associated with normal science—using established procedures and rules to complete the puzzle—provide a fertile medium in which classical empiricism, founded on the belief that only information gained through sensory experience provides true knowledge, can thrive and reproduce itself. The archaeological research carried out in the eastern Mediterranean from the Depression to the collapse of the postwar era of sustained growth in the late 1960s was overwhelmingly rooted in classical empiricism. These archaeologists, who were often quick to incorporate new techniques such as radiocarbon dating into their research, continued to accumulate facts. They largely avoided questioning their conceptual frameworks, however, and eschewed theoretical discussions about the formation, development, and structure of the societies whose remains they were excavating.

The Archaeological Institute of America, the organizational infrastructure of classical archaeology in the United States, contracted during the Depression as its membership and contributions declined. In 1934, it ceased publication of *Art and Archaeology*, a popular archaeology and fine arts magazine with an annual circulation of ten thousand (Sheftel 1979). Fewer field projects were undertaken in Greece, Asia Minor, and Cyprus, and some involved only a single season or two. Other projects were large and well financed, especially the Rockefeller-supported, multiseason excavations and restoration of the Agora in Athens directed by Leslie Shear (1936) of Princeton. Besides the continuing excavations at Corinth supported by the American School at Athens, the other long-term projects of the Depression era were Hetty Goldman's (1935) Bryn Mawr research at Tarsus, Carl Blegen's (1934) University of Cincinnati excavations at Troy, and Yale University's investigations at Dura-Europos in Syria, which were cosponsored with the French Academy of Inscriptions and Belles-lettres and directed by Michael Rostovtzeff, the Sterling Professor of Classical Archaeology and Ancient History, who had recently been hired away from the University of Wisconsin (Hopkins 1979).

Dura-Europos was a settlement on the middle Euphrates River where Greeks and orientals intermixed in the wake of Alexander's conquest of the Persian Empire to forge an "oecumenical civilization" that was active in the eastern provinces of the Roman Empire and that "formed the cultural background of the Byzantine Empire. But this Hellenistic Greek civilization ... [remained] the civilization of minorities, of the ruling class only, and never completely absorbed the ancient civilizations of the various parts of the Near East" (Rostovtzeff 1938, 6). Rostovtzeff's (1938, 9) goal was to "... throw light on the problem of the origin and growth of the Greco-Semitic civilization of Mesopotamia." The project stressed the importance of the cosmopolitan minorities at Dura-Europos. Furthermore, the excavations were undertaken at a time of rising Arab nationalism, particularly strong during the 1920s and 1930s in Syria, which was viewed as an avenue to oil-rich regions in Iraq and the Gulf. In the modern world, cosmopolitan minorities, reminiscent of those that thrived at Dura-Europos, would keep this avenue open to the Western oil companies, especially those centered in the United States and France.

The expedition to Dura-Europos may reveal wider understandings of U.S. society in the 1930s. Recall that archaeology was reconfigured in the late nineteenth century, so that Greece was linked with civilization, Christianity, the New Testament, and the white race, whereas the Ancient East was connected with the Old Testament,

Judaism, nonwhite Semitic buffer races, and oriental societies that were not quite as civilized as those of Greece or Rome. The Dura-Europos expedition took place at a time when U.S. political-economic interests were expanding rapidly in the oil-rich areas of the old oriental empires, when the indigenous peoples of the Middle East resisted the colonizing efforts of the French and English, and when a young archaeologist from Yale wondered whether a .22 caliber pistol would stop charging Arabs (Hopkins 1979, 9, 36). Symbolically, Dura-Europos was a Roman settlement, complete with Christian church and synagogue, that stood atop of the ruins of earlier Semitic civilizations and shrines dedicated to Semitic gods. Given the physical structure of the site as well as pervasive views about hierarchies of cultures and races in U.S. society, it must have seemed natural that a classical archaeologist and ancient historian rather than an orientalist would direct the project.

By turning their gaze toward the Near East in the 1930s, the classical archaeologists were able to ignore what was happening at the time in Central Europe (Arnold 1990; Schnapp 1981). At the least, they did not address the events in the pages of the *American Journal of Archaeology*. Before 1933, prehistoric archaeology in Germany was distinctly less important than research in the classical world or the Orient. However, once the National Socialists came to power, this changed. Classical and oriental studies were denigrated and marginalized, and prehistoric archaeology of Germany flourished as a rapidly growing number of practitioners tied their investigations to the new interests of the state, providing arguments that underwrote both its racism and territorial expansion.

U.S. archaeology flourished in the Near East during the 1930s. The Rockefeller-funded Oriental Institute at Chicago, directed by James Breasted until his death in 1935, "... was at work at strategic points along the entire Fertile Crescent." These included Anatolia, Syria, three projects in Iraq, Megiddo in Palestine, Persepolis in Iran, the prehistoric survey of the Nile Valley, and the epigraphic and architectural survey housed at Luxor, which was funded in part by Julius Rosenwald, a University of Chicago trustee and philanthropist interested mainly in Negro education (Breasted 1977, 391–92, 402). Other institutions also undertook archaeological expeditions in the Near East on a much more limited scale during the 1930s. For example, archaeologists sponsored by the University of Pennsylvania and Dropsie College worked at several localities on Cyprus as well as at Tepe Gawra in the oil-rich Mosul region of Iraq and Tepe Hissar in Iran (Winegrad 1993, 96–101). Archaeologists affiliated with the American School of Oriental Research in Jerusalem—alone and in collaboration with U.S. universities and seminaries as well as the British—undertook excavations at various sites in Palestine and conducted an extensive archaeological survey in the Levant (Glueck 1938; King 1983, 61–109).

William F. Albright of Johns Hopkins University was the driving force behind the American School of Oriental Research in Jerusalem and the reorientation of biblical archaeology in the United States during the 1920s and 1930s (Dever 1990, 12–23). Albright saw German biblical criticism (higher criticism) as a threat that could potentially undercut the historical foundations of faith in the Scriptures, especially in the books of the Old Testament. Much like other conservative and evangelical Protestants, he wanted to use archaeology to counter the challenge and to demonstrate the fundamental truth of the Bible. Like most archaeologists of his day,

Albright was also a classical empiricist who, in spite of his belief in the divine inspiration of the Scriptures, believed that the existence of facts was unproblematic and that they could be gathered systematically by using recognized procedures—in this instance, the excavation techniques devised by George Reisner earlier in the century. He sought evidence from sites dating to the second millennium B.C. to provide an authentic context for the Patriarchal Era of Genesis, to document the Mosaic age and Exodus, to situate the Israelite faith earlier than the biblical critics suggested, and to portray uniqueness of Israelite religion and its superiority to contemporary religious systems (Dever 1989).

In the context of the Fundamentalist-Modernist religious controversy of the 1920s and 1930s, Albright occupied a middle ground (Marsden 1980, 176). This controversy was waged largely in the Midwest where he went to school; the Fundamentalists were most prominent among groups that splintered from the Northern Baptists and Presbyterians, and the Baptist Divinity School at the University of Chicago was the country's leading center of Modernist views. Unlike the Fundamentalists, Albright was not particularly critical of the Modernists, except for their penchant for higher criticism, which undercut the historical basis of faith in the Bible; he was not profoundly disturbed by the linkages of Modernist views with Darwinism and evolutionism or even by their denial of the authority of church officials in hierarchically organized denominations (Cashdollar 1989, 276). His acceptance of classical empiricism and the use of scientific methods gave him credibility that was not usually granted to religious conservatives who were more openly critical of Modernist views.

The secularized biblical archaeology of Albright all but disappeared after the Fundamentalist-Modernist controversy wore itself out in the 1930s. Fundamentalism as an organized movement had collapsed because of the separatist tactics of its leaders, which moved their followers out of mainstream Protestant sects. The new conservative leaders who emerged after the war—Billy Graham, for instance—remained in the mainstream denominations. They portrayed the liberals as Congregationalists and Unitarians from Boston who had close ties with Eastern Establishment capitalism, who encouraged the participation and direct action of the clergy in the civil rights and antiwar movements, and who were either soft on communism or tried to steer a middle course between it and capitalism. The conservatives, of course, also opposed existentialists who treated the Bible as mythology (Wuthnow 1988, 142–48).

Biblical archaeology was slowly reconstituted in the postwar milieu shaped by the conservative-liberal religious debates. Its practitioners came to view it as a set of techniques—stratigraphy or pottery analysis, for instance—that were auxiliary to biblical studies. Biblical archaeologists were seminarians who had studied Semitic languages and Old Testament history and theology. They used archaeological techniques to increase understanding of the Scriptures and to demonstrate the historicity of biblical events by confirming that they had actually occurred and were represented by the fortifications, public buildings, or destruction layers of sites that linked with events and personages mentioned in the Old Testament. In the 1950s and 1960s, their interests and activities increasingly diverged from those of more secular colleagues in colleges and universities who did not share their theological interests and goals of reconstructing the Patriarchal Era or the Mosaic Age (Dever 1990, 19–23).

As a result, biblical archaeology increasingly became the domain of conservative Protestants drawn largely from the Core Culture. It thrived and expanded steadily during the 1950s and 1960s, judging by the growing popularity of the *Biblical Archaeologist,* first published in 1937, and the appearance of a steady stream of books concerned with the subject. Excavations conducted by the Israeli state at Masada in the mid-1960s further spurred interest in the United States in the culture and history of the ancient Israelites and Canaanites (Silberman 1989, 87–101). For the biblical archaeologists, the excavations confirmed that they had at least one shared interest with the Israeli state apparatus, a perception that provided some impetus for launching the *Biblical Archaeological Review* in 1974. Biblical archaeology associated with the New Testament was transformed into the archaeology of early Christianity and merged with classical archaeology as its center of gravity shifted from the Levant to Greece and Rome. These were preeminently the domains of Eastern Establishment archaeologists after the war.

In 1948, a group of scholars, including archaeologists affiliated with the Oriental Institute and various schools of the Archaeological Institute of America, met in Boston with a former U.S. Ambassador to Egypt and his Egyptian counterpart to lament the deplorable lack of knowledge and understanding Americans had about Egypt and the Near East. More importantly, they discussed the formation of a permanent research center in Cairo that would provide U.S. citizens with firsthand experience that differed in kind from that offered by the Middle Eastern "area program" at Princeton (Dow 1948). The American Research Center in Egypt was founded that year; its aims were to study not only "the living Muslim present" and the more remote periods of Egyptian culture, "the most venerable civilization on earth," but also the intervening periods influenced by developments in the Greek, Roman, Hellenistic, and Byzantine-Coptic worlds. With the exception of John Wilson of the Oriental Institute, who was named director of the new school, all of the other officers were affiliated with Eastern Establishment institutions located east of the Hudson River: Harvard, Yale, Columbia, and the Metropolitan and Brooklyn Museums.

Modest grants from the United States Educational Foundation established by the Fulbright Act and from the Bollingen Foundation supported two fellows each year at the American Research Center in Egypt, one in Islamic studies and the other in Egyptology. The center's first excavation was supported by U.S. government funds to record and preserve monuments in Nubia that would be inundated by the Aswan Dam. The project began in 1963 at Gebel Adda near Abu Simbel and focused initially on the history of the early Christian period and medieval Islamic architecture (Riefstahl 1962, 34). A matching grant of $500,000 from the U.S. government, a supplementary award from the National Geographic Society for the excavations at Gebel Adda, and increased financial support from the universities affiliated with the center underwrote expanded archaeological research throughout the 1960s (Riefstahl 1963).

The School for Classical Studies in Athens and Rome reopened soon after the war ended. New circumstances shaped their operations during the 1950s and 1960s as archaeological research programs sponsored by universities—notably Princeton, Harvard, Bryn Mawr, and Pennsylvania—became increasingly more important.

Shear's excavations at the Agora in Athens, which had been interrupted by the war, received additional Rockefeller funding and were opened again in the late 1940s during the unsettled conditions fomented by the Greek civil war; they continued through the 1960s, first under the direction of Homer Thompson and then Leslie Shear, Jr., whose father had initiated the project in the 1930s. Five of the twelve fellows appointed to the center in the late 1940s to work at the Agora or on other projects were women. In 1948, the Greek government issued a five-year moratorium limiting the number of excavations that could be conducted by foreign research institutes in the country. Although archaeologists continued to work on museum collections and materials from earlier excavations in Greece, this decision coincided with a marked increase in activity at the school in Rome and in Turkey, where excavation and export permits were easier to acquire.

The School of Classical Studies of the American Academy in Rome was reorganized in 1947. It accepted nineteen students in its summer program and appointed five fellows for the 1947–48 academic year. A year later, the school initiated its excavations at Cosa, which continued through the 1960s. By 1955, thirty-four students participated in the school's summer field program, roughly half of whom received Fulbright grants that year. Superficial observations suggest that the level of U.S. government funding for archaeological research, largely through its Fulbright and foreign currency programs, was greater in Italy than Greece in the postwar years. Because much of this research was focused on the Roman period, the corporatist U.S. government was, in effect, spending more money to investigate the activities of an early imperial state than those of the less centralized city-states in Greece with their intermittent traditions of participatory democracy.

Classical archaeology in Greece and Italy in the postwar years was partly text driven. Excavations provided objects and associations that verified, clarified, or expanded understanding of information provided by classical authors. This meant that archaeologists were heavily influenced by the observations of ancient writers and used the explanations provided, for example, by Homer concerning the destruction of Troy or by Julius Caesar and Tacitus about the migrations of Germanic peoples. It also meant that the classical archaeologists rarely, if ever, examined the implicit assumptions of the analytical categories they used, especially those concerned with the existence of cultural and racial hierarchies. These assumptions were widespread and their prevalence clearly revealed when archaeologists and other writers attempted to correlate linguistic evidence concerning early Indo-European languages with archaeological data and skeletal remains. They frequently assumed that race, language, and culture were inextricably linked and constructed elaborate theories to relate the Indo-European problem to the historic specificity of particular regions.

For example, R. A. Crossland (1971), who summarized the status of the Indo-European problem, wrote that most scholars believe that the early Indo-European language was spread by migrants from Mesopotamia, where agriculture was invented, to adjacent northern regions and that Semitic barbarians from poorer lands to the west, Syria, then moved into Mesopotamia in such numbers that their languages swamped and transformed the Sumerian language of southern Mesopotamia. Northern Indo-European speakers actually moved into Greece toward the end of the third millennium B.C., where they were responsible for major cultural and social changes. On the one hand, Crossland argues that scholars did not necessarily believe the immigrants were homogeneous in cultural or physical type; on the other hand, he suggests that these innovative migrants were responsible for the widespread destruction of many settlements at the beginning of the Middle Helladic Period and for the spread of Minyan pottery throughout Greece and parts of Anatolia. Claims that the immigrants can be recognized by their material culture and their physical type, as some anthropologists argued, seemingly contradict assertions about the extent of their cultural and physical heterogeneity.

The Indo-European problem was important, because it was necessary to account for the existence of civilizations that preceded those of the Greek and Aegean city-states of classical antiquity and seemingly arose from simple farming communities. The Indo-European problem is just one example of how notions of cultural hierarchy and cultural growth or development were linked with the ideas of an innovative race that thrived in the Pontic region or north of the Caucasus Mountains and diffusion from areas with high "potential" to areas with less. In a sense, the arguments of Kossinna and the eugenicists from the 1920s and 1930s were accepted with slight modification and little discussion; what was debated in the 1950s and 1960s was the location of the original Indo-European homeland.

DISCUSSION

Archaeology in the United States was reorganized again after World War II. Some archaeologists affiliated themselves with anthropology; others reaffirmed their connections with classics, oriental studies, or Old Testament theology. Archaeology's center of gravity shifted from museums, the American Schools established overseas, and the federal relief programs of the 1930s to academic departments in universities. The influx of students on the GI Bill in the 1940s and 1950s and the "Baby Boom" in the 1960s fueled a steadily increasing expansion in both the size and number of universities and departments in which some form of archaeology was taught.

This meant that university programs established before the war trained many of the first generation of postwar students, who subsequently accepted positions in departments and programs that were established or achieved after the war. As a result, the linkage between established archaeology programs and the newer ones founded after the war has been characterized as a colonizing process. For example, Americanist archaeologists trained at Harvard colonized Tulane University, and Michigan-trained archaeologists turned Louisiana State University into one of its outposts in the Southeast. When the established programs expanded, they often hired their own graduates or those from other established programs—for instance, there are multiple connections between Michigan and Chicago and between Harvard and the University of Pennsylvania. From the late 1950s through the 1960s, the existing graduate programs in anthropology were not able to meet the demand of new departments and universities for archaeologists trained in anthropology, that is, Americanist or Old World prehistoric archaeologists. This process continued until the early 1970s, when the expansion of both universities and departments with archaeology programs finally ground to a stop.

Archaeology expanded unevenly after the war because of its new connections with other academic disciplines. Anthropology flourished in the postwar milieu, whereas classics survived. New budgetary units were created in the postwar era in many universities—UCLA or Temple, for example—when joint anthropology and sociology programs divided and established their disciplinary autonomy. In addition, anthropology departments became more numerous in the 1950s and 1960s than classics or oriental studies programs that supported archaeology. Even within the same university, anthropology departments typically had more faculty and students than classics departments by the 1950s, and they employed more archaeologists. By placing themselves on the science side of the humanities versus the sciences debate, anthropologists positioned themselves to gain access to National Science Foundation funds as well as Fulbright and other kinds of federal support for their research investigations.

Before the war and immediately after it, archaeology in the United States was almost exclusively the domain of the college-educated, white middle and upper classes. Few members of buffer races from southern and eastern Europe, Native Americans, Asians or African Americans were employed as professional archaeologists before the late 1950s. Judging by the changing composition of the Archaeological Institute of America and the Society for American Archaeology during the postwar era, class and gender relations developed differently in classical archaeology from Americanist and prehistoric archaeology. In classical archaeology, class position was more important than gender in the postwar construction of the discipline, as both men and women trained at private institutions in the East continued to enter the profession. Of the twelve fellows appointed to the School of Classical Studies in Athens in the late 1940s, five were women; several of the women who had been fellows at the school in the 1930s continued their affiliation with it and remained prominent in the Archaeological Institute of America in the 1950s and 1960s. Roughly the same proportion of men to women belonged to the professional organization in the late 1950s and early 1960s as in the 1930s.

The Society for American Archaeology exhibited a different growth pattern during the 1950s, when the ratio of new male and female members was more than 13 to 1, and the percentage of women in the society actually declined slightly in the late 1950s. This reflected changes in the composition of the profession. Members of various buffer races that constituted the immigrant working class at the turn of the century entered college and the profession for the first time as Americanist archaeologists; however, given the gender bias of the GI Bill, most of those who did so were men. During the late 1950s and early 1960s, increasingly more men than women undertook graduate training in Americanist and prehistoric archaeology. They received a steadily increasing proportion of the doctorates in anthropology awarded for archaeological research. There was also differential gender discrimination during the postwar years, as some men trained in Americanist archaeology refused, for various reasons, to permit the participation of women graduate students in field research projects they directed. Others encouraged their participation and provided financial support for their efforts.

Two popular stereotypes of archaeologists already well developed in the early 1930s movie, *The Mummy,* were those of the older, obsessed professor and a younger counterpart, the adventurer striding across the desert or through the rain forest in search of lost cities or treasure. These stereotypes were captured in the 1980s by the movie characters of Indiana Jones and his father, who reflect the hypermasculinization of Americanist archaeology that occurred in the 1950s and 1960s, an era when *Playboy* appeared on the newsstands, crowds lined up at movie theaters to see James Bond films, and gunfighters, secret agents, and Green Berets filled a mythic landscape shaped by the Cold War (Slotkin 1992). Myriad sources fed the construction of these images. They include stories about the activities, real or presumed, of archaeologists who had served in Army or Navy Intelligence during World War I and the interwar years; accounts, some reaching epic proportions, of the experiences of those archaeologists who served in the Office of Strategic Services (OSS) during the Second World War; and the remembrances of wartime camaraderie and the perceptions of GIs who had been in Asia, North Africa, or the Pacific (Brunhouse 1971). These reminiscences underpin the image that white, heterosexual men, acting alone or in concert, are dominant actors and that all others—women, gay men, lesbians, and people of color—play passive, secondary, or oppositional roles at best. They coincided with massive campaigns waged in the media by corporations and the state to promote consumerism and to get women out of the work force (McLuhan 1951, 40, 70). These campaigns, which idealized family life and appropriate behaviors for men and women, were very successful. Their prescriptions were institutionalized in some universities and regions where archaeological investigations were carried out.

CHAPTER 5

The New Archaeology and the Neoliberal

State, 1969 to 1993

U.S. society was in crisis by the late 1960s. Economic growth had slowed almost to a standstill, real wages were declining, and social unrest was sweeping across the country. City dwellers took to the streets to complain about the effects of urban renewal, the construction of highways through their neighborhoods, and spiraling health costs. Antiwar and civil-rights demonstrators rallied to challenge the Vietnam War and racism; and college students occupied buildings to protest the war and the dehumanization of higher education. The origins of the crisis were rooted in the unwritten compromise reached by capital and labor in the late 1940s. The capitalist class, led by its international monopoly and finance sectors, settled for aspects of a welfare state, a managed Keynesian economic policy, inexpensive comprehensive education, a commitment to full employment, and marginalizing its own free-market elements in return for labor peace. Organized labor agreed to participate in a capitalist growth economy shaped by Cold War rhetoric and xenophobia. However, the foundations for the agreement were unstable from its inception and became steadily and noticeably more rickety in the 1960s as serious restructuring of the U.S. economy began and the logic underlying the established political parties disintegrated (Hall 1988, 36–41; O'Connor 1973; Phillips 1982, 1993, 3–31; Wolfe 1977, 1981).

The economies of the capitalist states were rapidly integrated into a single world system and reorganized after 1968. This was already called the "New International Economic Order" by 1980 (Kolko 1988; Marchak 1991). It signaled a shift from extractive industries to service economies and to the increasing importance of finance capital. Whereas the first transnational corporations, which developed after the turn of the century, were lured by petroleum and mineral resources, those that began to appear in the late 1960s were attracted to the Third World and parts of Europe by the availability of cheap, non-union labor and the ability to hide profits. U.S. corporations—notably electronics and semiconductor firms such as Fairchild, General Electric, and Intel—established overseas subsidiaries and factories. This process was facilitated by improved communications, computers, and containerized shipping. In the 1970s, ideologues at the World Bank and the International Monetary Fund (IMF) encouraged the less-developed nations to promote export-oriented economies, and private U.S. banks began to make high-interest, high-risk loans that enabled those nations to do so. In 1970, the banks made 40 percent of their profits abroad; six years later, 72 percent of their profits came from overseas. When the United States abrogated the Bretton Woods Agreement in 1971, all of the capitalist states were suddenly forced

"... to subordinate every aspect of economic policy to the defence of currency," and the banking and finance sectors quickly asserted their hegemony (van der Pijl 1984, 262).

An important political realignment also began during Richard Nixon's presidency from 1969 to 1974. The national and international capitalists found a new unity of interest in creating conditions that would ensure higher rates of profit. They were attracted in growing numbers to the Republican Party because of its efforts to diminish state control or regulation of the economy and to promote private-sector initiatives. These policies facilitated the restructuring of corporations through mergers and the movement of industry and capital to areas inside and outside the United States where cheap labor was available. Both processes promoted further capital flight, deregulation, and the appearance of self-appointed boards from the private sector, such as the Trilateral Commission or the Municipal Assistance Corporation of New York, to manage the economy and control expenditures by elected officials (Crozier, Huntington, and Watanuki 1975; Sklar 1980).

The Southern and Sunbelt strategies of the Republican Party articulated widespread discontent by attacking the peace, civil rights, and countercultural movements and various welfare and entitlement programs. These strategies simultaneously fed on and fueled racism, xenophobia, nativism, the resurgence of self-reliant individualism, and an uncritical patriotism that identified with power and subordinated contested differences. They shifted the Republican Party's center of gravity from the Northeast, where it had resided in the 1930s, to the South and the West, where there were large nonwhite or immigrant populations. They gained support in the predominantly white, working-class neighborhoods and suburbs of the deindustrializing cities in the Northeast and the Midwest, which had been historic strongholds of organized labor and the Democratic Party (Bennett 1988, 332–408; Davis 1986, 103–53). They also undergirded "law and order" platforms in the 1968 and 1972 presidential elections, which criminalized the actions of the poor, peace and civil rights activists, middle-class college protesters, and counterculture advocates, and which created heavily armed SWAT teams and expanded domestic surveillance. They also fueled the American Federation of Labor's defection from the Democratic Party in 1972 and the reactionary counterdemonstrations organized by the building trades and teamsters in the early 1970s.

Nixon's presidency was a transitional stage marked by contradictory policies and legislation. Old-style, corporatist regulatory legislation—such as the National Environmental Policy Act (1969)—was enacted to permit a limited degree of state control over industrial pollution and environmental issues; however, the provisions of the act as well as the regulatory powers of the Environmental Protection Agency were immediately attacked and steadily gutted by amendments added during the 1970s and 1980s. This regulatory legislation existed side by side with new-style, neoliberal policies that removed the federal government from certain public arenas. For example, the State and Local Federal Assistance Act (1972) transferred the burden of funding public assistance programs from the federal government to the states. During the next twenty years, this would ultimately bring many cities and states to the edge of bankruptcy and lead to austerity programs imposed by private boards, such as the Philadelphia Industrial Development Corporation or New York's Municipal Assistance Corporation, whose members are answerable to the finance sector rather than elected officials or voters. This also led to chronic underfunding and repeated attempts to dismantle social programs, including higher education, the costs of which were increasingly shifted back to the individual during the 1970s. It also promoted taxpayers' revolts, reduced unemployment compensation, and forced workers into unsafe or unpleasant employment at low wages with few, if any, benefits. Between 1968 and 1981, the typical worker with three dependents experienced a 20-percent decline in the real standard of living (Davis 1984, 34).

A new form of hegemony, dominated by banking and finance capital, was firmly in place by 1978. The banking industry was steadily deregulated during the 1970s; tax concessions granted by the federal government and the steadily higher interest rates banks charged for loans and debt servicing underwrote enormous profits by the middle of the decade. Banks had money to lend, and they sought high-risk loans to maximize profit rates. Large banks, like Chase Manhattan or CitiBank, became nodal points in the national industrial structure being created by mergers. Their officers sat on the boards of directors of corporations swallowed up and created by mergers. Officers from the same bank, serving on the corporate boards of different companies, created a web of interlocking directorates. By 1978, there were several dozen interlocked directorates, each clustered around a regionally based bank— Chase Manhattan and CitiBank in New York, First Boston, Mellon in Pittsburgh, BankAmerica in California, and others (Domhoff 1983, 56–81; Menshikov 1969). These and other banks provided the capital that financed mergers, fueled real estate speculation, refinanced risky loans, paid for debt servicing, and underwrote the massive expansion of military expenditures in the 1980s.

The specter of a major economic crisis loomed on the horizon by 1978; if the less-developed countries defaulted on loan repayments, the banks that had made the loans would be shaken to their very foundations and might even be forced to close. They succeeded in putting off the "savings and loan" crisis for nearly a decade with a three-pronged strategy: (1) refinancing some loans and writing off others; (2) abandoning both détente and the Trilateral Commission prescriptions for an interconnected three-region capitalist empire rooted in linkages between the United States and Latin America, Japan and Asia, and Europe and Africa in favor of all-out responses to the presumed threats posed by the Soviet Union, Grenada, and other newly recognized enemies of the United States; and (3) expanding military expenditures. This 180-degree policy shift occurred in the middle of Trilateralist Jimmy Carter's presidency and cost him reelection. In 1980, Ronald Reagan emphasized Carter's apparent vacillation and his softness toward Iran and the "Evil Empire." He emphasized the need for new supply-side economic policies that would provide tax concessions for the wealthy in order to stimulate investments, the benefits of which would quickly trickle down to the middle and working classes. He promised to end failed social programs and eliminate bloated bureaucracies.

What followed in the wake of the 1978 policy changes were a series of initiatives in the late 1970s and 1980s that wreaked havoc in Africa, Latin America, and the Eastern bloc. For example, the Latin American countries, which had a total combined debt of $220 billion in 1979, paid $365 billion in principal and interest during the 1980s; however, in 1990, they were even deeper in debt; they now owed more than $420 billion even though they had just paid an amount equal to 164 percent of their debt a decade earlier. More than 60 percent of its people now live in poverty, and probably no more than ten thousand individuals out of the 450 million people who live there benefited materially from the policies imposed by the International Monetary Fund, the World Bank, and the local governments forced to do their bidding. Similar, if not worse, conditions prevail throughout much of Africa. The policies promoted levels of military expenditure that effectively bankrupted the USSR and provoked important reorganizations of the class structures in states on the margins of the capitalist world—notably the former USSR and Eastern Europe. These processes have, in turn, sparked a series of genocidal nationalist struggles fueled, in large part, by Western capital.

The policies also underwrote a major episode of class formation in the United States that began in the late 1970s. It was launched by a combination of factors: the restructuring of the labor market, a 10- to 20-percent devaluation of the dollar in mid-1977 followed by declining real wages, rising prices and interest rates, and steadily growing unemployment coupled with smaller unemployment benefits covering shorter periods of time. It was sustained by the massive income redistribution facilitated by military expenditures and by the tax concessions enacted by Congress during the 1980s. This promoted the formation of an increasingly polarized, two-class society: one with money and the other impoverished. A fivefold increase in the number of millionaires in the late 1970s and early 1980s left the wealthiest 1 percent of the population in control of a steadily rising proportion of the wealth—40 percent and still climbing. In the same period, the percentage of the country's wealth held by the poorest 40 percent declined from about 11 percent to less than 8 percent. In the process, the middle classes were squeezed. A few moved into the moneyed tier, whereas a larger number was forced toward poverty (Domhoff 1983; Davis 1986). Many men and women turned increasingly to the rapidly expanding underground economy, which may have accounted for as much as 10- to 20-percent of the gross national product during the 1980s (Nonini 1988).

Class formation had many consequences in the 1980s, especially for those squeezed between declining real incomes on the one hand and inflation, rising prices, and taxes on the other. For example, significant increases in the numbers of small business start ups and failures provided sure signs of economic hard times in the early part of the decade. The number of single-parent households headed by women in the declining white middle classes grew dramatically. There was explosive growth of homelessness in the cities: the thirty homeless families recognized by New York City welfare agencies in 1969 had increased to five thousand by 1985 and 15,600 by 1988 (Susser 1993). Adolescent and young men of color experienced twice the rate of unemployment and three times the rate of poverty as their white contemporaries. Sixty percent of those who were employed worked in the lowest-paid jobs. A steadily growing percentage of adolescent and young men of color were incarcerated. The United States may, in fact, have jailed a greater percentage of its adolescent and young men during this period than any other country in the world.

What rapidly emerged during the 1980s was a split-level economy characterized by relatively fewer well-paying jobs and relatively more low-paying positions in health care, fast-food restaurants, and private police or security forces. The loss of industrial jobs, combined with the de-skilling of the work force and the expansion of service-sector employment, dramatically altered the opportunities and expectations of young working-class men and women entering the labor market during the 1980s (Weis 1990). Except for a miniscule number of entertainers and professional athletes who received high salaries, most of the better-paying jobs were located in the high-tech and pharmaceutical industries, the financial sector, or law firms that worked out the details of mergers. These positions typically required advanced college degrees, and the numbers of Masters in Business Administration (MBAs) and lawyers grew rapidly during the 1980s. They adopted the wheeling-dealing, free-market mentality of Wall Street. They embraced the Social Darwinist concerns with individual control and individualism advocated by antiwelfare, anti-union, New Right spokespersons who were heavily invested in oil and mineral exploration, real estate, and the emerging labor-intensive service sector. However, when crises loomed on the horizon, they sought and typically received special consideration from the federal government, a sort of socialism for the rich.

The Black movement that crystallized in the 1950s and 1960s reshaped the political landscape of the United States. Its participants argued that "race is not only a matter of politics, economics, or culture, but all of these 'levels' experienced simultaneously" (Omi and Winant 1986, 90). They argued that it was part of everyday life. In the face of efforts by the state to coopt, rechannel, and repress its members, the black movement fragmented in the 1960s into competing currents, some stressing entry into electoral politics, others advocating nationalist or socialist programs (San Juan 1992). Nevertheless, its success inspired all of the other social movements that emerged in the 1960s; the student, Chicano, Puerto Rican, Asian-American, Native American, women's, and gay movements have learned from its victories and defeats and modeled their programs on its experiences. The fascists of the New Right, many of whom lay claim to sole possession of authentic Christianity or religion, also learned from this history (Bennett 1988, 375–408).

The limited success of the black and other movements provoked opposition to the idea of equality and attempts to dismantle the gains made by racial minorities in the 1950s and 1960s. Racism was recharged and repackaged by the color-blind legislation of Congress and the Supreme Court and by the code words of virtually every political campaign in the 1970s and 1980s. Whereas the old buffer races of the 1890s—the Jews, the Italians, and the Poles from eastern and southern Europe—were absorbed into a white race that was redefined after World War II, new immigrants from Latin America, Asia, or the Middle East arrived in growing numbers and came to constitute the new buffer races of the United States (Sacks 1992). Ethnicity and the idea of a hierarchy of races and cultures were given a fresh breath of life in a social milieu that combined race and class issues with civil rights and discussed them increasingly in a language that revived the Social Darwinist rhetoric of the Gilded Age.

Cultural patterns were recast once again as social classes and communities decomposed and were reconstituted during the 1970s and 1980s. The cultures emerging from the processes of ethnogenesis set in motion by class formation gave voice to the sentiments and understandings of emergent groups who recognized a common identity derived from recognition of their shared place in the new class structure. In some instances, their adherents have created new sensibilities and infused old ones with alternative meanings that challenge established or hegemonic views. For exmple, consider the appreciation many African-American communities have of ancient Egypt, a fact not fully acknowledged and understood in the prevailing academic discourse. In other instances, the practices and sentiments of subordinated classes and communities—such as the tatoos appreciated by white working-class and gay men—have been appropriated by Madonna and other entertainers and turned into avant-garde commodity fetishes for new classes and communities of consumers. In still other instances, the elements of distinctive regional cultures have been exchanged for the homogenizing symbols of the hegemonic culture; for example, the silver belt buckles and turquoise jewelry once commonly seen at the annual meetings of the Society for American Archaeology have slowly been replaced by business suits, L. L. Bean chinos, and docksider shoes. As a result, the boundaries that separated the Eastern Establishment and Core Cultures under the corporatist state were rapidly blurred after the 1970s with the consolidation of the neoliberal state and the new class structure. This view lends credence to claims that postmodernism is the cultural logic of late twentieth-century capitalism (Harvey 1989; Jameson 1984, 1991).

THE REORGANIZATION OF ARCHAEOLOGY AND THE NEW ARCHAEOLOGY

The processes and contradictions that manifested themselves in the events of the 1970s and 1980s reshaped the organization of the profession and affected the content of archaeological discourse. These included important structural transformations in the labor market and the increased segmentation and de-skilling of the work force (Gordon, Edwards, and Reich 1982). Universities no longer provided the major source of employment. Many of the doctoral dissertations written during the period were increasingly specialized. Their authors dealt in greater depth with topics or areas defined in increasingly narrow terms, and many exhibited a reluctance or inability to address the broader kinds of questions and areas that some of their predecessors had examined a decade or two earlier.

The early 1970s was the heyday of the "New Archaeology," whose advocates stressed the importance of examining critically the concepts and methods used in the discipline (Leone 1972). It was also a time, reminiscent of the late 1930s, when agencies at various levels of government required the preparation of easily understood and comparable, and thus relatively standardized, statements about archaeological "resources" because of provisions in the Historic Sites Preservation Act (1966) and the Environmental Policy Act (1969). Given the demands of the state, it is not surprising that archaeologists were quick to adopt the language and framework of logical positivism—as Steward, Bennett, and Kluckhohn had advocated in the late 1930s—which focused attention on the concepts and methods used to organize information. It is also not surprising that, in this milieu, some of the New Archaeologists also adopted the problematic idiom of systems theory, which Robert Lilienfield (1978, 263) characterized as "... the 'natural' ideology of bureaucratic planners and centralizers."

Archaeologists in the colleges and universities had been incredibly successful at reproducing themselves in the 1950s and 1960s. Their success is reflected in a general way by the growth of the Archaeological Institute of America and the Society for American Archaeology during the 1960s and 1970s. As Table 2 shows, the Archaeological Institute of America grew steadily from 2,747 members in 1960 to 6,753 members in 1970. After a short-lived 10-percent loss in the mid-1970s, the membership rose rapidly to an all-time high of 9,680 in 1981, plummeted to 7,230 in 1988, and climbed again to 8,484 in 1990.

The Society for American Archaeology's membership rose, as Table 1 shows, from 1,176 individuals in 1960 to 1,794 individuals in 1969. The organization grew explosively during the next four years at an annual growth rate of more than 20 percent. The membership, which stood at 3,916 individuals by 1973, continued to grow, though at a steadily declining rate until 1981, when it reached an all-time high of 5,179 individuals. It subsequently declined to 4,277 in 1987, climbed briefly to 4,955 in 1988, and fell again to about 4,200 in 1991. In other words, the membership changes of the two organizations are virtually identical. Both grew regularly during the 1960s and 1970s, reached maxima in 1981, lost a quarter of their members by 1987 or 1988, briefly added members after the short-lived economic growth spurt in 1988, and lost members when real economic growth fell between 1989 and 1991.

This is not the whole story, however, because it does not reflect significant changes in the composition of the profession. Whereas women have historically constituted about 40 percent of the members of the Archaeological Institute of America since the late 1920s, this was not the case with the Americanist archaeologists. As Table 1 illustrates, both the number and percentage of women in the Society for American Archaeology rose slowly after the war until 1956, when the 133 women constituted 13.6 percent of the members. During the next four years, fourteen women and 186 men joined the society; as a result of this more than 13 to 1 ratio, the percentage of women actually declined to 12.5 percent in 1961. By 1969, the 263 women in the organization constituted 14.7 percent of its members. That is, during the 1960s, 5.9 men were inscribed on the membership list of the association for every woman.

A change occurred in the early 1970s, when the percentage of women in the Society for American Archaeology virtually doubled. By 1973, the 923 women in the society constituted 23.6 percent of its members. That is, for every woman who joined the association, 1.8 men were added to its roles. By 1976, the 1,440 women constituted 28.3 percent of the members. This meant that 1.3 men joined for each woman during this three-year period. The percentage of women members increased to about 35 percent by 1988, which means that, for every woman who joined the society after 1976, 1.5 men *left* the association. Virtually all of the women who joined the Society for American Archaeology after 1970 were baby boomers born after World War II; many undoubtedly had fathers who attended college on the GI Bill. Under the current conditions, it is reasonable to believe that women may, in fact, constitute a majority of the Society for American Archaeology's members by the second decade of the twenty-first century. In terms of popular images, it suggests that Indiana Jones is actually a young woman in disguise.

Colleges and universities with archaeology programs housed in various departments absorbed many of the individuals trained between the 1950s and the early 1970s. However, the employment opportunities afforded by colleges and universities had slowed to a standstill by the mid-1970s. State aid for higher education had leveled off or was actually declining, and the funds that were available were increasingly shifted away from academic programs to cover the costs of central administration. As a consequence, anthropology and classics departments stopped growing. New jobs were not created; vacant positions were not filled; and many untenured faculty saw their jobs evaporate as university promotions committees succumbed to internal pressures that made tenuring more difficult. An increasing number toiled in precarious, temporary positions whose very existence depended on whether or not soft money would be available for all or part of the coming year.

Given the relative proportion of men and women who entered the profession during the late 1950s and 1960s, this meant that the vast majority of the archaeologists hired during the 1960s and early 1970s were men, many of whom received tenure before the full effects of the economic downswing that led to the contraction of higher education were felt. Larger numbers and percentages of women entered the archaeological job market after the mid-1970s at precisely the time the number of academic positions available was plummeting. As a result, competition heightened for the few university positions that opened up in the late 1970s and 1980s, and a small percentage were filled by women. Under the current no- or slow-growth conditions, the situation of a relatively large number of older, tenured men and a smaller number of younger women concentrated in the untenured ranks will not change appreciably until the first decade of the next century. Furthermore, in light of the massive structural transformations of universities, underwritten by Social Darwinist and free-market ideologies that took place in the 1980s, there is no guarantee that positions vacated by retirements or deaths after the year 2000 will automatically be filled or even continue to exist.

Federal legislation passed between 1966 and 1974 also had a significant effect in reshaping the labor market for archaeologists in the mid-1970s (Schiffer and Gumerman 1977; Dworsky et al. 1983, 216–44). The Society for American Archaeology lobbied hard and successfully for the passage of legislation that followed in the footsteps of the Antiquities Act (1906) and the Historic Sites Act (1935), which were concerned with the preservation of historic buildings and lands. The Historic Sites Preservation Act (1966) created the National Register and the President's Advisory Council on Historic Preservation; Section 106 of the act granted a review function to the council whenever properties on the National Register would be affected by federal action. The National Environmental Policy Act (1969) required the preparation of environmental impact statements that contained up-to-date information about the archaeological resources that would be endangered by proposed federal actions. The Archaeological and Historical Conservation Act (1974) provided funds to preserve and recover significant archaeological information threatened by federal actions.

These laws established the federal-level infrastructure for Cultural Resource Management (CRM) archaeology in the United States. They also laid the foundations for the legislation and regulations that were written at the state level. By 1980, an estimated six thousand individuals were engaged in CRM archaeology. They were employed by various federal, state, county, or local-level agencies, which issued contracts for the various kinds of the archaeological studies required by law. Some contract archaeologists were employed by universities or museums—the Museum of

Northern Arizona, Southern Illinois University, the University of Pittsburgh, or Sonoma State University, for example—that established CRM research and degree-granting programs. The majority, however, were consultants or employees of private firms that supported themselves by bidding for state and federal funds and money from contractors and developers to prepare environmental impact statements assessing the significance of archaeological resources that would be affected by proposed activities (Rogge 1983, 8–16).

Hundreds of these companies came into existence in the mid-1970s, many of which were small and probably under-capitalized. Soon their numbers dwindled, as they disappeared or were purchased by larger, better capitalized firms. The self-employed entrepreneur of the mid-1970s became the salaried employee of the national or international corporation in the 1980s. By all estimates, the amount of money available to do archaeology in the United States increased enormously in the early and mid-1970s. The annual expenditure on CRM archaeological research in the United States approached $300 million by the late 1970s (Fitting 1982; Wendorf 1979). Contract archaeology had rapidly become a big business (King 1981).

The extent of CRM archaeology was enormous. For example, Eugene Rogge (1983, 16) writes that more than 1,600 reports were prepared to describe CRM projects carried out in Arizona in 1979–80. He reports that most of the CRM projects carried out in the late 1970s and early 1980s were small, typically costing less than $25,000. However, for every five hundred small projects, there would also be about a dozen that cost $100,000 or more and one with a budget in excess of $1 million. The total cost of the Dolores Project, which had an annual budget of $1.8 million in the late 1970s and early 1980s, exceeded $8 million. The annual cost of this project alone was nearly equal to the total amount awarded by the National Science Foundation for archaeological research in any given year since the late 1960s.

Given the amounts of money involved each year, it should not be surprising that CRM projects, especially the larger ones, were carefully scrutinized by various state and federal agencies, or that contractors and reporters occasionally claimed that the CRM investigations often resulted in multimillion-dollar delays. It should also not be surprising that, in the mid-1980s, CRM firms had visions of enormous financial windfalls every time "Star Wars" projects were mentioned, especially the widely discussed proposal to build a railroad network for movable guided missiles in the western United States. If implemented, there would have to be impact statements written for vast areas at costs in excess of $1 billion or so. The same firms also drooled when they talked about superfund legislation in 1989 at the First Joint Archaeological Congress in Baltimore and the opportunities that might be afforded by having their employees investigate and prepare impact statements on toxic waste dumps. It is significant that occupational health and safety issues were not part of that discussion.

Americanist archaeology was effectively transformed in the early 1970s. This was due partly to the rapid withering of the the labor market provided by colleges and universities during the 1950s and 1960s. It was also due partly to the employment opportunities afforded by various federal and state regulatory agencies and by the private sector. As a result, the interests and activities of archaeologists engaged in CRM investigations began to diverge from those of their academic colleagues (King

1971). This was reflected in the formation of a separate organization in 1975—the Society of Professional Archaeologists (Adams 1982; Brose 1983). Eight years later, its membership stood at 576 individuals. Subsequently, another special-interest group was formed: the American Society for Conservation Archaeology, which had about two hundred members in 1983.

The New Archaeology, hinted at earlier in the decade, burst full blown onto the scene in 1968 with the publication of *New Perspectives in Archeology* (Binford and Binford 1968). The ensuing debate centered less on whether the New Archaeology was really new or merely a more explicit restatement of what had been done for years and centered more on the necessity of explicitly formulating and testing hypotheses. The New Archaeologists' critique of classical empiricism and their concerns with scientific method understood in Baconian terms and with improving the methodological rigor of the field were not new; they had been previewed in the late 1930s and the early 1940s. Neither was their adoption of the historical functionalist and developmentalist strategies proposed by Leslie White, Julian Steward, and others in the 1950s, nor their acceptance of a conception of society that stressed the interrelatedness of the various aspects of culture. What was new was the emphasis the New Archaeologists placed on the process of discerning regularities. As philosopher of science Alison Wylie (1993, 9) notes:

> ... systematizing observables (saving the phenomena) is simply not the point of most science; ... systematization (discerning patterns [among observables], which often manifest themselves only under highly artificial laboratory conditions) is the means by which scientists gain access to, and test models of, underlying (largely unobservable) mechanisms and processes that *generate* the (messy) phenomena we observe around us. This seemed exactly the point the New Archaeologists wanted to make in the 1960s and 1970s: that archaeologists should shift their attention to the cultural/historical analogue of these underlying mechanisms and processes, and should treat the recovery and manipulation of archaeological material as a means to this end.

What was also new were the conditions that shaped and constrained the debates over the New Archaeology in the late 1960s and early 1970s. There were probably more college students taking courses in Americanist archaeology and archaeological method and theory than ever before or perhaps since. Many of them subsequently began careers in CRM archaeology, either as employees of various state and federal agencies or in one of the private contracting firms. Most importantly, many of the federal and state-level regulations written during the 1970s directly mirror the conceptual language and methodological concerns of the New Archaeology. While such philosophers of science as Alison Wylie (1981) and Merrilee Salmon (1982) analyzed the research program and pointed out its limitations, CRM archaeologists worked and wrote in terms of its guidelines. Admonitions in the early 1980s to do archaeology and stop philosophizing about it are commentaries indicating just how rapidly the New Archaeology became a hegemonic viewpoint in the Society for American Archaeology and among archaeologists trained in anthropology departments at U.S. colleges and universities (Flannery 1982).

Graduate training in archaeology was also transformed. Seminars continued to be an important vehicle, but their content changed. Although surveys of regional archaeology still played an important role, seminars concerned with topics—settlement patterns, agricultural origins, exchange, sociocultural evolution, or cultural resource management, for example—came to occupy central places in many curricula. As a result, some academics seem to have adopted, either explicitly or implicitly, Thomas Kuhn's (1970) view that scientific knowledge is cumulative only in periods of normal science and that a scientific revolution was taking place in the kinds of archaeology taught in anthropology departments.

Partly because of the dramatic expansion of the primary literature, students in areas courses relied increasingly on summaries or interpretations of primary sources rather than on the older materials themselves. In the topical courses, they made considerable use of collections of readings that focused on certain concepts or themes underlying debates rather than on the debates themselves (Leone 1972). Unlike their predecessors, they recognized and acknowledged the importance of their debt to the logical positivists. Their discussions of methodology increased in frequency, intensity, and perhaps acrimony. Their language became more scientistic, as a growing number accepted the ideas that the methodological procedures of the natural sciences could and should be directly adapted to archaeology and that archaeological investigations could be formulated in terms parallel to those of the natural sciences (Fay 1975, 11–69). These, of course, are features of the New Archaeology. As the academic job market tightened, archaeologists struggled to show that they had something new to offer and that their work was relevant to the rest of anthropology. This included the potential contributions of archaeology to resolving modern social problems such as undirected technological growth, environmental degradation, social disintegration, and population growth (Fritz 1973).

The study of cultural processes, not the results preserved in the archaeological record, was the crucial problem for the New Archaeologists. This was a fundamental innovation of their program. The problems they chose to examine derived from earlier concerns of archaeologists, such as the development of agriculture or the rise of the state. In their investigations, they focused attention on the processes and mechanisms that promoted stability and change in particular societies. They phrased their discussions in terms of universal laws of human behavior or in the idiom of ecology or systems theory (Flannery 1973; Fritz and Plog 1970; Watson et al. 1971, 1984).

The advocates of the two approaches—the quest for universal laws and human ecology/systems theory—retained the rationalist assumptions about human beings and social relations that are inherent in functionalism, ideas that human cultures are formed out of practical activity and utilitarian interest (Sahlins 1969, 1976). The implication of these assumptions is that culture is simultaneously the product of rational human subjects interacting with one another, each attempting to maximize or optimize his or her own interests, and an instrument for reproducing itself or for maintaining human population within certain Malthusian limits. From this perspective, society is an aggregate of equivalent items—economically rational, androgynous individuals—and one society is, in reality, very much like every other. By extension, all mirror the attitudes and social relations of bourgeois Western society. Thus, both approaches were univocal in the sense that each views complex social phenomena through a lens that can bring only one image into focus. They separated the study of society from the study of history and eliminated significant culturally meaningful distinctions between individuals and groups within a society; the systems theory approach also blurred important differences between the cultural and natural worlds.

The systems theory approach represented the revival during World War II of the ideas that analogies existed between the functions of living organisms and those of machines concerned with information, communication, goal-seeking through feedback, and computation, and that these parallels were worthy of further investigation (Heims 1975, 1991). Systems theory developed in a milieu that was overwhelmingly concerned with equilibrium, stability, homeostasis, social control, self-regulation, efficiency, operations management, and cost-benefit analysis to name only a few of the concepts that entered the social sciences under its aegis. Whereas ecology provided an organismic model that stressed interdependence, systems theory built on "... a mechanical metaphor more continuous with the technocratic consciousness and ... [that] embodies a humanistic imperative centered on the impulse to manage (dominate) the environment" (Lilienfield 1978, 263).

The New Archaeology was not an isolated phenomenon in the mid-1960s. Similar movements claiming to represent methodological and epistemological breaks with early practices arose at roughly the same time in fields as diverse as geography, English, and hotel management. The positivism underpinning these movements was linked with the generally optimistic climate of the early 1960s and with celebrating the success of U.S. imperialism (Trigger 1981, 1984; personal communication). However, by the late 1960s and early 1970s, the climate was decidedly less optimistic. The power and prestige of the U.S. state was challenged at all levels by protests at home, by revolutions abroad, by the expanded productivity of Western Europe and Japan, and by the sudden rise to prominence of finance capital. The United States' hegemony was undermined, and things appeared to be falling apart. By virtue of their position in the institutions of both the state and civil society, archaeologists were affected by forces hard to comprehend and beyond their ability to control. As they became increasingly dependent on federal and state agencies and the private sector for their livelihood and for the support of their research, their interests were increasingly intertwined and enmeshed with those of the state and the wider society. Given the milieu in which they emerged, the New Archaeologists' fascination with the role of managers and their initiation of change in response to external pressures to promote stability take on nuanced meaning (Flannery 1972; Wright 1969, 1977).

As economic growth slowed and the specter of the crisis of the 1970s began to haunt the West, the utility of the concepts of stability, continuity, and equilibrium were questioned. Society seemed to lack direction and appeared increasingly out of control. The response of some archaeologists was to adopt a new methodology aptly called catastrophe theory; its proponents proposed to use it to study the emergence of new forms of organizations in situations where the continuous accumulation of gradual changes suddenly leads to rapid transformations and where the system is so complex that it is impossible to identify all of the parts and their interrelationships; this, of course, was paralleled by the development of the theory of punctuated equilibrium in evolutionary biology. One archaeologist, perhaps after surveying the events of the late 1970s, observed perceptively:

For some human societies, stability (in the sense of peace and prosperity) is assured only by continuous growth. Zero growth does not represent for them a stable state, and negative growth can accelerate to disintigration [sic].

(RENFREW 1979, 489)

The New Archaeologists attempted to redefine the field and redirect inquiry to problems that they saw as relevant not only to anthropology but also to society as a whole. To accomplish this, they had to forge new alliances within anthropology and outside of it. They organized a number of interdisciplinary research projects that involved specialists from other academic professions—botanists, geologists, soil scientists, or palynologists. However, without more clearly conceptualized understandings of what they were studying, the participants in these projects often were forced to talk in terms of the lowest common denominator. In other words, the interdisciplinary projects witnessed and underwrote the resurgence of reductionist, determinist explanations, which tried to account for the properties of a complex entity, such as human society, by referring to the properties of its constituent parts.

Such reductionist accounts did not resonate particularly well with developments in sociocultural anthropology during the 1970s and 1980s, many of which were idealist and emphasized the historically contingent, systemic nature of human society and multivocality—that is, individuals or groups occupying different positions in a set of historically constructed social relations frequently have quite different understandings and appreciations of those structures. The fervor of the New Archaeology also never noticeably touched biblical and classical archaeology, whose respective research foci were the Old Testament and the civilized world—European, Christian, Greco-Roman, and white (Dyson 1981, 1985, 1993; Wright 1975). Biblical and classical archaeologists working in the eastern Mediterranean did not separate the study of history from the study of society. Classical archaeologists, except for the ancient historians, generally ignored the study of society and treated history as a succession of wars, leaders, or art styles, much as historians, steeped in the tenets of classical empiricism, have done throughout the twentieth century.

Americanist and classical archaeology were increasingly estranged during the 1970s. Only a handful of individuals belonged to both the Society for American Archaeology and the Archaeological Institute of America. In addition, mention of Americanist archaeology in the *American Journal of Archaeology,* the organ of the AIA, between 1969 and 1978 was limited to less than thirty book reviews and a "state of the field" article written by Gordon Willey in the early 1970s. There was a brief reconciliation between 1979 and 1985, when the journal published six annual summaries of current trends and developments in Americanist archaeology written by Robert Dunnell. The depth of the separation during the 1970s is reflected by a similar paucity of articles and reviews in *American Antiquity.* The only magazine that regularly printed articles and reviews that dealt with both classical and Americanist archaeology was *Archaeology,* which has been published consistently by the Archaeological Institute of America since 1947 and had a circulation of sixty thousand in 1985.

The fervor generated by the New Archaeology dissipated during the late 1970s. However, the search it promoted for a more explicit methodology continues, especially among archaeologists who are concerned with cultural resource management or who have adopted the scientism of the physicalizing aspects of the logical positivist's program (Raab and Goodyear 1984). It continues in the attempts to borrow approaches from other fields such as ecology and systems theory in the early 1970s and mathematics and theoretical biology in the early 1980s. It also persists in the efforts to clarify epistemological and ontological issues by those archaeologists who look to philosophy for inspiration and by those philosophers of science who base their research on what archaeologists say and do.

The New Archaeology was already hegemonic by the early 1980s among archaeologists employed in anthropology departments and cultural resource management. However, archaeology in general and the New Archaeology to the extent it was hegemonic were never uncontested during the 1970s. The challenges came from diverse sources. Many archaeologists concerned with culture-historical reconstruction rooted in classical empiricism chose to ignore the New Archaeology altogether; however, "they were swamped as the numbers of new academic archaeologists increased" in the late 1960s and early 1970s (Trigger, 1993; personal communication). Internalist critiques also challenged the novelty of the New Archaeology, its implicit assumptions and conceptual framework, or the inability of functionalist theories of change to deal with structural differentiation (Athens 1977; Dunnell 1980). There were both internal and external critiques of the practices of CRM archaeology (Lacy and Hasenstab 1983; MacDonald 1976; Morgan 1977; U.S. General Accounting Office 1981). Finally, other archaeologists rejected the reductionist-determinist explanations of the New Archaeology and sought, instead, to reunite the study of society with the study of history. They wrote from a number of theoretical perspectives (Patterson 1986b, 1989b, 1990). Some examined anomalies, where the available evidence did not support theoretically informed wisdom or predictions (Kohl and Wright 1977). Some romanticized the past, implicitly criticizing modern society (Coe 1980). Some embraced structuralism or symbolic anthropology, with their avoidance of the concept of power and suggestion that ancient peoples really were different in the ways they perceived their world (Glassie 1975; Leone 1986). Others were unabashedly Marxist in their theoretical perspective and built on the various currents in that problematic. These diverse viewpoints were conflated and called "postprocessual" archaeology by the mid-1980s; however, several of them, notably the Marxist approaches, were already evident in Americanist archaeology by the 1950s (McGuire 1993; Trigger 1993). The most important critiques of New Archaeology were those articulated with some possibility for political action.

Challenges came from diverse groups whose views were muted by the hegemonic and largely unstated assertions that there was a single correct and scientific way of looking at the world and that the ancient societies they studied were composed of interchangeable, essentially androgynous individuals. One group consisted of members of the old buffer races from southern and eastern Europe who entered Americanist archaeology for the first time in the 1950s and 1960s. A second group consisted of gays and lesbians whose sexual preferences and politics, while not immediately apparent in their writings, are evident in the safe havens and support they provided gay and lesbian archaeology students during the 1970s and 1980s (Duberman 1991; d'Emilio 1992). A third group, increasingly more vocal with time, was composed of the women who entered the profession in unprecedented numbers in the 1970s. Many had already read feminist writers or would do so in the near future, and a significant number became actively involved in women's political issues, such as gender equity and the Equal Rights Amendment (DuBois et al. 1987).

The most important challenge, however, came from outside the profession. It consisted of the efforts of Native Americans who, from the early 1970s onwards, challenged both the archaeologists' interpretations of pre-Columbian history and the ethics of their practices, especially the excavation and conservation of skeletal remains on museum shelves (Deloria 1992a; Trigger 1980a; Zimmerman 1989). Their activities led to the passage of significant federal legislation: the Archaeological Resources Preservation Act (1979), the National Museum of the American Indian Act (1989), and the Native American Graves Protection and Repatriation Act (1990), all of which affect the reburial and repatriation of Native American skeletal and artifactual remains. "As recently as 1989, the SAA [Society for American Archaeology] opposed federal legislation viewed as favorable to Native Americans...." (Powell et al. 1993, 16); realizing that public opinion was solidly behind the Native Americans and that its own membership was divided over the issues of reburial and repatriation, the executive committee of the Society for American Archaeology subsequently reversed its position.

The victories of Native Americans in the bitter struggles over reburial and repatriation currently serve as a backdrop and model for events that are unfolding in New York as this book is being written. The excavation of human remains at the African Burial Ground, located on federal land in lower Manhattan, has sparked front-page controversy and energized the diverse Black communities of the New York metropolitan area (Cook 1993; Harrington 1993). The dispute—the insensitivity of the forensic anthropologists, the ineptness of various government agencies, and the almost total disregard for law and decency shown by some contractors—seems to be the repeat performance of a bad play. African-American communities in the city, which have long histories of struggling against injustices in other arenas of everyday life, are reliving the experiences of Native Americans with respect to people whom they also count as ancestors to be revered and respected.

Archaeology flourished outside the universities during the 1980s, partly because of the expanded state and federal legislation and partly because of tax incentives granted to real estate developers who used historic preservation to construct and promote heritage themes. The bureaucratic structures associated with CRM archaeology expanded, reaching from the federal to county and even municipal levels. The various agencies responsible for overseeing CRM investigations and issuing contracts to private firms simultaneously diversified, carving out their own specialized niches, and asserted their autonomy and independence from sister agencies in the same level of the state apparatus. The number of employees involved in regulatory agencies expanded during the decade. In the mid-1980s, the various land management agencies of the federal government spent about $75 million a year on CRM archaeology (McManamon 1992; Keel et al. 1989). This figure does not include equal or larger amounts allocated each year by other federal agencies such as the Federal Energy Regulatory Commission, Housing and Urban Development, the Environmental Protection Agency, or the Department of Transportation. The most conservative estimate suggests that the level of federal support for CRM archaeology remained constant throughout the 1980s; other estimates suggest that the level of support actually grew because of increased allocations for cultural impact statements by the Federal Energy Regulatory Commission and the Department of Transportation. Although no one has any clear idea about the amounts land developers and contractors for CRM projects spent each year in the 1980s, the number of CRM archaeologists increased between 1980 and 1990. Consequently, it is safe to conclude that the annual expenditures for CRM were at least $300 million after 1980. It is also safe to conclude that private-sector CRM archaeology operates according to the laws of motion described by Karl Marx in *Capital* and, consequently, that the need for profits in a highly competitive market will, in the long term, override any commitment to the high-quality or value-free archaeology desired by some of its practitioners.

The overall increase in funding for archaeological research in the United States was accompanied by shifts in the source of funds available for overseas investigations. In 1968, the National Science Foundation's support for archaeology through its anthropology program in the Division of Behavioral and Neural Sciences did not increase; this was the first time since the inception of the archaeological research program fourteen years earlier that the foundation had failed to respond to the growing demands of the profession. Its 1992 allocation for archaeology is about $3.5 million. Given inflation and devaluation, its support has actually remained almost stationary since the Vietnam War (Dickson 1984; Smith 1973). The National Endowment for the Humanities established in 1965 began to support archaeological research in the mid-1970s; it currently awards about $700,000 annually for archaeological research.

Archaeologists conducting investigations overseas have also made use of foreign currency held by the U.S. government through Fulbright and other programs (Borden 1966). Since the late 1960s, however, they have frequently turned to multinational corporations such as Anaconda Copper Company in Chile from 1968 to 1972 and Carnation Milk or Southern Peru Copper Company in the 1970s for financial aid and logistical support. The extent and timing of their support in these years often reflected and depended on fluctuations in commodity prices or currency exchange rates. Under the neoliberal state, archaeologists have also relied increasingly on private philanthropies such as the National Geographic Society or the L. S. B. Leakey Foundation.

The division of labor between the National Science Foundation and the National Endowment for the Humanities in the 1980s has breathed new life into shopworn distinctions between the sciences and humanities and between peoples with history and those who lacked history. It also gave credence to distinctions that were drawn by individuals and politicians outside the profession between civilized peoples and races and those that were savages or barbarians or closer to nature. For instance, many of the projects supported by the National Endowment for the Humanities were concerned with the peoples of classical antiquity, European settlers in the American colonies or the Republic, and the literate ruling classes of buffer races, such as the Maya; these were peoples with history. The National Science Foundation has supported "prehistoric" archaeology in places or periods where the subjects had no written history and, consequently, could be studied "scientifically" as either part of or an extension of the natural world.

Of course, this division of labor was made in the 1880s, during the formative years of both the Archaeological Institute of America and the American Anthropological Association. The former focused on the civilized peoples, whereas the latter was concerned with primitive peoples who resided on the margins of the civilized world or were recently incorporated into it. The distinction was resurrected or reaffirmed again in the 1970s and 1980s. The Society for Historical Archaeology was established in 1968 to study the archaeology of the settler-colonists who arrived in the sixteenth and seventeenth centuries. Like the classical and biblical archaeologists, they studied peoples with history. The Archeology Division of the American Anthropological Association emerged during the restructuring and fragmentation of that organization in the mid-1980s. It currently has about 1,430 members, 38.2 percent of whom are women. Many of its members also belong to the Society for American Archaeology and are concerned to varying degrees with anthropological archaeology, traditionally the archaeology of primitive societies or peoples without history.

Although it is easy to describe the centers of gravity of both organizations, it is essential to recognize the significant differences of opinion regarding where those centers of gravity should be located and what implications the differences have for forging alliances. For instance, historical archaeologists currently offer four descriptions of their field and prescriptions for its development in the future: (1) James Deetz (1977) argues that the subject matter of historical archaeology is the archaeology of white settler-colonists; (2) Stanley South (1977) sees it as an extension of the New Archaeology into places and periods of time in which a portion of the population was literate; (3) Mark Leone and others (1987) argue that it is the archaeology of industrial capitalism; and (4) Robert Paynter (1988) and others view it as part of anthropology and suggest that it is, in fact, integral to the study of class and state formation (McGuire and Paynter 1991). In her 1993 keynote address to the Society for Historical Archaeology, Alison Wylie (1993) pointed out that historical archaeology has the potential to cross the boundaries between history and archaeology by developing a theoretically informed interrogation of two independent forms of evidence: written documents and material remains. Such a tack would allow it to redress silences in both kinds of evidence and to explore and develop radical critiques of the theory and practices of scientific New Archaeology.

The organization of classical archaeology in the United States remained relatively stable in some respects during the last twenty-five years. The centers of gravity of the Archaeological Institute of America are a number of local or regional chapters, the more established and larger of which are in Princeton, New York, Boston, Washington, and Chicago; less than 10 percent of its members are not affiliated with a chapter. A smaller percentage of its members than the Society for American Archaeology or the Archaeology Division are employed in full-time museum or university positions, and most of those who do teach are housed in classics departments with philologists, language teachers, literary critics, and possibly ancient historians (Cole 1989). As a result, there is still a basis for multiform tensions between text and object orientations and fetishes within the academic contexts in which classical archaeologists and ancient historians ply their crafts (Dyson 1989).

In other respects, real debates have been taking place within the classics profession. A women's caucus formed in 1972 at the annual meeting of the American

Philological Society; two years later, it sponsored a session on women in ancient myth and religion at an annual meeting held jointly with the Archaeological Institute of America (Hallett 1989). Its members have both protested and been parties in class action suits regarding issues of gender discrimination in the 1970s and 1980s (Gutzwiller 1989). The paucity of minorities in the profession was also raised in the 1980s (Haley 1989). Classicists as well as outsiders have also begun to examine the social construction of the profession and how its curricula resonate with wider issues in contemporary U.S. society (Bernal 1987; Bloom 1987; Figueira 1989; Halporn 1989; Hammond 1985).

There have also been significant alterations in biblical archaeology since the early 1970s. The American Schools of Oriental Research continue. They were established at the turn of the century, and their center of gravity was located along the Boston–Washington corridor, especially in the Oriental Clubs of New Haven, New York, and Philadelphia, whose members also supported Congregationalist and Presbyterian missions and schools in the Levant. The first overseas school was located in Jerusalem; a second facility was established in Baghdad following the First World War. After the 1967 war, another center was founded in Jordan. This allowed biblical archaeologists, mostly interested in the first and second millennia B.C.—the Old Testament—and mainly from bible colleges and seminaries in the United States to continue working in both Israel and Jordan under the watchful eyes of the two governments. The American Schools of Oriental Research maintains two publications series: the *Bulletin of the American Schools of Oriental Research* and the *Biblical Archaeologist.* The latter was established in 1937 and currently has a annual circulation of about 3,700.

A more significant change occurred with the formation of the Biblical Archaeology Society in Washington in the mid-1970s. The circulation of its magazine, *The Biblical Archaeology Review,* has risen from about 9,000 in 1977 to 212,000 in 1993. Its readers have identified themselves as college-educated, married, and overwhelmingly conservative, fundamentalist, or evangelical Protestants (*Biblical Archaeology Review* 1979, 1982). The magazine is mostly concerned with Old Testament studies, which it situates in the ancient Israelite states that were destroyed and are being resurrected out of the desert by the modern Israeli state. Its popularity is due in part to the rise of the New Right in the United States and to what Harold Bloom (1992) has described as the emergence of a post-Christian American religion.

One other feature of everyday life in the era of the neoliberal state affects archaeology. It results from the moneyed classes' increased demand for antiquities as investments and a hedge against the collapse of the monetary system. Thirty years ago, for instance, Moche-style portrait-head pottery vessels from the north coast of Peru, which cost $50 in the field or twice that amount in Lima shops, fetched $1,500 in the pre-Columbian galleries in New York's Upper East Side. By the 1970s, shops in New York and Los Angeles were charging ten or twenty times that amount for the same specimens. A decade later, these pieces brought $50,000 to $100,000. The increased demand for antiquities underwrote looting on a massive scale in the Third World and fueled the rapid growth of the illicit traffic and sale of antiquities in the United States (Adams 1971). Archaeologists have been involved on both sides of this issue. Some have lobbied for and helped to write United Nations' resolutions condemning the traffic and federal legislation that prohibits the importation of cultural remains. So far, however, the laws that have been enacted are notoriously difficult to enforce. Other archaeologists have actively supported the illicit traffic through such activities as authenticating pieces for collectors and dealers. By doing so, they perpetuate the market, drive up prices, promote further looting, and indirectly provide information to contemporary artists who create the forgeries occasionally purchased by individuals and museums. The art and antiquities markets have also spawned a cottage industry whose practitioners are increasingly concerned with developing detailed grammars of art styles and high-tech procedures that can be used to authenticate pieces and identify forgeries.

ARCHAEOLOGY IN THE NEW GILDED AGE

Some social critics call the 1970s and 1980s the New Gilded Age. They are referring to features of everyday life in the 1880s and 1890s that have been resurrected and recast by the rise of finance capital during the last twenty-five years. Perhaps the more notable are the new moneyed classes' rapacious behavior, insatiable appetites, and complete disregard for the sensibilities of others, epitomized on television by "Dallas'" J. R. Ewing and in real life by various real estate developers, junk-bond brokers, lawyers, and hotel owners who gained notoriety in the 1980s. Perhaps more important are the segmentation or increasing specialization of work and the alienation it produces (Doray 1988). This is reflected both by a quantum leap in the amount of information produced, and by the steady proliferation of increasingly specialized professional journals. It means that archaeologists working in different geographical areas or for different firms, governmental agencies, or universities become steadily less aware of and concerned with what colleagues are doing and the relations of their own activities to those of others. Looking at what has happened to archaeology since the late 1960s suggests that the illusion is not only accurate but also that archaeology is, in fact, an aspect of New Gilded Age, postmodern culture.

Let us briefly consider some of the substantive contributions and clarifications of the 1970s and 1980s and their linkages to wider issues and intellectual currents in the society. The problems archaeologists examined during this period were the same or derivative from the ones they had investigated in the 1950s and 1960s. For those in anthropology programs, these included human origins, the beginnings of food production and early village life, the rise of cities, class and state formation, motors of social development, and the linkage of history and society. The interconnections between artifactual and textual materials loomed larger for archaeologists who examined the rise and fall of early civilizations—states—in the Aegean, Mesoamerica, or the Near East. They had to confront the task of articulating their investigations of objects and associations with linguistic, literary, and historical studies. Keeping artifactual and textual information separate was, of course, one of the hallmarks of the methodology-laden orientation of much of the New Archaeology (Dyson 1993; Renfrew 1980; Snodgrass 1985). It is important to note that the relationships between the established and new perspectives are dialectical rather than linear;

archaeologists develop and refine their viewpoints in the context of ongoing debates, the new questions and evidence they engender, and the clarifications they produce.

The study of human origins was an important activity, an exceedingly well-funded area of inquiry, during the 1970s and 1980s. The "man the hunter" research agenda established by Sherwood Washburn and others in the late 1950s and 1960s built consciously on the United Nations Educational, Scientific, and Cultural Organization (UNESCO) concept of the "universal man"—that abstract individual who stood in the realm of the biological, behavioral, and social sciences that were both outside and removed from the realm of political debate. Racial equality and cooperation, the quintessential features of universal man, were rooted in biological structures and behaviors that were prerequisite for the development of bipedal loco-motion, tool use, and speech. The implications of the sexual differences underlying the social relations of demographic reproduction became apparent once hunting became the dominant way of life, events that coincided with appearance of the genus *Homo* and the transformation of the biologist's population into the anthropologist's social group (Haraway 1988). Glynn Isaac's (1978) essay on food sharing among early hominids was the clearest statement of this perspective. In this view, groups of early men, hunters and toolmakers who cooperated and communicated with each other, used stone tools to kill and butcher an animal, parts of which they brought back to share with their offspring and women, who foraged for plant foods around their camp or home base. He evoked a power image of male and female differences rooted in both behavior and physiology.

Criticisms of universal man and the man-the-hunter model appeared in the 1970s and 1980s. They came from a number of sources with diverse theoretical underpin-nings. Feminist anthropologists were among the first to point out that the model was problematic, since it incorporated and unconsciously built on the views of white, middle-class, male academics. Sally Slocum (1975) showed that the term "man" referred to males in some instances and to human beings of both sexes in others, that the model implied only male hunters cooperated and communicated, and that it excluded the possibility of asking how sexual differences were understood and how gender differences structured everyday life. Instead of rooting the sexual division of labor and sharing in the biological differences between males and females, Lila Leibowitz (1975, 1986) challenged the ideas that the stereotypical nuclear family of postwar U.S. society and the subordination of women could be projected back nearly two million years into the past; she argued instead that these characteristics were not part of some essentialist human nature but rather that they were social construc-tions characteristic of historically specific situations and forms of society. Using data drawn from primate studies and the archaeological record, she suggested that the ear-liest hominid populations may not have had a sexual division of labor apart from bio-logical reproduction.

From the mid-1970s onwards, Edward O. Wilson (1975, 1978) and other socio-biologists launched another kind of challenge to the theoretical underpinnings of the man-the-hunter model. Wilson adopted a cybernetic approach that blurred the bound-aries between animal and human and that saw society as a system composed of var-ious components that functioned according to some overall optimizing strategy. The relative efficiency of the various components could be measured in terms of the fitness or natural selection value that they afforded the system as a whole. It was identical to the neoclassical economist's market, where autonomous, androgynous individuals competed with one another as they bought and sold commodities to achieve some end (Haraway 1982). Thus, for Wilson and other sociobiologists, competition, not sharing, was the root of human nature; the development of cooperation was something that had to be explained.

From the late 1970s through the mid-1980s, Lewis Binford (1977, 1981, 1985) raised questions about the integrity of the archaeological deposits at early hominid sites and whether the associations of bones and tools in deposits that had been modified by various processes actually supported the man-the-hunter scenario given voice by Isaac and others. Pursuing a remark by Isaac that early hominids may also have procured meat by scavenging, Binford raised a series of technical questions concerning the evidence and the inferences drawn from it: Did the bones indicate hunting and butchering had taken place? Did they provide indications of having been moved from a kill site to a base camp? Did the remains support the idea of a sexual division of labor? What constituted the evidence for scavenging, and did the bone assemblages indicate it had occurred? Several studies were undertaken in the early 1980s—for example, Pat Shipman (1986)—to assess the relative importance of hunting and scavenging among the early hominids at Olduvai Gorge, Tanzania and Koobi Fora, Kenya. One outcome of the studies was that scavenging was clearly a more important food procurement activity among these populations than originally thought; as a result, the search for the man-the-hunter scenario, characterized by hunting moderate- to large-sized animals and the putative origins of cooperation and a sexual division of labor, was shifted to a later part of the human lineage (Blumenshine 1987; Gailey 1985).

During the 1980s, the search for the beginnings of cooperation and the sexual division of labor centered increasingly on the Middle to Upper Paleolithic transition, which has been more thoroughly studied in western Europe and the Levant than elsewhere. There has also been a persistent but not universal tendency since the early 1900s to equate the Middle Paleolithic with Neanderthals and the Upper Paleolithic with anatomically modern human beings and to view the transition as the consequence of the causal connection of biological evolution, behavioral and neurological changes, and cultural development (Clark and Lindly 1989). Others have viewed this transition as an outcome of population growth (for example, Gilman 1984). Tendencies toward typological thinking were abetted in the late 1980s by popular media representations and distortions of the significance of mitochondrial DNA studies. Descriptions of Eve as the first anatomically modern woman whose descendants migrated out of the Garden of Eden and pictures portraying Neanderthals as hairy, heavy-browed individuals who scavenged for a livelihood and the white-skinned, Cro-Magnon families that succeeded them conveyed powerful, if not ambiguous, messages at a time when racism, the idea of racial and cultural hierarchies, debates over family values, and attacks on social programs such as aid to the homeless or unemployed were on the rise in U.S. society. Archaeologists were not only consumers of these understandings, they also helped to produce them.

At the same time, archaeologists undertook research in the 1980s that disassembles these images. They produced evidence indicating significant continuities across the boundary between the Middle and Upper Paleolithic; that the timing and duration of transition varied significantly from one region to another; that skeletal remains classified as Neanderthal were associated with Upper Paleolithic tools in western Europe; that anatomically modern human remains were found with Mousterian assemblages in the Near East; and that the archaic and anatomically human fossils, which coexisted in the Levant for forty thousand or fifty thousand years and for a shorter period in eastern Europe, represent a single, highly varied population rather than two typologically distinct populations or races, one of which replaced the other following a scenario similar to the one popularized by Jean Auel's *Clan of the Cave Bear* (Bar-Yosef 1989; Chase 1989; Wolpoff 1989). More importantly, they provided evidence showing that human beings cooperated with each other before, during, and after the transition. They participated in hunting drives that could only be carried out collectively; they shared the products of their labor with one another; the members of groups at Shanidar Cave and in France cared for two individuals, one badly injured and the other with severe arthritis; and they made objects that probably identify individuals with particular social groups and others that express the individuality or creativity of the artist. What perhaps remains to be demonstrated more decisively is how a division of labor based on gender, extending beyond demographic reproduction, became, along with age, a factor in structuring social relations within and between groups.

In the years immediately following World War II, Robert Braidwood devised an empirical test for Childe's "neolithic revolution" hypothesis, which linked the development of agrarian production with the rise of the year-round settlements and autonomous village communities. In Childe's view, increasing aridity forced people into river valleys and oases, where plants and animals that could be domesticated were found. However, finding little evidence for environmental change in the Zagros, Braidwood (1963) argued that food production—agriculture and herding—emerged as communities residing in these favorable habitats experimented with and ultimately domesticated the plants and animals around them. This underwrote increasingly localized subsistence activities and settlement, larger group size, and the creation of surpluses that allowed some members of the population to engage in full-time craft specialization. Structurally, Braidwood's argument is rooted in the tradition of classical political economy derived from Adam Smith, which asserts that economic development occurs when communities initiate changes in the productive forces.

During the 1960s, archaeologists challenged the relations postulated between the development of agriculture and the rise of permanently settled village life. Archaeologists working on the central coast of Peru showed that the relationship between the appearance of agriculture and permanently occupied villages was complex. The richness of marine resources afforded groups that lived in close proximity to them opportunities for year-round settlement before the development of agricultural food production (Lanning 1967; Moseley 1975; Patterson and Lanning 1964). They argued this in narrow utilitarian terms, a perspective that ultimately derives from neoclassical economics, which was originally launched as a critique of classical political economy (Clarke 1982). Anthropologists—notably Clifford Geertz (1956, 1963)—had already begun to phrase arguments about cultural change in neoclassical terms by the late 1950s; rejecting materialist conceptions of history concerned with growth, Geertz and the ecological anthropologists focused instead on the evolution of the ecosystems in which cultural development took place; they sought to specify more precisely the relations between certain human activities and·their surroundings (Patterson 1987).

The New Archaeologists consolidated the neoclassical critique of classical political economy in anthropological archaeology during the 1970s. At the same time, they severed studies of the processes involved in plant and animal domestication from those concerned with the development of permanent settlements or early village communities. For example, Binford (1968) and Kent Flannery (1969) argued that incipient cultivation was the end product of a strategy that involved the increasingly intense exploitation of seasonal resources, which permitted sedentism and population growth in optimal areas followed by emigration into less well-endowed neighboring areas where the new residents introduced and manipulated the wild crops and animals they had exploited earlier. By doing so, the communities had selected from an array of possible strategies, thereby achieving their goal of reestablishing equilibrium. This perspective underwrote repeated efforts from the late 1970s onwards to apply models and theories derived from evolutionary ecology to archaeology (Ford 1977; Gall and Saxe 1977; Keegan and Diamond 1987; Kirch 1980; Reidhead 1980; Rindos 1984).

Rejecting claims that societies ever successfully establish or reestablish equilibrium conditions, Mark Cohen (1975, 1977, 14–15) argued that agriculture—which he views as a new relationship between societies and their natural environments rather than a new understanding of the natural world—was an unsuccessful effort to do so. Population growth was the motor that drove communities to shift from extensive foraging subsistence activities to more intensive agricultural pursuits. In his view, the impetus for population growth was a naturally determined variable originating outside the social system. The pressures it generated—the natural Malthusian tendency for populations to increase and outstrip the available food supply—were mediated through the economic base. Thus, Cohen presented one version of the cultural materialist alternative to the ecosystems perspective of the New Archaeology (Kohl 1981; Llobera 1979; Oakes 1981; Price 1982). Although archaeologists critically examined the empirical and theoretical foundations of neo-Malthusian arguments (Brumfiel 1976; Cowgill 1975a, 1975b), they neither acknowledged nor discussed the implications of Malthusian ideas in a social milieu that was already experiencing the rapid resurgence of scientific racism (Chase 1980; Nell 1979).

Reconstructions of ancient social organization did not orginate with the New Archaeologists: Such studies were already being made in the 1950s (for example, Adams 1966; Deetz 1965; MacNeish 1972; Menzel 1959). Nevertheless, they were favorably disposed to these investigations and began to develop this line of inquiry in the late 1960s. They were particularly receptive to the functionalist conceptual frameworks proposed in the 1960s by Elman Service (1962) and Morton Fried (1967), both of whom were concerned with social evolution, the development of political society. In their works, Service and Fried viewed societies as aggregates of essentially androgynous individuals that were easily interchangeable with one another, rather than as complexly textured webs of social relations that were structured by age, gender, life experience, kinship, or class. As a result, the New Archaeologists who adopted their conceptual frameworks had to identify the archaeological correlates of the various types of societies they discussed. Did a particular set of archaeological assemblages reflect a band, ranked society, tribe, chiefdom, or state? In the process, they began to recognize and appreciate the assets and liabilities of the categories as they were originally defined and as they were subsequently deployed and used by archaeologists (Earle 1987; Feinman and Neitzel 1984; Peebles and Kus 1977).

In spite of the shortcomings of their conceptual framework, the New Archaeologists made significant contributions to the study of ancient social organization. Flannery's (1967) study of scheduling laid important foundations for discussing time and space as operating factors in production. Various essays in *The Early Mesoamerican Village* acknowledged differential burial practices and technical divisions of labor both within and between households, patio groups, and villages in the Oaxaca Valley, which were attributable to differences in age, sex, or social position within the community (Flannery 1976). Their reconstructions of ancient social organization occurred at the same time as those of other archaeologists who did not share its logical positivism and systems theory. Thus, René Millon's (1967, 1976) study of social relations at Teotihuacán, William Haviland's (1967) examination of stature differences among Maya burials, or Dorothy Menzel's (1976) study of burial practices at Old Ica, none of which were particularly inspired by the New Archaeology, provided clear indications that other issues of ancient social organization, such as class formation and ethnicity, could also be addressed.

Like the cultural evolutionists, some New Archaeologists tended to view state-level organization as the highest form of social development. It was the end product of a gradual unfolding of the community's potential to optimize or approach the goal of stability; this happened through accommodations to successive dynamic equilibria or adaptive states. Unlike the cultural evolutionists who were economic determinists, the New Archaeologists held that the political-juridical and ideological superstructures determined the economic base and that the natural role of the state was to maintain equilibrium and protect the society from systemic pathologies—such as meddling, usurpation, or hypercoherence—which promoted stress and instability. In the idiom of systems theory, the flow of energy or information was regulated by a hierarchy of specialized components, each of which promotes homoeostasis. "... the highest, most abstract, and most unchanging of these ... lie in the highest-order (or 'governmental' controls), which deal in policy more often than commands" (Flannery 1972, 409). Thus, in this view, the policies of the state are the motors for cultural development; the state is the creator of culture as well as its censor; the undifferentiated masses are both the producers of the surpluses that sustain the state's personnel and the audience for its performances.

The New Archaeologists viewed change as gradual and directional; adaptations, once they were achieved by the purposive behavior of goal-seeking social systems, were relatively long-lived. This meant that class-stratified, state-based societies were immediately preceded by hierarchically organized, prestate societies— chiefdoms, in Service's terms—that had existed for several centuries before the new adaptive state emerged (Wright 1977, 1986). However, cultural materialists—such as William Sanders and David Webster (1978) or Barbara Price (1978)—challenged the universality of the New Archaeology's essentially unilineal typology. They argued, instead, that societies in environments with varying degrees of diversity, risk, and productivity follow different developmental trajectories. As a result, whereas some chiefdoms were stepping stones on the path to state formation, others were evolutionary dead ends whose potential for further development was constrained by a combination of demographic and ecological factors. Furthermore, whereas pristine states developed autochthonously, many others were secondary: They were derived historically from earlier, preexisting states or were imposed in areas where states had not existed previously.

Thus, once again theoretical differences between the communications and ergonomics systems perspective of the New Archaeologists and cultural materialism led to different understandings of social evolution in the 1970s. The divergent viewpoints of the two theoretical frameworks had other dimensions as well. For example, New Archaeologists viewed state formation as a process that affected and homogenized all of the societies in a region, molding them into a modular lattice composed of a single social type—the state. The cultural materialists viewed cultural evolution in terms of the interplay of environmental and demographic constraints that impinged from the outside to affect the natural unfolding of a society's developmental potential. This produced mosaics composed of different types of societies. However, in at least one area the New Archaeologists and the cultural materialists were in accord: the importance of exchange and trade.

Sudden increases in external trade, according to Colin Renfrew (1984, 86–87) and the archaeologists who followed his lead, were responsible for the rise of civilization and the origin of states. Trade, they argue, brings "... in its wake new wealth, new craft specialisations, new weapons and defensive needs, ... [as well as] the transformation of a village subsistence economy into an urban society" (Renfrew 1969, 158). Expanded commerce was viewed as an emergent condition, a response to the intensification of social life. It was both the product and the source of new human needs. As a consequence of the expansion of market exchange, the traders who traveled over well-trod paths to ply their wares visited artisans who congregated in the new urbanized centers to peddle the commodities they produced in the marketplace. These achievements signaled the rise of civilization and the formation of clusters of early states, each "with a stratified organisation for exchange," that were held together by trade as remote interaction and peer polity interaction (Renfrew 1984, 105). In other words, once trade and markets emerged, different kinds of societies were unified and enmeshed in steadily more complex webs of social relations; more importantly, the enveloped communities were increasingly regulated by the optimizing rationality and capitalist logic of neoclassical economics.

Both the cultural materialists and the New Archaeologists who adopted a systems theory perspective in the 1970s were involved in constructing new images of nature and what it meant to be human. The cultural materialists were attempting to build "theories about culture that incorporate lawful regularities occurring in nature," laws that both regulate human behavior and that human beings can never change (Harris 1979, 56–57). These laws operate at the level of the individual who is trying to satisfy biopsychological needs—such as eating, sex, or expending less energy. Thus, the individual becomes the unit of cultural evolution, which occurs when "... individual men and women ... respond opportunistically to cost-benefit options" calculated in terms of the capitalist logic and the rationality of neoclassical economic models (Harris 1979, 61).

At the core of the cultural materialist problematic is the neo-Malthusian argument that cultural evolution is a response to the population pressure that results when individuals, operating to satisfy their sexual desires, have too many babies. When this happens, the law of diminishing returns begins to operate. The marginal productivity of labor declines relative to other factors in a fixed economy, and the quality of everyday life begins to fall. These circumstances can only be turned around, if there are technological innovations that increase productivity and allow the population to expand to its natural limit. In this view, individual human beings are essentially prisoners of their appetites; their only hope for salvation is a technological fix provided by scientific elites that have the ability to look through the cultural overlay and to suspend their desires, at least momentarily, while they locate the appropriate remedy.

The New Archaeology advocates of systems theory also reworked nature and culture. By treating human beings as components in hierarchically organized information systems whose relative efficiencies could be measured under conditions of stress, they blurred the boundaries separating humans from animals, organisms from machines, and the organic from the physical. In doing so, they populated the archaeological landscape with cyborgs—those machine-organism hybrids, crafted by scientists, that lack culturally constituted identities (Haraway 1991, 1, 149–82). Nature and culture are no longer opposed or conceptually distinct domains. Cyborgs are the essentially interchangeable, androgynous individuals that aggregate and form the lower-level components of a society. They act ergonomically in accordance with the optimizing or maximizing policies of the higher-order components, policies that incorporate the rationality of neoclassical economics and repackage it as a law of nature. In this view, the ability of individuals to make their own history is as constrained as it is in the cultural materialist problematic. As individuals achieve their own ends, the collectivity of which they are parts makes successively closer approximation of its goal of systems maintenance and increased stability. Thus, historical change can only proceed along a single developmental pathway with a fixed end product called the capitalist state. From the viewpoint of scientists steeped in logical positivism and in least-common-denominator answers, histories and behaviors in different areas are infinitely predictable and easily compared.

Both theories are reductionist and determinist. They assert that real social change is either impossible or beyond the capacity of all but the elites who monopolize and control knowledge and power. The essentially Hobbesian and Malthusian arguments of the cultural materialists assume that everyday life takes place on a level playing field and that each individual starts with the same amount of wealth and capabilities as her or his competitors; they do not consider what happens when wealth is not evenly distributed, how individuals came to have different amounts, or why the impoverished are disadvantaged relative to the more affluent members in circumstances where appetites are satisfied by buying and selling in the market. The systems theorists assume that such inequalities are ultimately inherent in the social system itself because of the hierarchical organization of the cybernetic components that send and receive information. In spite of their differences, both theories have been appealing to elites, who explain the advantages they possess in terms of heightened acumen or a Social Darwinist gene that is better expressed in some individuals or more representative of one population than another.

Both theories are ultimately despairing. They claim that social inequality is natural and, because social change is a natural process culminating in the capitalist state, it is ultimately impossible to remedy this fact and the circumstances that issue from it. In other words, social relations are fixed, and people have little or no chance of changing their circumstances. These theories have not been particularly appealing to individuals and groups in the society who believe that social relations and conditions are historically constructed and that, under some circumstances, people have in fact succeeded in changing the conditions of everyday life; they have made their own history but not under circumstances of their own choice.

DISCUSSION

The distinctions between the Eastern Establishment and Core Culture were blurred economically by corporate mergers and politically by the voter realignments orchestrated by the Republican Party and the American Federation of Labor in the 1970s. The distinctions no longer bear the same cultural meaning and significance they had before 1970. Nevertheless, residuals of the two historic blocs are still in place. For instance, the old hegemony of Eastern Establishment culture still weighs heavily in the organization of the Archaeological Institute of America, and Core Culture concerns appear to persist in biblical archaeology. Residuals of the two blocs also remain for archaeologists trained in anthropology—those who belong to the Archeology Division of the American Anthropological Association or the Society for American Archaeology—however, they no longer have the same shaping effects they had in the 1950s. As a result, both organizations, as well as the classicists in the Archaeological Institute of America, are receptive to increasingly frank discussions of women's issues. Nevertheless, many members in both groups continue to harbor views that gender hierarchy and patriarchal social relations, such as the ones depicted in the Old Testament, are natural rather than culturally constructed.

Since the late 1960s, finance capital—the articulation of banks and industrial firms with the dominance of the former—has been the economic motor driving both the privatization and institutionalization of archaeology in the United States. This was evidenced by the era of mega-museum exhibits beginning in the 1970s. These included the King Tut exhibit, "The Treasure of Tutankhamun," which moved with tremendous publicity from the Metropolitan Museum of New York to other museums across North America (Hoving 1978). As Robyn Gillam (1989, 78–79, 87) pointed out, the fifty-five objects in the exhibit were brought from Egypt to the United States by the U.S. Sixth Fleet in the wake of the Camp David accords. The Camp David agreement marked Egypt's shift from the Soviet to the U.S. sphere of influence and the appearance of new investment for U.S. firms. Once in New York, the objects were turned over to Exxon, an oil company with close ties to the Rockefeller banks in New York, which "... provided the form and vehicle for this event" (Gillam 1989, 78). The exhibit generated $259 million, only about $7 million of which was returned to the Egyptian Antiquities Organization to refurbish exhibits in the Cairo museum and to promote tourism.

The same banks also underwrote the recycling and redlining of real estate in the 1970s and 1980s. These activities were fueled by the Environmental Protection Act

(1969) and the Historic Sites Preservation Act (1966), which created the National Register. Tax exemptions granted in the 1970s and 1980s turned wastelands with a few old buildings into areas with exploding land values. Buildings placed on the National Register were restored; they not only enhanced real estate values in these new developments but also gave them a stamp of authenticity, providing an instantaneous heritage rooted in some local, regional, or national historical tradition. In Philadelphia, for instance, the only thing that remained after the restoration of one building on the National Register—the Wanamaker House, where the former postmaster general lived—was its facade. In another development, objects removed from excavations in a historic district were placed in an exhibit case in the lobby of the new commercial building erected on its ruins. The exhibit was then portrayed as a museum and was used by the building's owners as the basis for claiming further tax exemptions as a nonprofit organization serving the public.

The New Archaeology evolved rapidly in the conditions that emerged in the New Gilded Age. It was initially a challenge to archaeologists to clarify the concepts and methods they used to discern regularities in the archaeological record and in the development of ancient societies. Many advocates, especially those concerned with ecological modeling and optimal foraging strategies, quickly adopted the idiom of the finance capitalists on the Trilateral Commission and, later, in the World Bank, who also spoke of maximizing and optimizing strategies that were rooted in the natural behavior of individuals. The cultural materialist explanations rooted in neo-Malthusianism were framed in the same language as claims concerning overpopulation that were made by the officials at the Ford Foundation. In the change, arguments framed in terms of historical stages of development received less emphasis than they had a generation earlier in the 1950s.

The New Archaeology inherited a legacy: the distinction between civilized and noncivilized societies. Lamentably, it strengthened the unfortunate dichotomy drawn between prehistory and history. In this view, civilized peoples—those with states and writing systems—have history; the remainder of the world's societies, most of humanity, lacks history. Their history becomes part of natural history, or it is relegated to myth. In either case, it is accessible only to the tools of the archaeological scientist who is the only one qualified to fill in the silences.

Many New Archaeologists gradually dropped their early claims that archaeology should be relevant. However, diverse groups during the 1970s and 1980s, whose members included archaeologists, firmly believed that archaeology did, in fact, have relevance for explaining contemporary social relations and, thus, for exploring the potential and implications of alternative courses of action in the future. In archaeology, the members of these diverse groups have been lumped together and called "post-processual" archaeologists. The label is unfortunate to the extent that it is understood as ascribing a unity of view to individuals who, in fact, defend quite different positions under some conditions but not in others. In the next chapter, let us examine these social constructivist perspectives in more detail, how they relate to the issues of relevance and to circumstances that emerged during the neoliberal era, and how substantive contributions based on them have added significant new dimensions to the practice of archaeology in the United States.

CHAPTER 6

Archaeology and Multiculturalism: Race, Class, and Gender in the Neoliberal State

Immigration has been one of the most significant features of U.S. society during the past twenty-five years. Nearly ten million persons have entered the United States legally since 1969. Another three million seized the window of opportunity afforded by the amnesty provisions of the Immigration Reform and Control Act (1986) to legalize their status. Several million more, who entered the country illegally or over-stayed visas, have successfully disappeared and now support themselves in the under-ground economy. As a result, the United States now has the largest immigrant population in the world. Not since the heyday of immigration between 1900 and 1910, when almost nine million persons entered the United States and the foreign-born constituted nearly 15 percent of its total population, have so many strangers come to its shores (Rumbaut 1991).

Whereas 95 percent of the immigrants at the turn of the century came from Europe, more than 75 percent of the legal arrivals today are from Latin America and Asia. The new arrivals constitute an internally diverse population: well-educated Koreans and Chinese; impoverished second-wave Cambodian and Hmong families; and working-class men and women from Mexico, the Caribbean, and Central America. Although they have settled across the country, nearly 70 percent are con-centrated in a few metropolitan areas such as New York, Los Angeles, Miami, or the San Francisco-Oakland-San Jose triangle. More than 20 percent of the current population in each of these metropoles is foreign-born (Rumbaut 1991). In the pro-cess, new neighborhoods have been forged inside or on the margins of those already established. In Philadelphia, for instance, which has a significant immigrant popula-tion but is not one of the large magnet regions, Little Saigon now sits next to the Italian Market, and both are wedged between a small Mexican barrio and an African-American neighborhood that emerged on the edge of the district, the residents of which in the 1950s were largely Jews whose parents or grandparents came from east-ern Europe before the First World War.

The arrival of the first massive waves of Asian- and Latin American immigrants in the 1970s coincided with the simultaneous, and not unrelated, reorganization of the U.S. class structure and ethnogenesis, the appearance of new groups composed of previously disconnected individuals who were beginning to sense that they had some-thing in common. Taken together, these processes marked the development of iden-tity politics. The immigrants constituting the new "people classes" were acutely aware of the fact that women, American Indians, Chicanos, Puerto Ricans, and gays and lesbians, to name only a few, were demanding recognition of rights and claims based on their identities. They participated in and were affected to varying degrees and in different ways by the new social movements. The politics of many of the movements, like those of some civil rights activists in the 1960s, celebrated differences and demanded equal recognition and rights because of them. Their goal was to ensure the survival of the community. In some instances, the new immigrants followed their lead and adopted similar tactics.

Opposition to the collectivist goals of the new social movements appeared almost immediately. The opponents rooted their claims in another strand of liberal thought. They gave precedence to the rights of the individual and demanded that differences be ignored (Taylor 1992). This view was embodied in the 1974 Bakke decision of the U.S. Supreme Court. The judges held that the admissions policies of a medical school, which set aside a certain number of places for members of groups that were under-represented in the profession, discriminated against a white male who was denied admission, even though he had higher test scores than some minority-group members accepted into the program.

Such claims and counterclaims, as well as equally intense debates that raged within and across various movement groups, were the starting points from which new forms of social consciousness and identity were constructed in the 1970s and 1980s. Economically, they were buttressed by the massive immigration and changing complexion of the large cities, coupled with deindustrialization, growing unemployment, the flight of capital to states with large supplies of cheap labor and permissive work laws, the reconstitution of the class structure, and the steady erosion of U.S. influence in world affairs. Politically, the debates were sustained by a dense, interconnected web of policies, laws, and court rulings that were promulgated at all levels of government and that were selectively enforced or ignored by various parts of a state apparatus that worked together to ensure their own continuity even when they might oppose each other on specific issues.

These are the foundations of the culture wars that have raged in the United States for the past twenty-five years (Berman 1992; Hunter 1991; Takaki 1993; West 1993). Multiculturalism, Eurocentrism, Afrocentrism, women's studies, cultural heritage, political correctness, antiracism, and antisexism involve a lot more than words in a time when the overall thrust of the state has been to sever the tenuous links forged between political equality and democracy. What has been constructed since 1969 are a new social hierarchy and a new understanding of what America means. However, neither has yet been firmly set in place, since these visions are being contested. What the advocates of different views dispute are (1) how novel or different this hierarchy is from previous ones; (2) identifying the social categories that belong in this hierarchy; (3) how to define or characterize them; and (4) and determining what place each occupies in the grand scale. What is not being explored sufficiently are the bases for claiming that such a hierarchy actually exists in the first place!

Multiculturalism is the way that many academics and bureaucrats occupying relatively privileged positions in the class structure chose to acknowledge the formation of the new social hierarchy in the 1980s. Multiculturalism recognizes cultural diversity. That is, different communities have different cultural values and practices, which they have a right to defend. Multiculturalism, as it is discussed today, has a lot to do with what is viewed as the imposition of one culture on another and with the assumed superiority of those who claim the power to impose their vision (Taylor 1992, 63). However, multiculturalism often distorts the issue of power relations by representing inequalities between communities as problems of backwardness or individual practices (Wetherell and Potter 1992, 138). It confuses racism, sexism, homophobia, and class struggle when it reduces the discrimination and oppression associated with social hierarchy to individual prejudice. It frequently ignores institutional, financial, or legal arrangements that buttress these and other practices and the beliefs that sustain them.

Roger Kimball (1991, 13) has succinctly characterized the new social hierarchy:

> ... The choice facing us today is not between a "repressive" Western culture and a
> multicultural paradise, but between culture and barbarism. Civilization is not a gift, it is
> an achievement—a fragile achievement that needs constantly to be shored up and
> defended from besiegers inside and out.

The claim of a social hierarchy that differentiates civilization from barbarism and the West from the rest is buttressed by more than words. For instance, in 1991, Yale University accepted a $20-million gift from a recent alumnus to strengthen its commitment to studying the institutions, ideas, and traditions of Western civilization (Carby 1992, 16, 18). In accepting the gift, Yale's president remarked that the university

> ... will be able to renew its commitment to the study and teaching of Western
> civilization at a time when critical understanding of the West has never been more
> important.... This generous gift enables us to reaffirm the central importance of the
> study of the Western tradition, the major source of the institutions and ideas that have
> shaped our nation.

> (YALE UNIVERSITY, OFFICE OF PUBLIC AFFAIRS 1991)

Needless to say, the primary beneficiaries of this gift are the young men and women who will attend this already well-endowed educational institution. From the president's view, the students will gain more textured appreciations of the transcendental connection between the civilizations of Greece and Rome and contemporary U.S. society and of the equally enduring, timeless distinction between them and non-Western civilizations and cultures around the world. In Kimball's view, they will learn the difference between civilization, an achieved stage of cultural refinement characteristic of a Western elite, and the barbarism that is typical of the rest of the world's people.

What is so striking about the words and ideas of Kimball and Yale's ex-president, on the one hand, and the multiculturalists, on the other, is that they are couched in the language of archaeology. This points to where and how archaeologists have contributed to the culture wars of the past and how they participate, consciously or not, in those of the 1980s and 1990s. Archaeologists have helped to erect and sustain an analytical framework that uses certain concepts to organize particular bodies of evidence and to answer questions about them. This framework operates in a predictable manner—by the same rules—from one case to another. It integrates numerous, varied, and occasionally even contradictory elements into a single whole. It circumscribes and contains diversity within certain flexible but manageable limits. It filters out unwanted or unacceptable events, understandings, or implications (Belich 1986, 311–13). It predicts civilization as the inevitable end product of human history. Consequently, when archaeologists endorse, repeat, or amplify the existing framework, they entrench it more deeply in the emerging public discourse.

Simply put, the current debates about social hierarchy revive arguments, ideas, and attitudes that were hegemonic during the era of massive immigration at the turn of the century. Their popularity waned but never disappeared during the Depression and the years following World War II. There are still buffer races, but they are no longer the same as the ones that existed a century ago. The old buffer races composed of immigrant groups—the Irish, Jews, Italians, and Slavs, to name only a few—who formed the lower layers of the historically organized, stratified working class that emerged before the First World War were partially transformed with the social mobility of the "melting pot" in the late 1940s and 1950s.

More than two million men, overwhelmingly white and many from the old European buffer races, attended college on the GI Bill. As a result, they acquired knowledge of the high culture and refinement previously claimed as the domain of ruling class and educated layers of the middle class. Many took the kinds of jobs that had been closed to their fathers and uncles and that were not open to their less-educated brothers and sisters. They filled vacant positions and newly created ones in the rapidly expanding U.S. economy. Higher education made class boundaries somewhat more porous, and those possessing college degrees were able to pass through the membrane and to attach themselves in varying degrees and different ways to the dominant classes and their hegemonic culture. In the process, these socially and spatially mobile individuals and groups forged new ties with their kin and reconstituted old identities in new ways as they moved to the new, overwhelmingly white middle-class suburbs that were sprouting up across the country (Fields 1990, 90; Sacks 1992; Wynn 1976).

Buffer races have been re-created in the context of class formation during the 1970s and 1980s. This milieu was shaped by a constricting, stagnant economy and rising poverty. The new buffer races include the Asian model minorities—the affluent, well-educated additions to the professional classes—and exclude the large numbers of Asian refugees who joined the most impoverished layers of the working class. They include Hispanics, modeled after the middle- and upper-class Cuban refugees of the early 1960s, but exclude the Mariel "boat people" and the hundreds of thousands of immigrants from Puerto Rico, Mexico, and other countries in Latin America. They include the anticommunist immigrants from Eastern Europe granted political asylum but probably exclude Muslim refugees from war-torn regions in the same area. They may soon include some members of the white ethnic groups organized by downwardly mobile professional and skilled workers who lost their jobs and the standards of living they once knew as they swept into that internally diverse group that social scientists homogenize and call the urban underclass.

Different logics have underpinned the idea of race during the last two centuries. Around 1800, Johann Blumenbach, the philosopher Immanuel Kant, and their contemporaries believed that no precise criteria existed that allowed one to distinguish and classify races, because the "innumerable varieties of mankind run into one another by insensible degrees" (Gossett 1965, 37). Even though Blumenbach thought that racial classifications were arbitrary, he nevertheless divided humanity into five races on the bases of behavioral and physical attributes: Caucasian, Mongolian, Ethiopian, American, and Malay. A century later, the scientific racism of Louis Agassiz, Frederick W. Putnam, and their contemporaries was rooted in the idea of immutable pure types that were related hierarchically. The eugenicists claimed these lower races—as well as the working class, female, and criminal populations of their own Western societies—constituted contemporary primitive societies (Allen 1983; Pick 1989); they proclaimed the biological inferiority of these lower races and worried about what they viewed as the deleterious consequences of interbreeding. As the millennium approaches, the analytical category of race is increasingly reconstituted, once again, around the logic of class, culture, and the constraints imposed by poverty.

Of course, these are not the only logics undergirding the concepts of race and white supremacy and the practices of racism. Cornel West (1988, 22–23) points to the Judeo-Christian logic emanating from the biblical account of Ham, whose disrespect and rejection of paternal authority were divinely punished by the darkening of his descendants. West and Joel Kovel (1984) point to the psychosexual logic that treats people of color as inanimate others associated with acts of subordination and violence. They show that such ideas and theories about race, which may be rejected or of marginal importance in academic and professional communities, persist and remain effective in wider social discourses (Wetherell and Potter 1992, 20). This is especially true at a time when many of the New Right participants in those debates proclaim the inerrancy of the Bible and make no distinction between fact and faith.

The analytical categories used by archaeologists—civilization, culture, prehistoric, primitive, formative, or religion, to name only a few—have complex histories in which new meanings have been added and others have become less important in certain contexts (for example, Haraway 1991, 127–48; Williams 1983). However, meanings are rarely ever completely erased. Some became secondary, others archaic. These concepts resembled giant snowballs perched on a hilltop, susceptible to the slightest pressure that would send them hurtling down the slope, picking up everything in their path before smashing into the bottom. When heavily laden concepts—such as civilization and race—splatter, all of the diverse meanings that they picked up through time suddenly appear and are deployed simultaneously with differing emphases in public discourse.

THE REACTIONS OF ARCHAEOLOGISTS IN AND TO THE 1970S AND 1980S

Archaeologists were neither completely insulated from the culture wars of the 1970s and 1980s nor completely unaffected by the issues they raised. Whereas many archaeologists were indifferent or even cynical towards the social movements of the 1970s and 1980s and a few were openly hostile, especially when they were affected personally, others were genuinely touched by the issues they raised. They tri to integrate these issues into their everyday lives. As a result, they began to ask questions about the problems of discrimination, oppression, domination, and exploitation. Racism and race, sexism and gender, and the state and class structures were issues that would begin to shape the questions they asked. For instance, Robert Schuyler (1970, 88) wrote that

> ... just as Kathleen G. Aberle ... has called upon ethnography to study not only conquered non-Western cultures but also the process of imperialism itself, so Historic Sites Archaeology can make a major contribution to modern anthropology by studying the processes of European expansion, exploration, and colonization as well as those of culture contact and imperialism, that underlie one of the most dynamic periods of world history....

The stimuli for their inquiries systematically came from outside the profession, because few, if any, inside it were directly confronting these issues. In practice, this meant engaging with groups and individuals in the social movement organizations of the 1970s—such as the civil rights, antiwar, peace, or women's movements—whose major interests and aims were not archaeology. This does not mean that the participants in various movement groups and coalitions were disinterested in archaeology or that they even saw it as irrelevant to their concerns. They most certainly did not, although some archaeologists at the time did, in fact, boast about how disconnected their work was from the "real world." For those who connected in different ways and varying degrees with the social movements of the 1960s through the 1980s, it also meant developing perspectives and languages to deal with the issues addressed to the wider society and then extending the insights they gained by participating in those debates to the theory and practice of archaeology.

The formation of historical archaeology as a semi-autonomous discipline coincided with the appearance of hyphenated Americans and ethnic studies programs in the early 1970s. It also coincided with the decline of various assimilationist programs and agendas and with steadily increasing criticism about the validity and utility of the melting pot metaphor (Gleason 1992; Sollors 1986). This shift followed in the wake of the African-American struggle for civil rights. It occurred as legislation and programs rooted in the recognition of cultural differences were blocked and claims rooted in color-blindness came to the fore. The melting pot and color-blind perspectives implied that indigenous and immigrant peoples were naturally and unproblematically assimilated into the mainstream of American social life. However, as Kathleen Deagan (1983, 3–4) noted:

> Excavations at colonial and postcolonial sites have led Robert Schuyler (1976, 35) and James Deetz (1977, 135) to suggest instead that the formation of American
> ~~~~ ~rocess of systematic exclusion of non-Anglo groups from the
> ican life. This also suggests that the essential denial of any non-
> ur heritage—reflected today in its exclusion from traditional
> al history—is not just a contemporary phenomenon.
>
> 10 took this issue seriously examined precisely those groups
> m traditional constructions of American heritage. As a result,

Charles Fairbanks and his associates began to excavate the cabins of Black slaves, plantations, and creole communities in the late 1960s and early 1970s (Ascher and Fairbanks 1971; Fairbanks 1974; McGuire 1982; Orser 1990). Their concerns led at least one ethnohistorian working in the southeastern United States to inquire whether the spatial patterning found at some pre-Columbian sites in the region might not be the product of ethnogenesis—the formation of ethnic identities in circumstances shaped by the development or recomposition of class structures (Willis 1980).

In the 1950s and 1960s, a few archaeologists testified in land claims cases brought by various Native American peoples. These cases were concerned with property rights; they also involved the issues of ethnic or tribal identity and the use of archaeological remains to establish identity or to demonstrate continuity between the contemporary and aboriginal communities of particular areas. However, the relations between archaeologists and Native Americans deteriorated rapidly beginning in the late 1960s, when a resolution suggesting that archaeologists needed to show greater respect toward American Indians was not even discussed at the business meeting of the Society for American Archaeology in 1968. The downhill slide continued through the mid-1980s as Native Americans expressed concerns with increasing frequency over the excavation of cemeteries and sought the repatriation and reburial of skeletal remains housed in museums (Rosen 1980). These relations reached their nadir in 1984, when a majority of the Society for American Archaeology passed a resolution opposing reburial except in situations where lineal descendants wanted the remains reburied (Hammil 1987; Powell et al. 1993, 13–15).

Some of the contentious issues separating archaeologists and Native Americans were resolved in the late 1980s by the passage of federal legislation: the National Museum of the American Indian (1989) and the Native American Graves Protection and Repatriation Act (1990). Others have been ameliorated to some extent by a series of frank discussions between archaeologists and Native Americans, first at a heavily attended SAA meeting in 1986, then at the World Archaeological Congress (WAC) held later that year, and subsequently at a WAC Inter-Congress held in South Dakota in 1989 (Hubert et al. 1989). At the 1992 plenary session of the SAA annual meeting, Indian-rights activist Vine Deloria (1992b) opened the door for further improving relations between archaeologists and Native Americans.

By the mid-1970s, a few U.S. archaeologists were beginning to raise questions about the theoretical frameworks they used to examine and discuss state-based societies (Crumley 1976, 1979; Kus 1982, 1983). The issue they brought to the table for discussion was cultural complexity (Kohl 1981; McGuire 1983; Wenke 1981). The cultural evolutionary theories of the New Archaeologists were built on poorly developed understandings of social stratification and the class structures characteristic of states. They exhibited even less understanding of oppression and exploitation, on the one hand, and their mirror images, resistance and class struggle, on the other. They conflated technical divisions of labor, which reflected task specialization, with the social division of labor, which was rooted in the unequal distribution of social product and structural inequalities. Some of the New Archaeologists seemed to view social inequality as the end product of natural processes rather than as socially constructed relations (Flannery 1972; Johnson 1982). The deficiencies of such theories became steadily more apparent in a milieu where the wars of national liberation in Africa and Asia, the civil rights struggles and urban rebellions in the United States, the police riot at the Democratic Convention in 1968, the Vietnam War, and the Watergate scandals were regular fare in television new shows and other media.

As a result, some began to engage Marxist and Third World writers concerned with oppression, exploitation, class, and political economy on their own terms rather than filtered through the views of V. Gordon Childe (Kohl 1975, Smith 1976). These laid the foundations for subsequent studies of power relations, inequality, and domination and resistance (McGuire and Paynter 1991; Patterson and Gailey 1987). Archaeologists produced them for diverse reasons and in different ways. To some they were an extension of the concerns of various antiwar, peace, or solidarity groups and an indication of their engagement with those movements. Other archaeologists saw the analytical power of Marxist social theory for dealing with issues of oppression, exploitation, and ideology; however, they decanted political engagement from Marxist praxis for various reasons (Leone 1982, 757). Some of their concerns—such as job security—were, in fact, real; several archaeologists were indeed fired, and others encountered various difficulties from their employers and professional peers precisely because of their *involvement* in political movements rather than the language they used.

By the mid-1970s, a small but steadily increasing number of archaeologists began to address issues raised by feminist writers in the women's movement. Feminists refined their arguments and views during the 1970s and 1980s; consequently, the issues they addressed shifted through time. Their first explorations in the late 1960s and early 1970s were rooted in the language of class and political engagement largely because of the influence of the civil rights and peace movements. By the mid-1970s, they focused increasingly on issues of oppression, control of women's sexuality, and male violence. By the end of the decade, women of color had shown clearly that the initial understandings of gender had to be expanded in order to incorporate those facets of identity that were constructed in racial or ethnic terms (Hall 1992, 1–40).

Those archaeologists concerned with women's issues confronted two problems (Conkey and Spector 1984; Gero 1983, 1985; Conkey and Gero 1991; Wylie 1991). The first involved the circumstances and employment opportunities of the large number of women who entered the profession in the early 1970s, just as the economy was souring and the job market was rapidly transforming. As a result, the issues of employment equity and discrimination in hiring and promotion were major foci of their inquiries and activities in the 1970s. This resulted in the formation of the Committee on the Status of Women in Anthropology (COSWA) in the American Anthropological Association and the accumulation of statistical information that showed that women were, and still are, under-represented in the tenured ranks at universities and disproportionately represented in non-tenure-track positions (Vance 1975; Kramer and Stark 1988). A Committee on the Status of Women in Archaeology (COSWA) was formed by the executive committee of the Society for American Archaeology in the late 1970s and disbanded a few years later. However, renewed concerns in the late 1980s led to the formation of committees on the status of women in the Society for American Archaeology, the Archeology Division of the American Anthropological Association, and the Society for Historical Archaeology; they also led to the organization of heavily attended symposia at various national meetings and the highly successful Chacmool conference on "The Archaeology of Gender" organized by graduate students at the University of Calgary (Walde and Willows 1991).

The second problem involved developing a more textured appreciation of gender differences, more refined ways of recognizing gender distinctions in the archaeological record, and greater understanding of their significance and implications. Gender differences refer to the ways in which sexual differences that are perceived as natural are constructed. There are two levels of construction. The first is concerned with what is defined as constituting "natural." Biology, occupation, sexual preference, age, and possession of female essence are only a few of the criteria mentioned in the ethnographic and historical literature that have been used to circumscribe and give substance to the meaning of *natural*. The other level attaches significance to the sexual differences that have been used to constitute men, women, or other genders.

Archaeologists concerned with gender issues have provided empirical evidence that simultaneously places females in the archaeological record and points out the limitations of existing premises. They have challenged some basic assumptions in the field and begun to deconstruct notions such as biological constraints on behavior, which are based on slender and highly selected ethnographic and historical evidence. They have also shown how historical records built on analytical categories in Western social thought portray the work of females as nondynamic, an element to be acknowledged and then ignored in reconstructing processes of social change. They have challenged the utility of logical positivism, with its emphasis on particular methods of testability and verification, as a means of examining questions about social constructions such as gender because logical positivism dismisses these constructions as untestable, of marginal interest, or not relevant. They ask us to pay more attention to the contemporary intellectual and sociopolitical contexts and meanings of analytical categories we deploy to interpret the archaeological record (Gero and Conkey 1991).

The concerns over racism, domination and resistance, and sexism developed as parallel yet separate currents in archaeology that were capable of uniting at the slightest provocation. Just such a provocation occurred in the mid-1980s around the World Archaeological Congress held in Southampton, England, in 1986. The congress, originally sponsored by the International Union of Prehistoric and Protohistoric Sciences (IUPPS), was arranged by a local British organizing committee. After considerable debate, the members of the British committee recognized the requests of the British anti-apartheid movement to honor United Nations resolutions calling for academic and cultural sanctions against South Africa and Namibia. They withdrew their invitations to scholars from South Africa and Namibia. The IUPPS quickly withdrew its recognition and support of the British committee, whose members moved ahead with their plans. Several archaeologists in the United States organized a boycott of the World Archaeological Congress on the grounds that it violated academic freedom. While they succeeded in blocking travel grants for U.S. participants, the boycott was not completely successful from the perspective of its organizers. Several hundred archaeologists from the United States went to the congress, which put the issues of racism, domination and oppression, and sexism squarely on the table for discussion in various symposia and caucuses as well as at a plenary session attended by several thousand participants from more than one hundred countries (Ucko 1987). Many came away from the World Archaeological Congress with the realization that they had just participated in perhaps the most exciting and thought-provoking archaeological conference of the twentieth century.

One consequence of the intellectual fervor created by the World Archaeological Congress was a series of symposia and conferences organized around the theme of postprocessual archaeology. The term *postprocessual* is most accurately described as an umbrella that attempts to cover individuals with divergent viewpoints and commitments (Kohl 1985; Patterson 1989b, 1990). The center of gravity for the development of postprocessual archaeology in the late 1980s was clearly among visitors to or from Cambridge, England (Hodder 1985; Shanks and Tilley 1987a, 1987b). There are several strands of postprocessual archaeology. One strand is an effort to confront the issue of human agency, which was largely ignored by the overly deterministic theories of the New Archaeology (Trigger 1991). Another strand is a commentary on and critique of the highly centralized, hierarchical organization of the British archaeological community; of the high levels of marginal employment experienced by recently trained archaeologists; and of the neoliberal transformation of British society during the Thatcher years. At least the appeals of young British archaeologists to Nietzsche and Foucault's arguments about knowledge and power, Derrida's postmodernism, Lyotard's view of knowledge as a language game, or Baudrillard's simulacrum begin to make sense when viewed from this perspective. However, as yet, neither strand of postprocessual archaeology has been easily or successfully transferred to the United States. In this milieu, archaeology continues to have multiple, dispersed, almost hermetically sealed centers of gravity with disparate or even diverging interests, judging by the laments of that handful of classical archaeologists in the Archaeological Institute of America who are still attempting to interest their colleagues in the New Archaeology!

The participants in the panels and conferences in postprocessual archaeology organized in the United States have typically included four categories of individuals: those who discuss race, those who examine class and exploitation, those who explore gender, and those from England (for example, Preucel 1991). Whereas the participants of these symposia had political and theoretical concerns that intersected in Southampton, the areas of overlap quickly evaporated when academic and theoretical matters were brought to the fore and the real political issues were moved to the side. A vast chasm separated the materialist concerns of those processual and postprocessual archaeologists who had appropriated Marxist and feminist social thought from those of their postprocessual colleagues who had opted for idealist perspectives.

Nevertheless, once political issues were put on the table for discussion, real opportunities developed for their interests to merge and rapidly form into a single current, as they did at the World Archaeological Congress and have done in less public ways at other conferences since then. For example, several hundred members with diverse interests were outraged when they discovered that the program committee for the 1993 annual meeting of the Society for American Archaeology had systematically excluded invited sessions submitted by women and Latin American students. They protested this reprehensible act to the organization's executive committee, whose members recognized their sensitivities and agreed that issues of social justice and responsibility belong squarely on the SAA's agenda along with congressional lobbying and other activities on behalf of the profession.

Today, interest in the subject of archaeology is widespread and falls across a broad spectrum of groups. This claim is supported, on one hand, by the steady stream of articles appearing in newspapers and periodicals, such as the *National Geographic*, and special programs on public broadcasting stations and commercial television channels (Gero and Root 1990). On the other, it is evidenced by the extensive gray literature on the margins of the profession that has been called cult or fantastic archaeology by some authors with professional certification (Cole 1980; Harrold and Ewe 1987; Williams 1991). These labels point to the existence of differing interpretations across the spectrum of groups utilizing archaeological information and indicate perceived power relations and hegemonic viewpoints. Although authors from the profession convey something about how these groups deploy archaeological information, they tell us almost nothing about who belongs to the organizations, how they are situated, and the roles they play in the contemporary class and cultural structures of the United States.

This breadth of interest in archaeology is also evidenced by the central role it has played in three important debates about racism, sexism, oppression, and exploitation in the last decade: the contribution of Martin Bernal's (1987) *Black Athena* to the multiculturalism debate; the various Columbus quincentenary celebrations, countercelebrations, and publications (Chilcote and Dugan-Abbassi 1992; Cohen 1993; Foster 1992); and the controversies over mother goddesses and the structure of early European society (Barstow 1976). What is most noticeable about them is the virtual absence of professional archaeologists at the centers of the controversies, given the centrality of their subject matter in the debates. For the most part, professional archaeologists have remained on the sidelines, publishing essays on the consequences of the European invasion or reviews in professional journals and mainstream periodicals, such as *Archaeology* or the *Mediterranean Journal of Archaeology, The New York Times Book Review,* or *The New York Review of Books* (for example, Thomas 1989–91). Only a few have forayed across the boundary separating journals associated with the profession from magazines with more overtly political and analytical aims, and even fewer professionals have their work cited in the latter (for example, Sued-Badillo 1992a, 1992b). When their work is cited, it often acquires nuanced meanings and is deployed in new ways in the more overtly political contexts.

In other words, as far as the major cultural debates of the late twentieth century are concerned, a majority of the professional archaeologists in the United States have positioned themselves in a very narrow band of the total spectrum of opinion. They have generally refrained from engaging with other perspectives outside narrowly circumscribed professional arenas, including those that might even be called mainstream positions. This stands in marked contrast to the position occupied by practitioners of archaeology, such as Thomas Jefferson, at the end of the eighteenth century or first-generation professional archaeologists, such as Frederick Ward Putnam or George Breasted, a century later.

CONCLUSION

The subject of archaeology provokes intense curiosity. It addresses those fundamental questions raised more than two centuries ago by Jean Jacques Rousseau in
the *Second Discourse on the Origins of Inequality among Men*: What activities
define the social life of past peoples, how are these activities interrelated, how do
they communicate, and what is the material evidence for their social history and
history as a species? Archaeology is also potentially one of the more hopeful of
the historical and social sciences. It shows both that societies change and that
there are ways of organizing everyday social life and culture that differ fundamentally from our own. However, as a result, the potential of archaeology is like
that of a double-edged sword. A movement in one direction buttresses the existing social order; a slight movement in the other delivers a devastating critique of
contemporary civilization.

Depending on the question, interest in a given issue may be as wide as the class
structure itself or confined to specialized groups occupying some particular, narrowly
defined position in that structure. The debates that follow from this fact are consequently waged on terrains of varying width. The heated arguments over the recognition and significance of the Devonian Period (the time between 410 and 360 million
years ago) in England during the 1830s and 1840s were waged almost entirely by
gentlemen-specialists within the confines of the Geological Society and the British
Association (Rudwick 1985). However, fierce debates about evolution in England
and Scotland during the same decades extended far beyond professional societies and
the academy; views and exchanges about evolution and its significance erupted
across the social spectrum, as Adrian Desmond (1989) showed, and these varied
understandings were frequently linked with equally diverse beliefs about the formation and structure of the contemporary social relations. In general, the questions
Rousseau posed provoked opinions from groups located across the entire social spectrum; however, an unfortunate but all too frequent effect of professionalism is to
restrict participation in the debates and even to limit access to the arenas where they
take place (Gaventa 1980).

Throughout this book, I have historicized the development of archaeology in the
United States. I have examined its practice in light of the shifting political-economic,
social, and cultural contexts in which it developed. I have indicated that these contexts
were the same ones in which various understandings of the United States itself were
fabricated, reproduced, and adjusted or discarded in the face of new historical circumstances. I have argued that interpretations of archaeological evidence and past
societies have played central roles in the construction of powerful images and
metaphors concerning the place of U.S. society and the state in the world today and
their relationships with past societies and those in other parts of the world.

This is not the first effort to historicize the development of a historical or social
science in the United States. A few years ago, Dorothy Ross (1991) asserted that
American social science received many of its distinctive characteristics from the
ideology of American exceptionalism—a claim that the United States occupies a
unique place in world history because of its particular form of government and the
economic opportunities it has afforded immigrants and their descendants. She

explored how the ideology of American exceptionalism—which has its roots in the worldviews of the colonial period and early republic—was reconstituted in the wake of the transformations that followed the Civil War and Reconstruction. By examining linkages between ideology and practice, she revealed how the values and logic of American exceptionalism were incorporated into the models and explanations of the newly professionalizing disciplines of political economy, history, and sociology during the Gilded Age and Progressive Era.

Before that, David Noble's (1977, 321) study of corporate engineers during and after the Progressive Era also historicized the activities and beliefs of an American profession. His inquiry revealed how corporate engineers simultaneously strove to standardize science and industry, routinize research, and transform education. He also showed how the engineers took for granted the very social order they had created. They increasingly represented the social relations they had helped to create as part of the natural order. Noble (1984) subsequently showed how the technological determinism of the engineers—their belief that machines rather than people make history—is both cryptic and mystifying. This ideology, which still underpins most arguments about the benefits of technological progress, masks the fact that technological development is a social process.

The generally positive valuations attached to the idea of progress make it difficult for both the engineers and the wider public to ask critical questions about its consequences. While uncritical acceptance of the idea of progress is pacifying, avoidance of the crucial questions is escapist. The combination places the solution to all contemporary social problems in the future and suggests that the only route toward their remedy is the "natural" one involving a technological fix. The idea that the achievement of science was an end in itself and the way to find order in the historical flux of everyday life is scientism. Scientism, as Ross (1991, 467) observed, is a paradigm

> ... modeled on physical science and presumably rooted in the necessities of nature and human nature, that exempted American exceptionalism from history, at least any other than the track of perpetual liberal progress that could be extrapolated from the paradigm itself.

Scientism was added to the mix composing the collective cultural and historical conscience of U.S. society during the late nineteenth and early twentieth centuries. There, it coexisted in tension, in a dialectical relation, with American exceptionalism and with the strong antimodernist sentiments described by T. Jackson Lears. Antimodernism, in Lears's view, was simultaneously a lament about the passing of the old social order and a longing, albeit an ambivalent one, for its regeneration or at least for the re-creation of certain of its physical, moral, and spiritual elements in the social and cultural fabric that was then being woven on the loom of everyday life. It overlapped with a more up-to-date agenda of revitalization in a milieu shaped by accommodation to the increasingly routinized work regimes and bureaucratic rationality of U.S. capitalism at the turn of the century. Antimodernism, including its retreat into ancient, medieval, and oriental cultures and its re-creation of self-sufficiency through the Arts and Crafts movement, eased the transition to the consumption orientation of twentieth-century U.S. society (Lears 1981, xiii–xviii). For Lears (1981, 50, 301), the embourgeoisment associated with antimodernist sentiments at the turn of the century also helped the established elite to become a self-conscious ruling class and to retain and reinforce its cultural hegemony.

The fundamental importance of Lears' work is its recognition of a dialectical relation between class structure and culture. As a result, he portrays cultural transformation as far more subtle and generally messier processes than functionalist or structuralist social scientists, who too often view it in reductionist, mechanistic terms that evoke images of the growth of living organisms or the endlessly intermeshing gears of some perpetual-motion machine. He also understands that cultural transformation is much more complex than the machinations of some "... ruling-class committee conspiring to impose dominant values on hapless workers" (Lears 1981, xiii).

One of the two main deficits of Lears's work derives from the distinctions he draws among elite, mass, and popular culture, which embody power relations. These have been misread to imply that cultural innovation is a process initiated at the top of the class structure or by the state, which slowly filters down to the working class. The other weakness is his view that bourgeoisification of the middle classes was a universal process that proceeded along the same route and ended with approximately the same results in different parts of the United States; it overlooks the significance of differences in the various regional cultures that witnessed, underpinned, and underwrote this process. The limitations imposed by these deficits have been overcome to some extent by John Bodnar's (1992) examination of what happens when groups in different parts of the country decide to commemorate their past and encounter the contradictions of U.S. society as they are manifested in the areas where they live.

It is important to reiterate that the professionalization of archaeology occurred in a cultural milieu where American exceptionalism, scientism, and antimodernism were juxtaposed, fused, and opposed. Archaeology was simultaneously represented as a science that studied the natural history of society and as a humanistic discipline that studied the history and accomplishments of civilization. As scientists, archaeologists either studied those precivilized peoples who lived in the far distant past before the advent of writing or the ancestors of peoples who lived on the periphery of the expanding imperial U.S. state. They relegated these societies, which were examined with the methods of science, to the realm of nature; they viewed them as a baseline against which civilization and rate of progress could be measured. As students of civilization, they studied the material accomplishments of the Greek and Roman worlds described by classical writers who were viewed as quintessentially white and Western. As students of the civilizing process that underpinned the rise of Western and Christian civilization, they studied material remains from the Holy Land that enhanced understanding of and made contextual the accounts in the Old and New Testaments but did not achieve the levels of sophistication attained in Europe, which was quintessentially Western, Christian, and civilized. All of these tendencies and contradictory strands are still evident even today in the profession. Because of its demonstrated capacity for incorporating diverse groups into a single metanarrative, archaeology has to be taken seriously both as a part of cultural hegemony and as a set of practices for creating that hegemony.

As a result, archaeology became an increasingly well-financed activity in the United States during the twentieth century. How it came to be that way is a fairly complicated story. It is not a result of the unfolding of some innate propensity in human nature to satisfy curiosity or some other rational choice, nor is it a product of the steady forward march of science; it is instead a consequence of the actions of particular men and women who were able to make a little history given their own circumstances and relations to peoples and institutions around them. Why archaeology has remained and continues to be a well-financed set of practices and interpretations is a different story that also involves the interplay of people and institutions rather than the mechanical unfolding of some over-determined natural process.

It contributes to hegemony of the state and a regionally segmented ruling class by virtue of its authority over certain historical metanarratives and analytical categories. Judging by television, textbooks, and popular literature, it presents fairly standardized, straightforward accounts that fulfill the expectations of its listeners and readers. These accounts are more simple and monolithic than debates within the profession. The most important are perhaps the idea that there are hierarchies of societies, cultures, and races and the idea that there are sharp distinctions between peoples without history and those societies in the West that have produced written accounts of their heritage. U.S. archaeologists point to differences between primitive and civilized societies, simple and complex cultures, and, in increasingly audible stage whispers, to more advanced and less advanced human races. In their writings and in the museum exhibits they organize, they continue to represent human history outside the West and the Holy Land—in Africa, the Orient, and the Americas—largely as natural history or as myth. The past and present peoples of most of the world are depicted as part of the natural realm. Their societies are understood as adaptations to environmental changes or to Malthusian pressures, also rooted in nature, that have evolved slowly and gradually over time. Their social relations—which are actually cultural constructions that often involve complex intersections of class, gender, and race—are portrayed as natural rather than human provisions. The only regions whose inhabitants have human history rather than adaptations to their natural habitats and whose cultures are in fact cultured rather than naturally adapted are in the West, variously defined but always meaning northwestern Europe, areas occupied by European settler-colonists from that part of the world, and areas of the Middle East occupied by Jewish or Christian communities. These regions have human actors from the West who make history.

Depicting people such as Native Americans, Asians, and Africans as both divorced from history and part of the natural landscape and portraying others as having history separates both groups from their own histories and historical relations with each other. It is a mirror that distorts and deforms the truth about both (Huggins 1991). Although archaeology has at times perpetuated myths, it has also produced evidence that undermines the bases for those myths. For instance, in the nineteenth century, the absence of chronological evidence was used to portray Indian societies as static and unchanging; the construction of chronologies in the twentieth century effectively eliminates this particular stereotype of Native American societies and their history. However, not addressing the issues of racism, sexism, and exploitation that are the bedrock foundations of U.S. society and its relations with peoples on the margins rebuilds the deforming mirror of truth and perpetuates the myth.

The authority archaeologists possess regarding the meaning and interpretation of certain metanarratives and complex analytical categories—such as primitive cultures, civilization, or societal development—and their silence make it difficult for others to use them in order to understand what is happening in the world. This is especially true when the others who are attempting to formulate understandings of history, class, gender, race relations, or environmental issues are women, minorities, or oppressed groups, rather than the mainstream media, which constitute a multibillion-dollar industry controlled by a steadily decreasing number of transnational corporations (Herman and Chomsky 1988; Kellner 1990; Rogin 1987).

Archaeologists have not always adopted the view that they should remain silent and not participate in the cultural debates of the day. Cultural hegemonies, as Lears pointed out, are transitory and ultimately unstable in societies, especially in capitalist ones predicated on the continual transformation of the means of production and the continual creation of new forms of consumption. Archaeologists seem to have adopted the view that silence is golden with regards to the debates of the late twentieth century. Perhaps they learned this rule when their authority and interpretations were used to buttress existing cultural hegemonies. However, such a standpoint is potentially dangerous during periods when cultural hegemonies are being transformed and reconstituted. When class and state structures are being reorganized and cultural hegemonies reformed, it is conceivable that archaeologists might wake up one morning in the future and discover that everyone now takes their silence for granted. There will either be no one to talk to, or, even worse, no one who has the interest or time to listen. At that moment, the meaning of the fact that archaeology, like all other scientific practices, is a historically contingent activity becomes transparent as the new reality forces its way to the surface of our collective consciousness.

This book is not a claim that archaeologists have little to offer or that their labors during the last two centuries have produced little of import. Quite the contrary. Their investigations have eliminated the foundations for certain powerful stereotypes, and their work has surely shown that certain lines of inquiry are not likely to be particularly fruitful even if we keep completely open minds on the subject. As the biologist Richard Lewontin (1985) once quipped, "For all I know, we are being visited daily by extraterrestrial creatures. There is certainly nothing in the laws of physics to prevent it. But I really do require more than out-of-focus snapshots to make me take the possibility seriously."

This book is a call for archaeologists to situate their work and to understand its implications for the cultural debates of the late twentieth century. It is also a call to participate honestly and with integrity in the construction of a genuine politics that challenges a social order that has entrenched racism, sexism, oppression, and exploitation as integral aspects of everyday life and uses the metanarratives of archaeology to maintain their existence in an increasingly unstable and globalized society. Such a politics must be dialectical and dialogical, not absolutist. As the Canadian archaeologist Bruce Trigger (1989, 410) warns, it must begin with seeing the past as it was, not as we wish it might have been. Doing so will force us to confront the deforming mirror of truth as we strive to construct the new metanarratives we need to explain the world we live in and to provide insights about what might be possible in the future. It also requires us to locate our own positions in the social, cultural, and power structures of U.S. society, to recognize the historic specificity of their claims, and historicize the operation of their views.

BIBLIOGRAPHY

Abu-Lughod, Janet L.
  (1989) *Before European hegemon: The world system A.D. 1250–1350*. Oxford: Oxford University Press.

Adams, Richard E. W.
  (1982) Incoming presidential remarks. *American Antiquity, 47*(4), 830–32.

Adams, Robert McC.
  (1956) Some hypotheses on the development of early civilizations. *American Antiquity, 21*(3), 227–32.
  (1960) The evolutionary process in early civilization. In Sol Tax (Ed.), *Evolution after Darwin*, (Vol. 2, pp. 153–58). Chicago: University of Chicago Press.
  (1966) *The evolution of urban society: Early Mesopotamia and prehispanic Mexico*. Chicago: Aldine Publishing Company.
  (1971) Illicit international traffic in antiquities. *American Antiquity, 36*(1), ii–iii.

Agard, Walter A.
  (1957) Classics on the Midwest frontier. In Walker D. Wyman and Clifton B. Kroeber (Eds.), *The frontier in perspective* (pp. 165–83). Madison: University of Wisconsin Press.

Allen, Garland
  (1976) Genetics, eugenics and society: Internalists and externalists in contemporary history of science. *Social Studies of Science, 6*(1), 105–22.
  (1983) The misuse of biological hierarchies: The American eugenics movement, 1900–1940. *History and Philosophy of the Life Sciences 5*(1), 105–28.
  (1986) The Eugenics Record Office at Cold Spring Harbor, 1910–1940: An essay in institutional history. *Osiris, 2*, 225–64.
  (1987) The role of experts in scientific controversy. In H. Tristam Engelhardt, Jr., and Arthur L. Caplan (Eds.), *Scientific controversies: Case studies in the resolution and closure of disputes in science and technology* (pp. 169–202). Cambridge: Cambridge University Press.

American Oriental Society
  (1851) Redraft of the constitution and by-laws of the American Oriental Society, adopted May 16, 1849, and catalogue of members in 1850. *Journal of the American Oriental Society, 2*, xix–xxvii.

Anbinder, Tyler
  (1992) *Nativism and slavery: The Northern Know Nothings and the politics of the 1850s*. Oxford: Oxford University Press.

Appleby, Joyce
  (1992) *Liberalism and republicanism in the historical imagination*. Cambridge: Harvard University Press.

Aptheker, Herbert
  (1966) *A history of the American people: The colonial era* (2nd ed.). New York: International Publishers.
  (1976) *A history of the American people: Early years of the Republic from the end of the Revolution to the first administration of Washington (1783–1793)*. New York: International Publishers.

Arnold, Bettina
  (1990) The past as propaganda: Totalitarian archaeology in Nazi Germany. *Antiquity, 64*(244), 464–78.

Arnove, Robert F.
  (1980) Introduction. In Robert F. Arnove (Ed.), *Philanthropy and Imperialism; The foundations at home and abroad* (pp. 1–23). Boston: G.K. Hall and Company.

Ascher, Robert, and Fairbanks, Charles H.
  (1971) Excavations of a slave cabin: Georgia, U.S.A. *Historical Archaeology, 3*(1), 3–17.

Athens, J. Stephen
  (1977) Theory building and the study of evolutionary process in complex societies. In Lewis R. Binford (Ed.), *For theory building in archaeology: Essays on faunal remains, aquatic resources, spatial analysis, and systemic modeling* (pp. 353–84). New York: Academic Press.

Baldwin, John D.
  (1871) *Ancient America*. New York: Harper and Brothers.

Bancroft, Hubert H.
  (1886) *The native races of the Pacific states [1875–1876]* (5 vols.). San Francisco: The History Company.
  (1889) *History of the north Mexican states and Texas* (Vol. 2). San Francisco: The History Company.

Bandelier, Adolph F.
  (1892) Final report of investigations among the Indians of the southwestern United States carried on mainly in the years from 1880 to 1885 (Pt. 2). *Papers of the Archaeological Institute of America, American Series* (Vol. 4). Cambridge, MA: John Wilson and Son.

Banning, Lance
  (1980) *The Jeffersonian persuasion: Evolution of a party ideology*. Ithaca, NY: Cornell University Press.

Barstow, Anne
  (1976) The uses of archeology for women's history: James Mellaart's work on the neolithic goddess at Çatal Hüyük. *Feminist Studies, 4*(3), 7–18.

Bar-Yosef, O.
  (1989) Geochronology of the Levantine Middle Paleolithic. In Paul Mellars and Chris Stringer (Eds.), *The human revolution:*

Behavioural and biological perspectives on the origins of modern human beings (pp. 589–610). Princeton: Princeton University Press.

Beckwith, Jonathan R.
   (1989)   The science of racism. In John Trumpbour (Ed.), *How Harvard rules: Reason in the service of empire* (pp. 243–47). Boston: South End Press.

Beetham, David
   (1985)   *Max Weber and the theory of modern politics.* Cambridge, U.K.: Polity Press.

Beider, Robert E.
   (1986)   *Science encounters the Indian, 1820–1880: The early years of American ethnology.* Norman: University of Oklahoma Press.

Belich, James
   (1986)   *The New Zealand wars and the Victorian interpretation of racial conflict.* Auckland: Auckland University Press.

Benedict, Ruth
   (1945)   *Race; Science and politics.* New York: Viking Press.

Benison, Saul
   (1953)   *Railroads, land and iron: A phase in the career of Lewis Henry Morgan.* Unpublished doctoral dissertation, Columbia University, New York.

Bennett, David H.
   (1988)   *The party of fear: From nativist movements to the New Right in American history.* Chapel Hill: University of North Carolina Press.

Bennett, John W.
   (1943)   Recent developments in the functional interpretation of archaeological data. *American Antiquity, 9*(3), 208–19.
   (1946)   Empiricist and experimentalist trends in Eastern archaeology. *American Antiquity 11*(2), 198–200.

Bennett, Wendell C. (Ed.)
   (1948)   A reappraisal of Peruvian archaeology. *Memoirs of the Society for American Archaeology, 4.*

Bennett, Wendell C., and Bird, Junius B.
   (1949)   Andean culture history. *American Museum of Natural History Handbook Series, 15.* New York.

Bensel, Richard F.
   (1984)   *Sectionalism and American political development.* Madison: University of Wisconsin Press.
   (1990)   *Yankee Leviathan: The origins of central state authority in America, 1859–1877.* Cambridge: Cambridge University Press.

Bercovitch, Sacvan
   (1975)   *The Puritan origins of the American self.* New Haven: Yale University Press.
   (1978)   *The American jeremiad.* Madison: The University of Wisconsin Press.
   (1993)   *The rites of assent: Transformations in the symbolic construction of America.* New York: Routledge.

Berkhofer, Robert F., Jr.
   (1978)   *The white man's burden: Images of the American Indian from Columbus to the present.* New York: Alfred A. Knopf.

Berman, Paul (Ed.)
   (1992)   *Debating P.C.: The controversy over political correctness on college campuses.* New York: Dell Publishing.

Bernal, Ignacio
   (1980)   *A history of Mexican archaeology: The vanished civilizations of Middle America.* London: Thames and Hudson.

Bernal, Martin
   (1987)   *Black Athena: The Afroasiatic roots of classical civilization: Vol. 1. The fabrication of ancient Greece, 1785–1985.* London: Free Association Books.

Biblical Archaeology Review
   (1979)   Who are BAR readers? *Biblical Archaeology Review, 5*(3), 5.
   (1982)   In America, Biblical archaeology was—and still is—largely a Protestant affair. *Biblical Archaeology Review 8*(4), 54–56.

Binford, Lewis R.
   (1962)   Archaeology as anthropology. *American Antiquity 28*(2), 217–25.
   (1964)   A consideration of archaeological research design. *American Antiquity 29*(4), 425–41.
   (1965)   Archaeological systematics and the study of culture. *American Antiquity 31*(2), 203–10.
   (1968)   Post-Pleistocene adaptations. In Sally R. Binford and Lewis R. Binford (Eds.), *New perspectives in archeology* (pp. 313–41). Chicago: Aldine Publishing.
   (1972)   *An archaeological perspective.* New York: Seminar Press.
   (1977)   Olorgesailie deserves more than a normal book review. *Journal of Anthropological Research, 33*(4), 493–502.
   (1981)   *Bones: Ancient men and modern myths.* New York: Academic Press.
   (1985)   Human ancestors: Changing views of their behavior. *Journal of Anthropological Archaeology, 4*(3), 292–327.

Binford, Sally R., and Binford, Lewis R. (Eds.)
   (1968)   *New perspectives in archeology.* Chicago: Aldine Publishing.

Bledstein, Burton
   (1976)   *The culture of professionalism: The middle class and the development of higher education in America.* New York: W.W. Norton.

Blegen, Carl W.
   (1934)   Excavations at Troy 1933. *American Journal of Archaeology, 38*(2), 223–48.

Bliss, Frederick J.
   (1906)   *The development of Palestine exploration, being the Ely Lectures for 1903.* New York: Charles Scribner's Sons.

Bloom, Allan
   (1987)   *The closing of the American mind: How higher education has failed democracy and impoverished the souls of today's students.* New York: Simon and Schuster.

Bloom, Harold
   (1992)   *The American religion: The emergence of the post-Christian nation.* New York: Simon and Schuster.

Blumenshine, Robert J.
   (1987)   Characteristics of an early hominid scavenging niche. *Current Anthropology, 28*(3), 383–406.

Bock, Kenneth E.
   (1963)   Evolution, function, and change. *American Sociological Review, 28*(2), 229–37.

Bodnar, John
   (1992)   *Remaking America: Public memory, commemoration, and patriotism in the twentieth*

century. Princeton: Princeton University Press.

Boehmer, George H.
(1880) Index to papers on anthropology published by the Smithsonian Institution, 1847 to 1878. *Annual report of the Board of Regents of the Smithsonian Institution... for the year 1879* (pp. 476–83). Washington, DC: U.S. Government Printing Office.

Boggs, Carl
(1992) *Intellectuals and the crisis of modernity*. Albany: State University of New York Press.

Bondanella, Peter
(1987) *The eternal city: Roman images in the modern world*. Chapel Hill: University of North Carolina Press.

Borden, Charles E.
(1966) The Smithsonian foreign-currency program in archaeology and related disciplines. *American Antiquity, 31*(4), 452–53.

Bowdoin, James
(1785) A philosophical discourse, publickly addressed to the American Academy of Arts and Sciences. *Memoirs of the American Academy of Arts and Sciences 1*, 1–7. Boston.

Bowersock, G. W.
(1978) The rediscovery of Herculaneum and Pompeii. *The American Scholar, 47*(3), 461–70.

Braidwood, Robert J.
(1952) *The Near East and the foundations of civilization: An essay in appraisal of the general evidence*. Eugene: Oregon State System of Higher Education.
(1963) *Prehistoric men* (6th ed.). Chicago: Field Museum of Natural History.

Braidwood, Robert J., and Braidwood, Linda
(1953) The earliest village communities of southwestern Asia. *Journal of World History, 1*(2), 278–310.

Braidwood, Robert J., and Willey, Gordon R.
(1962) Courses toward urban life: Archeological considerations of some alternatives. *Viking Fund Publications in Anthropology 32*. New York.

Brain, Jeffrey P.
(1988) The great mound robbery. *Archaeology, 41*(3), 18–25.

Breasted, Charles
(1977) *Pioneer to the past: The story of James Henry Breasted, archaeologist* [1943]. Chicago: University of Chicago Press.

Brecher, Jeremy
(1979) *Strike!* Boston: South End Press.

Brew, John O.
(1959) Committee for the Recovery of Archaeological Remains. *American Antiquity, 24*(4), 450.
(1968) Introduction. In John O. Brew (Ed.), *One hundred of anthropology* (pp. 5–25). Cambridge: Harvard University Press.

Briggs, Ward W., Jr., and Benario, Herbert W. (Eds.)
(1986) *Basil Lanneau Gildersleeve*. Baltimore: The Johns Hopkins University Press.

Brose, David S.
(1983) Professionalism and performance in archaeological organizations: A disputation of the incoming presidential remarks of Richard E. W. Adams. *American Antiquity, 48*(4), 817–20.

Brown, Jerry W.
(1969) *The rise of biblical criticism in America 1800–1870: The New England scholars*. Middletown, CT: Wesleyan University Press.

Bruce, Robert V.
(1987) *The launching of modern American science, 1846–1876*. Ithaca, NY: Cornell University Press.

Brumfiel, Elizabeth M.
(1976) Regional growth in the eastern Valley of Mexico: A test of the "population pressure" hypothesis. In Kent V. Flannery (Ed.), *The early Mesoamerican village* (pp. 234–49). New York: Academic Press.

Brunhouse, Robert L.
(1971) *Sylvanus G. Morley and the world of the ancient Maya*. Norman, OK: University of Oklahoma Press.

Burns, Edward M.
(1954) The philosophy of history of the Founding Fathers. *The Historian 16*(2), 142–68.

Carlson, Leonard A.
(1981) *Indians, bureaucrats, and land: The Dawes Act and the decline of Indian farming*. Westport, CT: Greenview Press.

Cashdollar, Charles D.
(1989) *The transformation of theology, 1830–1890: Positivism and Protestant thought in Britain and America*. Princeton: Princeton University Press.

Cass, Lewis
(1840) Review: Antiquités mexicaines: Relation de trois expéditions du Capitaine Dupaix... . *The North American Review, 51*(109), 396–443.

Casson, Stanley
(1939) *The discovery of man: The story of the inquiry into human origins*. New York: Harper and Brothers.

Cayton, Andrew R.
(1986) *The frontier republic: Ideology and politics in the Ohio country, 1780–1825*. Kent, OH: Kent State University Press.

Caughey, John W.
(1946) *Hubert Howe Bancroft: Historian of the West*. Berkeley: University of California Press.

Chase, Allan
(1980) *The legacy of Malthus: The social costs of the new scientific racism*. Urbana: University of Illinois Press.

Chase, Philip G.
(1989) How different was Middle Paleolithic subsistence? A zooarchaeological perspective on the Middle to Upper Paleolithic transition. In Paul Mellars and Chris Stringer (Eds.), *The human revolution: Behavioural and biological perspectives on the origins of modern human beings* (pp. 321–37). Princeton: Princeton University Press.

Chauvenet, Beatrice
(1983) *Hewett and friends: A biography of Santa Fe's vibrant era*. Santa Fe: Museum of New Mexico Press.

Chilcote, Ronald H., and Dugan-Abbassi, Jennifer (Eds.)
(1992) 500 years of Colón-ization: Struggles for emancipation and identity. *Latin American Perspectives, 19*(3).

Childe, V. Gordon
  (1929) *The Danube in prehistory.* Oxford: Oxford University Press.
  (1934) *New light on the most Ancient East: The Oriental prelude to European prehistory* (2nd ed.). London: Kegan Paul.
  (1936) *Man makes himself,* 1st ed. London: Watts and Company.
  (1942) *What happened in history.* Harmondsworth, U.K.: Penguin Books.
  (1951) *Social evolution.* London: Watts and Company.
Clark, Geoffrey A., and Lindly, J.M.
  (1989) The case of continuity: Observations on the biocultural transition in Europe and Western Asia. In Paul Mellars and Chris Stringer (Eds.), *The human revolution* (pp. 626–76). Princeton: Princeton University Press.
Clarke, David L.
  (1968) *Analytical archaeology.* London: Methuen, MA.
Clarke, Simon
  (1982) *Marx, marginalism and modern society from Adam Smith to Max Weber.* London: Macmillan Press.
Coe, Michael D.
  (1962) *Mexico.* New York: Frederick A. Praeger.
  (1980) *The Maya,* 2nd ed. London: Thames and Hudson.
Cohen, Mark
  (1975) Population pressure and the origins of agriculture. In Stephen Polgar (Ed.), *Population, ecology, and social evolution* (pp. 79–121). Chicago: Aldine Publishing.
  (1977) *The food crisis in prehistory: Overpopulation and the origins of agriculture.* New Haven, CT: Yale University Press.
Cohen, Walter
  (1993) An interview with Martin Bernal. *Social Texts, 35,* 1–24. Durham, NC.
Cole, Douglas
  (1985) *Captured heritage: The scramble for Northwest Coast artifacts.* Seattle: University of Washington Press.
Cole, John R.
  (1980) Cult archaeology and unscientific method and theory. In Michael B. Schiffer (Ed.), *Advances in Archaeological Method and Theory* (Vol. 3, pp. 4–37), New York: Academic Press.
Cole, Susan G.
  (1989) Taking classics into the twenty-first century: A demographic portrait. In Phyllis Culham, Lowell Edmunds, and Alden Smith, (Eds.), *Classics: A discipline and profession in crisis* (pp. 15–24). Lanham, MD: University Press of America.
Commager, Henry S.
  (1975) The American Enlightenment and the ancient world [1971]. In *Jefferson, nationalism, and the Enlightenment* (pp. 125–39). New York: George Braziller.
Compton, Karl T., and Bush, Vannevar
  (1942) *Scientists face the world of 1942.* New Brunswick, NJ: Rutgers University Press.
Conkey, Margaret W., and Gero, Joan M.
  (1991) Tensions, pluralities, and engendering archaeology: An introduction to women and prehistory. In Joan M. Gero and Margaret W. Conkey (Eds.), *Engendering archaeology: Women and prehistory* (pp. 3–30). Oxford: Basil Blackwell.
Conkey, Margaret W., and Spector, Janet
  (1984) Archaeology and the study of gender. In Michael B. Schiffer (Ed.), *Advances in Archaeological Method and Theory* (Vol. 7, pp. 1–38) New York: Academic Press.
Cook, Karen
  (1993, May 4) Black bones, white science: The battle over New York's African Burial Ground. *The Village Voice,* p. 1.
Coon, Carleton
  (1939) *The races of Europe.* New York: Macmillan and Company.
  (1962) *The origin of races.* New York: Alfred A. Knopf.
  (1965) *The living races of man.* New York: Alfred A. Knopf.
Cowgill, George L.
  (1975a) On the causes and consequences of ancient and modern population changes. *American Anthropologist, 77*(3), 505–25.
  (1975b) Population pressure as non-explanation. In Alan Swedlund (Ed.), Population studies in archaeology and biological anthropology. *Memoir of the Society for American Archaeology, 30,* 127–31, Washington, DC.
Cronon, William, Miles, George, and Gitlin, Jay (Eds.)
  (1992) *Under an open sky: Rethinking America's Western past.* New York: W.W. Norton.
Cross, Whitney R.
  (1950) *The burned-over district: The social and intellectual history of enthusiastic religion in western New York, 1800–1850.* Ithaca: Cornell University Press.
Crossland, R. A.
  (1971) Immigrants from the north. In I.E.S. Edwards, C.J. Gadd, and N.G.L. Hammond (Eds.), *The Cambridge ancient history: Vol. I, Pt. 2. Early history of the Middle East* (pp. 824–76). Cambridge: Cambridge University Press.
Crozier, Michel, Huntington, Samuel P., and Watanuki, Joji
  (1975) *The crisis of democracy: Report on the governability of democracies on the Trilateral Commission.* New York: University Press.
Crumley, Carole L.
  (1976) Toward a locational analysis of state systems of settlement. *American Anthropologist, 78*(1), 59–73.
  (1979) Three locational models: An epistemological assessment for anthropology and archaeology. In Michael B. Schiffer (Ed.), *Advances in Archaeological Method and Theory,* (Vol. 2, pp. 143–74). New York: Academic Press.
Curti, Merle
  (1964) *The growth of American thought* (3rd ed.). New York: Harper and Row.
Dall, William H.
  (1877) On succession in the shell-heaps of the Aleutian Islands. In *Contributions to North American ethnology* (Vol. 1, pp. 41–91). Washington, DC: U.S. Department of the Interior.
Daniel, Glyn
  (1981) *A short history of archaeology.* London: Thames and Hudson.

Darnell, Donald G.
(1975) *William Hickling Prescott*. Boston: Twayne Publishers.

Darnell, Regna
(1970) The emergence of academic anthropology at the University of Pennsylvania. *The Journal of the History of the Behavioral Sciences, 6*(1), 80–92.
(1988) Daniel Garrison Brinton: The "fearless critic" of Philadelphia. *University of Pennsylvania Publications in Anthropology, 3*.

Darnovsky, Marcy
(1992) Stories less told: Histories of US environmentalism. *Socialist Review, 22*(4), 11–56.

Darrah, William C.
(1951) *Powell of the Colorado*. Princeton: Princeton University Press.

Davis, Mike
(1984) The political economy of late-imperial America. *New Left Review, 143*, 6–38.
(1986) *Prisoners of the American dream*. London: Verso.
(1990) *City of quartz: Excavating the future of Los Angeles*. London: Verso.

Deagan, Kathleen
(1983) *Spanish St. Augustine: The archaeology of a colonial Creole community*. New York: Academic Press.

Deason, Gary B.
(1986) Reformation theology and the mechanistic conception of nature. In David C. Lindberg and Ronald L. Numbers (Eds.), *God and nature: Historical essays on the encounter between Christianity and science* (pp. 167–91). Berkeley: University of California Press.

Deetz, James
(1965) The dynamics of stylistic change in Arikara ceramics. *University of Illinois Series in Anthropology, 4*.
(1977) *In small things forgotten: The archeology of early American life*. New York, NY: Anchor Books/Doubleday.

Deloria, Vine, Jr.
(1992a) *God is red: A native view of religion* (2nd ed.). Golden, CO: Fulcrum Publishing.
(1992b) *Indians, archaeologists, and the future*. *American Antiquity 57*(4): 595–98.

d'Emilio, John
(1992) *Making trouble: Essays on gay history, politics, and the university*. New York: Routledge.

Denning, Michael
(1987) *Mechanic accent: Dime novels and working-class culture in America*. London: Verso.

Desmond, Adrian
(1989) *The politics of evolution: Morphology, medicine, and reform in radical London*. Chicago: University of Chicago Press.

Dever, William G.
(1989, January 5–9) *American Palestinian and biblical archaeology: End of an era?* Paper presented at the First Joint Archaeological Congress, Baltimore, MD.
(1990) *Recent archaeological discoveries and biblical research*. Seattle: University of Washington Press.

Dickson, David
(1979) Science and political hegemony in the 17th century. *Radical Science Journal, 8*, 7–38.

(1984) *The new politics of science*. New York: Pantheon Books.

Diehl, Carl
(1978) *Americans and German scholarship, 1770–1870*. New Haven, CT: Yale University Press.

Diggins, John P.
(1988) *The proud decades: America in war and peace, 1941–1960*. New York: W.W. Norton.

DiMaggio, Paul
(1982a) Cultural entrepreneurship in nineteenth-century Boston: The creation of an organizational base for high culture in America. *Media, Culture and Society, 4*(1), 33–50.
(1982b) Cultural entrepreneurship in nineteenth-century Boston. Part II: The classification and framing of American art. *Media, Culture and Society, 4*(4), 303–22.

Dinsmoor, William B.
(1943) Early American studies of Mediterranean archaeology. *Proceedings of the American Philosophical Society, 87*(1), 70–104.

DiPeso, Charles C.
(1951) *The Babocomari village site on the Babocomari River, southeastern Arizona*. (Report No. 5). Dragoon, AZ: The Amerind Foundation.
(1956) *The Upper Pima of San Cayetano del Tumacacori: An archaeohistorical reconstruction of the Ootam of Pimeria Alta*. (Report No. 7). Dragoon, AZ: The Amerind Foundation.

Domhoff, G. William
(1983) *Who rules America now? A view for the '80s*. New York: Simon and Schuster.

Donohue, A. A.
(1985) One hundred years of the *American Journal of Archaeology*: An archival history. *American Journal of Archaeology, 89*(1), 3–30.

Doray, Bernard
(1988) *From Taylorism to Fordism: A rational madness [1981]* (David Macey, Trans.). London: Free Association Books.

Dow, Sterling
(1946) Report of the President. *Bulletin of the Archaeological Institute of America, 37*, 1–19.
(1948) The founding of an American Research Center in Egypt. *Archaeology, 1*(2), 136–45.

Drinnon, Richard
(1980) *Facing west: The metaphysics of Indian-hating and empire-building*. New York: New American Library.

Duberman, Martin
(1991) *Cures: A gay man's odyssey*. New York: E.P. Dutton.

DuBois, Ellen C., Kelly, Gail P., Kennedy, Elizabeth L., Korsmeyer, Carolyn W., and Robinson, Lillian S.
(1987) *Feminist scholarship: Kindling in the groves of academe*. Urbana: University of Illinois Press.

DuBois, W. E. B.
(1935) *Black Reconstruction*. New York: Harcourt Brace.

Dunnell, Robert
(1980) Evolutionary theory and archaeology.

Advances in Archaeological Method and Theory, 3, 38–100.

Dupree, A. Hunter
  (1957) *Science in the federal government.* Cambridge: The Belknap Press of Harvard University Press.
  (1972) The Great Instauration of 1940: The organization of scientific research for war. In Gerald Holton (Ed.), *The twentieth century sciences: Studies in the biography of ideas* (pp. 443–67). New York: W.W. Norton.

Dworsky, Donald, McVarish, Virginia, Perry, Kate M., and Robinson, Susan M.
  (1983) Federal law. In Christopher J. Duerksen (Ed.), *A handbook on historic preservation law* (pp. 191–342). Baltimore: The Conservation Foundation and The National Center for Preservation Law.

Dyson, Stephen L.
  (1981) A classical archaeologist's response to the New Archaeology. *Bulletin of the American Schools of Oriental Research, 242,* 7–13.
  (1985) Two paths to the past: A comparative study of the last fifty years of *American Antiquity* and the *American Journal of Archaeology. American Antiquity, 50*(3), 452–63.
  (1989) Competency and crisis in late twentieth-century classical archaeology. In Phyllis Culham and Lowell Edmunds (Eds.), *Classics; A discipline and profession in crisis* (pp. 211–20). Lanham, MD: University Press of America.
  (1993) From new to new age archaeology: Archaeological theory and classical archaeology—a 1990s perspective. *American Journal of Archaeology, 97*(2), 195–206.

Earle, Timothy K.
  (1987) Chiefdoms in archaeological and ethnohistorical perspective. *Annual Review of Anthropology, 16,* 279–308.

Ekirch, Arthur A., Jr.
  (1969) *Ideologies and utopias: The impact of the New Deal on American thought.* Chicago: Quadrangle Books.

Erb, Claude C.
  (1982) *Nelson Rockefeller and United States—Latin American relations, 1940–1945.* Unpublished doctoral dissertation, Clark University, Worcester.

Fagan, Brian
  (1977) *Elusive treasure: The story of early archaeologists in the Americas.* New York: Scribner's.

Fagette, Paul H., Jr.
  (1985) *Digging for dollars: The impact of the New Deal on the professionalization of American archaeology.* Unpublished doctoral dissertation, University of California, Riverside.

Fairbanks, Charles H.
  (1974) The Kingsley slave cabins in Duval County, Florida, 1968. *Conference on Historic Site Archaeology Papers, 7,* 62–93.

Fay, Brian
  (1975) *Social theory and political practice.* London: George Allen and Unwin.

Feierman, Steven
  (1990) *Peasant intellectuals: Anthropology and history in Tanzania.* Madison: University of Wisconsin Press.

Feigl, Herbert
  (1969) The Wiener Kreis in America. In Donald Fleming and Bernard Bailyn (Eds.), *The intellectual migration: Europe and America, 1930–1960* (pp. 630–673). Cambridge: Harvard University Press.

Feinman, Gary, and Neitzel, Jill
  (1984) Too many types: an overview of prestate societies in the Americas. *Advances in Archaeological Method and Theory, 7,* 39–102.

Field, James A., Jr.
  (1969) *America and the Mediterranean world, 1776–1882.* Princeton: Princeton University Press.

Fields, Barbara J.
  (1990) Slavery, race and ideology in the United States of America. *New Left Review, 181,* 95–118.

Figueira, Thomas
  (1989) The prospects for ancient history. In Phyllis Culham, Lowell Edmunds, and Alden Smith (Eds.), *Classics: A discipline and profession in crisis* (pp. 369–81). Lanham, MD: University Press of America.

Finnie, David H.
  (1967) *Pioneers east: The early American experience in the Middle East.* Cambridge: Harvard University Press.

Fisher, David H.
  (1975) *The Federalist Party in the era of Jeffersonian democracy.* New York: Harper and Row, Publishers.

Fitting, James E.
  (1982) The status of rescue archeology in North America. In Rex L. Wilson and Gloria Loyola (Eds.), *Rescue archeology: Papers from the first New World conference on rescue archeology* (pp. 173–90). Washington, DC: The Preservation Press.

Flannery, Kent V.
  (1967) The vertebrate fauna and hunting patterns. In Douglas S. Byers (Ed.), *The prehistory of the Tehuacán Valley* (Vol. 1, pp. 132–78). Austin: University of Texas Press.
  (1969) Origins and ecological effects of early domestication in Iran and the Near East. In Peter Ucko and G. W. Dimbleby (Eds.), *The domestication and exploitation of plants and animals* (pp. 73–102). Chicago: Aldine Publishing Company.
  (1972) The cultural evolution of civilizations. *Annual Review of Ecology and Systematics, 3,* 399–426.
  (1973) Archeology with a capital S. In Charles L. Redman (Ed.), *Research and theory in current archeology* (pp. 47–53). New York: John Wiley and Sons.
  (1982) The golden marshalltown: A parable for the archeology of the 1980s. *American Anthropologist, 84*(2), 265–78.

Flannery, Kent V. (Ed.)
  (1976) *The early Mesoamerican village.* New York: Academic Press.

Foner, Eric
  (1978) Class, ethnicity, and radicalism in the

Gilded Age: The Land League and Irish America. *Marxist Perspectives, 1*(2), 6–55.

(1980) *Politics and ideology in the age of the Civil War.* Oxford: Oxford University Press.

(1988) *Reconstruction; America's unfinished revolution, 1863–1877.* New York: Harper and Row.

Ford, James A.
(1938) *Report of the conference on Southeastern pottery typology.* Ceramic Repository, Museum of Anthropology. Ann Arbor: University of Michigan.

(1954) The type concept revisited. *American Anthropologist, 56*(1), 42–54.

Ford, Richard
(1977) Evolutionary ecology and the evolution of human ecosystems: A case study from the midwestern U.S.A. In James N. Hill (Ed.), *Explanation of prehistoric change* (pp. 153–84). Albuquerque: University of New Mexico Press.

Foster, John (Ed.)
(1992) Columbus and the New World Order, 1492–1992. *Monthly Review 44*(3).

Franklin, Francis
(1943) *The rise of the American nation, 1789–1824.* New York: International Publishers.

Freedman, David N.
(1972) William Foxwell Albright in memoriam. *Bulletin of the American Schools of Oriental Research, 205,* 3–13.

Fried, Morton
(1967) *The evolution of political society.* New York: Random House.

Fritz, Henry E.
(1963) *The movement for Indian assimilation, 1860–1890.* Philadelphia: University of Pennsylvania Press.

Fritz, John
(1973) Relevance, archaeology and subsistence theory. In Charles L. Redman (Ed.), *Research and theory in current archaeology* (pp. 59–82). New York: John Wiley and Sons.

Fritz, John, and Plog, Fred T.
(1970) The nature of archaeological explanation. *American Antiquity, 35*(4), 405–12.

Furner, Mary O.
(1975) *Advocacy and objectivity: A crisis in the professionalization of American social science, 1865–1905.* Lexington: The University of Kentucky Press.

Furniss, Norman F.
(1954) *The fundamentalist controversy, 1918–1931.* New Haven, CT: Yale University Press.

Gailey, Christine W.
(1985) Sex and gender in human origins: Lila Leibowitz on early Homo populations. Paper presented at the annual meeting of the American Ethnological Society.

Gall, Patricia L., and Saxe, Arthur A.
(1977) The ecological evolution of culture: The state as predator in succession theory. In Timothy K. Earle and Jonathon E. Ericson (Eds.), *Exchange systems in prehistory* (pp. 255–68). New York: Academic Press.

Gallatin, Albert
(1845) Notes on the semi-civilized nations of Mexico, Yucatan, and Central America. *Transactions of the American Ethnological Society, 1,* 1–352.

Gardiner, C. Harvey
(1969) *William Hickling Prescott: A biography.* Austin: University of Texas Press.

Gaventa, John
(1980) *Power and powerlessness: Quiescence and rebellion in an Appalachian valley.* Urbana: University of Illinois Press.

Gedicks, Al
(1975) American social scientists and the emerging corporate economy: 1885–1915. *The Insurgent Sociologist, 5*(2), 25–48.

Geertz, Clifford
(1956) *The development of the Javanese economy: A sociocultural approach.* (Document C/56-18). Economic Development Program. Cambridge: Massachusetts Institute of Technology, Center for International Studies.

(1963) *Agricultural involution: The process of ecological change in Indonesia.* Berkeley: University of California Press.

General Accounting Office
(1981) *Are agencies doing enough or too much for archeological preservation? Guidance needed.* (CED-81-61). Washington, DC: U.S. Government Printing Office.

Gerbi, Antonello
(1973) *The dispute of the New World: The history of a polemic, 1750–1900* [1955]. Pittsburgh: University of Pittsburgh Press.

Gero, Joan M.
(1983) Gender bias in archaeology: A cross cultural perspective. In Joan M. Gero, David Lack, and Michael L. Blakey (Eds.), *The sociopolitics of archaeology* (Research Report 23:51–57). Amherst: University of Massachusetts, Department of Anthropology.

(1985) Socio-politics and the women-at-home ideology. *American Antiquity, 50*(3), 342–50.

Gero, Joan M., and Conkey, Margaret W.
(1991) Tensions, pluralities, and engendering archaeology: An introduction to women and prehistory. In Joan M. Gero and Margaret W. Conkey (Eds.), *Engendering archaeology: Women and prehistory* (pp. 3–30). Oxford: Basil Blackwell.

Gero, Joan M., and Root, Dolores
(1990) Public presentations and private concerns: Archaeology in the pages of *National Geographic.* In Peter Gathercole and David Lowenthal (Eds.), *The politics of the past* (pp. 19–37). London: Allen Unwin.

Gibbs, George
(1862) Instructions for archaeological investigations in the United States. *Annual Report of the Board of Regents of the Smithsonian Institution... for 1861* (pp. 392–94). Washington, DC: U.S. Government Printing Office.

Gildersleeve, Basil L.
(1896) Classical studies in America. *The Atlantic Monthly, 57*(470), 728–37.

Gillam, Robyn
(1989) Disco Tut: Postmodern exhibitionism. *Canadian Journal of Political and Social Theory, 13*(3), 73–88.

Gilman, Antonio
(1984) Explaining the Upper Paleolithic revolution. In Matthew Spriggs (Ed.), *Marxist perspectives in archaeology* (pp. 115–26). Cambridge: Cambridge University Press.

Gladwin, Winifred, and Gladwin, Harold S.
(1928) *A method for the designation of Southwestern pottery types* (Medallion Papers No. 7). Gila Pueblo, Globe.

Glassberg, David
(1990) *American historical pageantry: The uses of tradition in the early twentieth century.* Chapel Hill: University of North Carolina Press.

Glassie, Henry
(1975) *Folk housing in middle Virginia: A structural analysis of historic artifacts.* Knoxville: The University of Tennessee Press.

Gleason, Philip
(1992) *Speaking of diversity: Language and ethnicity in twentieth-century America.* Baltimore: Johns Hopkins University Press.

Glueck, Nelson
(1938) Archaeological exploration and excavation in Palestine, Transjordan, and Syria during 1937. *American Journal of Archaeology, 42*(2), 165–76.

Godoy, Ricardo
(1977) Franz Boas and his plans for an International School of American Archaeology and Ethnology in Mexico. *The Journal of the History of the Behavioral Sciences, 13*(3), 228–42.

Goetzmann, William H.
(1959) *Army exploration in the American West, 1803–1863.* New Haven, CT: Yale University Press.
(1966) *Exploration and empire: The explorer and the scientist in the winning of the American West.* New York: W.W. Norton.

Goldfield, Michael
(1991) The color of politics in the United States: White supremacy as the main explanation for the peculiarities of American politics from colonial times to the present. In Dominick LaCapra (Ed.), *The bounds of race: Perspectives on hegemony and resistance,* (pp. 104–33). Ithaca: Cornell University Press.

Goldman, Eric F.
(1960) *The crucial decade and after: America, 1945–1960.* New York: Vintage Books.

Goldman, Hetty
(1935) Preliminary expedition to Cilicia, 1934, and excavations at Gözlü Kule, Tarsus, 1935. *American Journal of Archaeology, 39*(4), 526–49.

Goldmann, Lucien
(1968) *The philosophy of the Enlightenment: The Christian burgess and philosophy.* Cambridge: MIT Press.

Goodman, Paul
(1960) *Growing up absurd: Problems of youth in the organized system.* New York: Random House.

Goodwyn, Lawrence
(1976) *Democratic promise: The populist movement in America.* Oxford: Oxford University Press.

Gordon, David M., Edwards, Richard, and Reich, Michael
(1982) *Segmented work, divided workers: The historical transformation of labor in the United States.* Cambridge: Cambridge University Press.

Gossett, Thomas F.
(1965) *Race: The history of an idea in America.* New York: Schocken Books.

Gould, Stephen Jay
(1981) *The mismeasure of man.* New York: W.W. Norton.

Grabill, Joseph L.
(1971) *Protestant diplomacy and the Near East: Missionary influence on American policy, 1810–1927.* Minneapolis: University of Minnesota Press.

Graebner, William S.
(1991) *The age of doubt: American thought and culture in the 1940s.* Boston: Twayne Publishers.

Gramsci, Antonio
(1971) The intellectuals. In *Selections from the prison notebooks* (pp. 3–23). New York: International Publishers.

Green, Martin
(1966) *The problem of Boston: Some readings in cultural history.* New York: W.W. Norton.

Greene, Jack P.
(1988) *Pursuits of happiness: The social development of early modern British colonies and the formation of American culture.* Chapel Hill: University of North Carolina Press.

Greene, John C.
(1984) *American science in the Age of Jefferson.* Ames: Iowa State University Press.

Greenhalgh, Michael
(1989) *The survival of Roman antiquities in the Middle Ages.* London: Gerald Duckworth.

Gregory, Frederick
(1977) Scientific versus dialectical materialism: A clash of ideologies in nineteenth-century German radicalism. *Isis, 68*(242), 206–23.

Griffin, James B.
(1985) An individual's participation in American archaeology, 1928–1985. *Annual Review of Anthropology, 14,* 1–23.

Guralnick, Stanley M.
(1979) The American scientist in higher education, 1820–1910. In Nathan Reingold (Ed.), *The science in the American context; New perspectives* (pp. 93–142). Washington, DC: Smithsonian Institution.

Gusfield, Joseph R.
(1966) *Symbolic crusade: Status politics and the American temperance movement.* Urbana: University of Illinois Press.

Guthe, Carl E.
(1940) The basic needs of American archaeology. *Science, 90*(2345), 528–30.
(1967) Reflections on the founding of the Society for American Archaeology. *American Antiquity, 32*(4), 433–40.

Gutzwiller, Robert
(1989) Classics in the courts. In Phyllis Culham, Lowell Edmunds, and Alden Smith (Eds.), *Classics: A discipline and profession in crisis,* pp. 351–61. Lanham, MD: University Press of America.

Haag, William G.
   (1965)   William Snyder Webb, 1882–1964. *American Antiquity, 30*(4), 470–73.

Hahn, Steven
   (1983)   *The roots of Southern populism: Yeoman farmers and the transformation of the Georgia Upcountry, 1850–1890.* Oxford: Oxford University Press.

Haley, Shelley P.
   (1989)   Classics and minorities. In Phyllis Culham, Lowell Edmunds, and Alden Smith (Eds.), *Classics: A discipline and profession in crisis* (pp. 317–20). Lanham, MD: University Press of America.

Hall, Catherine
   (1992)   *White, male and middle class: Explorations in feminism and history.* New York: Routledge.

Hall, Stuart
   (1988)   The toad in the garden: Thatcherism among the theorists. In Cary Nelson and Lawrence Grossberg (Eds.), *Marxism and the interpretation of culture* (pp. 35–57). Urbana: University of Illinois Press.

Haller, John S.
   (1971)   *Outcasts from evolution: Scientific attitudes of racial inferiority, 1859–1900.* Urbana: University of Illinois Press.

Hallett, Judith P.
   (1989)   The Women's Classical Caucus. In Phyllis Culham, Lowell Edmunds, and Alden Smith (Eds.), *Classics: A discipline and profession in crisis* (pp. 339–50). Lanham, MD: University Press of America.

Halporn, James W.
   (1989)   Foreign scholars and American classical education. In Phyllis Culham, Lowell Edmunds, and Alden Smith (Eds.), *Classics: A discipline and profession in crisis* (pp. 305–316). Lanham, MD: University Press of America.

Hamby, Alonzo L.
   (1985)   *Liberalism and its challengers: F.D.R. to Reagan.* Oxford: Oxford University Press.

Hammil, Jan
   (1987)   Cultural imperialism: American Indian remains. *World Archaeological Bulletin, 1,* 36–37.

Hammond, Mason
   (1985, December, 10-13) The Indo-European origin of the concept of a democratic society. *Symbols,* a publication of the Peabody Museum and the Department of Anthropology. Harvard University, Cambridge.

Handy, Robert T. (Ed.)
   (1981)   *The Holy Land in American Protestant life, 1800–1848: A documentary history.* New York: Arno Press.

Haraway, Donna
   (1982)   The high cost of information in post-World War II evolutionary biology: Ergonomics, semiotics, and the sociobiology of communication systems. *The Philosophical Forum, 13*(2–3), 244–78.
   (1988)   Remodelling the human way of life: Sherwood Washburn and the new physical anthropology, 1950–1980. In George W. Stocking, Jr. (Ed.), *History of Anthropology* (Vol. 5, pp. 206-59). Madison: University of Wisconsin Press.

   (1991)   *Simians, cyborgs, and women: The reinvention of nature.* New York: Routledge.

Harding, Sandra
   (1991)   *Whose science? Whose knowledge? Thinking from women's lives.* Ithaca: Cornell University Press.

Harmon, George D.
   (1941)   *Sixty years of Indian affairs: Political, economic, and diplomatic, 1789–1850.* Chapel Hill: University of North Carolina Press.

Harrington, Spencer P. M.
   (1991)   The looting of Arkansas. *Archaeology, 44*(3), 22–31.
   (1993)   Bones and bureaucrats. *Archaeology, 46*(2), 28–38.

Harris, Marvin
   (1979)   *Cultural materialism: The struggle for a science of culture.* New York: Vintage Books.

Harris, Neil
   (1962)   The Gilded Age revisited: Boston and the Museum Movement. *American Quarterly, 16*(4), 545–66.

Harrold, Francis B., and Eve, Raymond A. (Eds.)
   (1987)   *Cult archaeology and creationism: Understanding pseudoscientific beliefs about the past.* Iowa City: University of Iowa Press.

Hart, Kevin R.
   (1976)   *Government geologists and the early man controversy: The problem of "official" science in America, 1879–1907.* Unpublished doctoral dissertation, Kansas State University, Manhattan.

Harvey, David
   (1982)   *The limits to capital.* Chicago: University of Chicago Press.
   (1989)   *The condition of postmodernity.* Oxford: Basil Blackwell.

Haskell, Thomas L.
   (1977)   *The emergence of professional social science: The American Social Science Association and the nineteenth-century crisis of authority.* Urbana: University of Illinois Press.
   (1979)   Deterministic implications of intellectual history. In John Higham and Paul K. Conklin (Eds.), *New directions in American intellectual history* (pp. 132–48). Baltimore: Johns Hopkins University Press.

Haven, Samuel
   (1855)   *Archaeology of the United States. Or sketches, historical and bibliographical, of the progress of information and opinion respecting vestiges of antiquity in the United States.* Smithsonian Contributions to Knowledge. Philadelphia: T. K. and P. G. Collins, Printers.

Haviland, William A.
   (1967)   Stature at Tikal, Guatemala: Implications for ancient Maya demography and social organization. *American Antiquity, 32*(3), 316–25.

Hawkins, Hugh
   (1979)   University identity: The teaching and research functions. In Alexandra Oleson and John Voss (Eds.), *The organization of knowledge in modern America, 1860–1920* (pp. 285–312). Baltimore: Johns Hopkins University Press.

Heale, M. J.
  (1990) *American anticommunism: Combating the enemy within, 1830–1970.* Baltimore: Johns Hopkins University Press.
Heims, Steve J.
  (1975) Encounter of behavioral sciences with new machine-organism analogies in the 1940s. *The Journal of the History of the Behavioral Sciences, 4*(4), 316–34.
  (1991) *The cybernetics group 1946–1953: Constructing a social science for postwar America.* Cambridge: MIT Press.
Heller, Agnes
  (1978) *Renaissance man.* New York: Routledge and Kegan Paul.
Hempel, Carl
  (1965) *Aspects of scientific explanation and other essays in the philosophy of science.* Glencoe, IL: Free Press.
Hencken, Hugh
  (1946) Future aims and methods in research in prehistoric Europe. *American Journal of Archaeology, 50*(1), 52–59.
Henshaw, Henry W.
  (1883) Animal carvings from the mounds of the Mississippi Valley. *Second Annual Report of the Bureau of American Ethnology, Smithsonian Institution, 1880–1881.* Washington, DC
Herbst, Jürgen
  (1965) *The German historical school in American scholarship.* Ithaca: Cornell University Press.
Herman, Edward S., and Chomsky, Noam
  (1988) *Manufacturing consent: The political economy of the mass media.* New York: Pantheon Books.
Hewett, Edgar L.
  (1910) Second annual report of the managing committee of the School of American Archaeology. *Bulletin of the Archaeological Institute of America, 1,* 170–92.
Heyl, Barbara S.
  (1968) The Harvard "Pareto Circle." *The Journal of the History of the Behavioral Sciences, 4*(4), 316–34.
Higgs, Robert
  (1987) *Crisis and Leviathan: Critical episodes in the growth of American government.* Oxford: Oxford University Press.
Higham, John
  (1957) Anti–Semitism in the Gilded Age: A reinterpretation. *The Mississippi Valley Historical Review, 42*(4), 559–78.
  (1965) The reorientation of American culture in the 1890's. In John Weiss (Ed.), *The origins of modern consciousness* (pp. 25–48). Detroit: Wayne State University Press.
  (1979) The matrix of specialization. In Alexandra Oleson and John Voss (Eds.), *The organization of knowledge in modern America, 1860–1920* (pp. 3–18). Baltimore: Johns Hopkins University Press.
  (1981) *Strangers in the land: Patterns of American nativism, 1860–1925.* New York: Atheneum.
Hilprecht, Herman V. (Ed.)
  (1903) *Explorations in the Bible lands during the 19th century.* Philadelphia: A. J. Holman.

Hinsley, Curtis M., Jr.
  (1979) Anthropology as science and politics: The dilemmas of the Bureau of American Ethnology, 1879–1904. In Walter Goldschmidt (Ed.), The uses of anthropology. *Special publication of the American Anthropological Association* (Vol. 11, pp. 15–32). Washington, DC: American Anthropological Association.
  (1981) *Savages and scientists: The Smithsonian Institution and the development of American anthropology, 1846–1910.* Washington, DC: Smithsonian Institution Press.
  (1984) Wanted: one good man to discover Central American history. *Harvard Magazine, 87*(2), 64A–64H.
  (1985a) Hemispheric hegemony in early American anthropology, 1841–1851: Reflections on John Lloyd Stephens and Lewis Henry Morgan. In June Helm (Ed.), Social contexts of American ethnology, 1840–1984. *1984 Proceedings of the American Ethnological Society,* (pp. 28–40). Washington, DC: American Ethnological Society.
  (1985b) From shell-heaps to stelae: Early anthropology at the Peabody Museum. In George W. Stocking, Jr. (Ed.), *History of Anthropology* (Vol. 3, pp. 49–74). Madison: University of Wisconsin Press.
  (1986) Edgar Lee Hewett and the School of American Research in Santa Fe, 1906–1912. In David J. Meltzer, Don D. Fowler, and Jeremy A. Sabloff (Eds.), *American archaeology past and future: A celebration of the Society for American Archaeology, 1935–1985,* pp. 217–33. Washington, DC: Smithsonian Institution Press.
Hodder, Ian
  (1985) Postprocessual archaeology. In Michael B. Schiffer (Ed.), *Advances in Archaeological Method and Theory* (Vol. 8, pp. 1–26). New York: Academic Press.
Hoebel, E. Adamson
  (1960) William Robertson: An 18th century anthropologist-historian. *American Anthropologist, 62*(4), 648–55.
Hofstadter, Richard
  (1955) *Social Darwinism in American thought, 1860–1915,* 2nd ed. Boston: Beacon Press.
Holmes, William H.
  (1893) A question of evidence. *Science, 21*(527), 135–36.
  (1897) Primitive man in the Delaware Valley. *Proceedings of the American Association for the Advancement of Science, 46,* 364–70.
  (1904) Introduction. In Mexican and Central American antiquities, calendar systems, and history; twenty-four papers. *Bureau of American Ethnology Bulletin* (Vol. 28, pp. 9–10).
Hoopes, Alban W.
  (1932) *Indian affairs and their administration with special reference to the Far West, 1849–1860.* Philadelphia: University of Pennsylvania Press.
Hooton, Earnest A.
  (1946) *Up from the ape.* New York: Macmillan.

Hopkins, Clark
(1979) *The discovery of Dura–Europos.* New Haven, CT: Yale University Press.
Horowitz, Helen L.
(1976) *Culture and city: Cultural philanthropy in Chicago from the 1880s to 1917.* Lexington: University of Kentucky Press.
Horsman, Reginald
(1981) *Race and Manifest Destiny: The origins of American racial Anglo–Saxonism.* Cambridge: Harvard University Press.
Hoving, Thomas
(1978) *Tutankhamun: The untold story.* New York: Simon and Schuster.
Howe, Barbara
(1980) The emergence of scientific philanthropy, 1900–1920: Origins, issues and outcomes. In Robert F. Arnove (Ed.), *Philanthropy and imperialism: The foundations at home and abroad* (pp. 25–54). Boston: G.K. Hall.
Hrdlička, Aleš
(1907) Skeletal remains suggesting or attributed to early man in North America. *Bureau of American Ethnology Bulletin, 33.*
Hrdlička, Aleš, in collaboration with Holmes, W. H., Willis, Bailey, Wright, Frederick E., and Fenner, Clarence N.
(1912) Early man in South America. *Bureau of American Ethnology Bulletin, 52.*
Hubert, Jane, Doumas, Christos, Mbunwe-Samba, Patrick, and Zimmerman, Larry
(1989) WAC Inter-congress. *World Archaeological Bulletin, 4,* 14–28.
Huddleston, Lee E.
(1967) *Origins of the American Indians: European concepts, 1492–1729.* Austin: University of Texas Press.
Huggins, Nathan I.
(1991) The deforming mirror of truth: Slavery and the master narrative of American history. *Radical History Review, 49,* 25–48.
Humphreys, R. A.
(1954) William Robertson and his "History of America." *Diamante II,* pp. 5–28. London: The Hispanic and Luso-Brazilian Councils.
Hunter, James D.
(1991) *Culture wars; The struggle to define America.* New York: Basic Books.
Hunter, Michael
(1971) The Royal Society and the origins of British archaeology: I. *Antiquity, 45*(178), 113–22.
(1975) *John Aubrey and the realm of learning.* New York: Science History Publications.
Isaac, Glynn
(1978) The food sharing behavior of protohuman hominids. *Scientific American, 238*(4), 90–106.
Jaher, Frederic C.
(1972) Nineteenth-century elites in Boston and New York. *Journal of Social History, 6*(1), 32–77.
Jameson, Fredric
(1984) Postmodernism, or, the cultural logic of late capitalism. *New Left Review, 146,* 59–92.
(1991) *Postmodernism, or, the cultural logic of late capitalism.* Durham, NC: Duke University Press.

Jefferson, Thomas
(1955) *Notes on Virginia [1785].* Chapel Hill: University of North Carolina Press.
Jennings, Francis
(1988) *Empire of fortune: Crowns, colonies, and tribes in the Seven Years' War in America.* New York: W.W. Norton.
Jessop, Bob
(1990) *State theory: Putting capitalist states in their place.* University Park: Pennsylvania State University Press.
Jessup, Philip C.
(1938) *Elihu Root,* 2 vols. New York: Dodd, Mead and Company.
Johnson, Frederick
(1955) Report of the Committee for Recovery of Archaeological Remains. *American Antiquity, 20*(2), 200–202.
(1961) A quarter century of growth in American archaeology. *American Antiquity, 27*(1), 1–6.
Johnson, Frederick, Haury, Emil W., and Griffin, James B.
(1945) Report of the Planning Committee. *American Antiquity, 9*(2), 142–44.
Johnson, Gregory A.
(1982) Organizational structure and scalar stress. In Colin Renfrew, Michael J. Rowlands, and Barbara A. Segraves (Eds.), *Theory and explanation in archaeology: The Southampton conference* (pp. 389–422). New York: Academic Press.
Jones, W. R.
(1971) The images of the barbarian in medieval Europe. *Comparative Studies in Society and History, 13*(4), 376–407.
Katz, Friedrich
(1981) *The secret war in Mexico: Europe, the United States, and the Mexican Revolution.* Chicago: University of Chicago Press.
Keegan, William F., and Diamond, Jared M.
(1987) Colonization of islands by humans: A biogeographical perspective. In Michael B. Schiffer (Ed.), *Advances in Archaeological Method and Theory* (Vol. 10, pp. 49–93). New York: Academic Press.
Keel, Bennie C., McManamon, Francis P., and Smith, George S.
(1989) *Federal archeology: The current program; annual report to Congress on the Federal Archeology Program FY 1985 and FY 1986.* Washington, DC: National Park Service, Department of the Interior.
Keen, Benjamin
(1971) *The Aztec image in Western thought.* New Brunswick: Rutgers University Press.
Kellner, Douglas
(1990) *Television and the crisis of democracy.* Boulder, CO: Westview Press.
Kelly, Arthur R.
(1940) Archaeology in the National Park Service. *American Antiquity, 5*(4), 274–82.
Kennedy, John M.
(1968) *Philanthropy and science in New York City: The American Museum of Natural History, 1868–1968.* Unpublished doctoral dissertation, Yale University, New Haven.
Kerber, Linda
(1970) *Federalists in dissent: Imagery and ideology*

in Jeffersonian America. Ithaca: Cornell University Press.

Kevles, Daniel J.
(1977) The National Science Foundation and the debate over postwar research policy, 1942–1945. *Isis, 68*(241), 5–26.

Kidder, Alfred V.
(1932) Annual Report of the Chairman of the Division of Historical Research. *Carnegie Institution of Washington Year Book 31*, 89–127.

Kidder, Alfred, II
(1954) Wendell Clark Bennett, 1905–1953. *American Anthropologist, 56*(2), 269–73.

Kildahl, Phillip A.
(1959) *British and American reactions to Layard's discoveries in Assyria (1845–1860)*. Unpublished doctoral dissertation, University of Minnesota, Minneapolis.

Kimball, Roger
(1991, January) "Tenured radicals": A postscript. *New Criterion*, pp. 4–13.

King, Michael L.
(1981, July 21) Land development unearths a mission for archaeologists. *The Wall Street Journal*, p. 1.

King, Philip J.
(1983) *American archaeology in the Mideast: A history of the American Schools of Oriental Research*. Philadelphia: The American Schools of Oriental Research.

King, Thomas F.
(1971) A conflict of values in American archaeology. *American Antiquity, 36*(3), 255–62.

Kirch, Patrick
(1980) The archaeological study of adaptation: Theoretical and methodological issues. In Michael B. Schiffer (Ed.), *Advances in Archaeological Method and Theory* (Vol. 3, pp. 101–57). New York: Academic Press.

Kluckhohn, Clyde
(1939) The place of theory in anthropological studies. *Philosophy of Science 6*(3), 328–44.
(1940) The conceptual structure in Middle American studies. In Clarence L. Hay, Ralph L. Linton, Samuel K. Lothrop, Harry L. Shapiro, and George C. Vaillant (Eds.), *The Maya and their neighbors* (pp. 41–51). New York: Appleton-Century.

Kohl, Philip L.
(1975) The archaeology of trade. *Dialectical Anthropology, 1*(1), 43–50.
(1981) Materialist approaches in prehistory. *Annual Review of Anthropology, 10*, 89–118.
(1985) Symbolic cognitive archaeology: A new loss of innocence. *Dialectical Anthropology, 9*(1–4), 105–18.

Kohl, Philip L., and Wright, Rita P.
(1977) Stateless cities: The differentiation of societies in the Near East. *Dialectical Anthropology, 2*(4), 271–83.

Kolakowski, Leszek
(1969) *The alienation of reason: A history of positivist thought*. New York: Doubleday.

Kolko, Gabriel
(1963) *The triumph of conservatism: A reinterpre-tation of American history, 1900–1916*. New York: Free Press.

Kolko, Joyce
(1988) *Restructuring the world economy*. New York: Pantheon Books.

Kovel, Joel
(1984) *White racism: A psychohistory* (2nd ed.). New York: Columbia University Press.

Kramer, Carol, and Stark, Miriam
(1988) The status of women in archeology. *Anthropology Newsletter, 29*(9), 11–12.

Krieger, Alex D.
(1944) The typological concept. *American Antiquity, 9*(3), 271–88.

Kubrin, David
(1981) Newton's inside out! Magic, class struggle, and the rise of mechanism in the West. In Harry Woolf (Ed.), *The analytic spirit: Essays in the history of science in honor of Henry Guerlac* (pp. 96–121). Ithaca: Cornell University Press.

Kuhn, Thomas S.
(1970) *The structure of scientific revolutions [1962]* (2nd ed.). Chicago: University of Chicago Press.

Kuklick, Bruce
(1977) *The rise of American philosophy, Cambridge, Massachusetts, 1860–1930*. New Haven, CT: Yale University Press.

Kus, Susan
(1982) Matters material and ideal. In Ian Hodder (Ed.), *Symbolic and structural archaeology* (pp. 47–62). Cambridge: Cambridge University Press.
(1983) The social representation of space: Dimensioning the cosmological and the quotidian. In Arthur Keene and James Moore (Ed.), *Archaeological hammers and theories* (pp. 277–98). New York: Academic Press.

Kusmer, Kenneth L.
(1979) The social history of cultural institutions: The upper class connection. *Journal of Interdisciplinary History, 10*(1), 137–46.

Lacey, Michael J.
(1979) *The mysteries of earth-making dissolve: A study of Washington's intellectual community and the origins of American environmentalism in the late nineteenth century*. Unpublished doctoral dissertation, George Washington University, Washington, DC

Lacy, David M., and Hasenstab, Robert J.
(1983) The development of least effort strategies in CRM: Competition for scarce resources in Massachusetts. In Joan M. Gero, David Lacy, and Michael L. Blakey (Eds.), *The socio-politics of archaeology* (Research Report 23), Department of Anthropology, University of Massachusetts, 31–50.

Lanning, Edward P.
(1967) *Peru before the Incas*. Englewood Cliffs, NJ: Prentice-Hall.

Larco Hoyle, Rafael
(1948) *Cronología arqueológica del norte del Perú*. Buenos Aires: Sociedad Geográfica Americana.

Larrabee, Stephen A.
(1957) *Hellas observed: The American experience of Greece, 1775–1865*. New York: New York University Press.

Leacock, Eleanor B.
(1979) Lewis Henry Morgan on government and property. In Madeline B. Léons and Frances Rothstein (Eds.), *New directions in political economy: An approach from anthropology* (pp. 308–31). Westport: Greenwood Press.

Lears, T. Jackson
(1981) *No place of grace: Antimodernism and the transformation of American culture, 1880–1920.* New York: Pantheon Books.

Leibowitz, Lila
(1975) Perspectives on the evolution of sex differences. In Rayna R. Reiter (Ed.), *Toward an anthropology of women* (pp. 20–35). New York: Monthly Review Press.
(1986) In the beginning . . .: The origins of the sexual division of labour and the development of the first human societies. In Stephanie Coontz and Peta Henderson (Eds.), *Women's work, men's property: The origins of gender and class* (pp. 43–75). London: Verso.

Leone, Mark P.
(1982) Some opinions about recovering mind. *American Antiquity, 47*(4), 742–60.
(1986) Symbolic, structural, and critical archaeology. In David J. Meltzer, Don D. Fowler, and Jeremy A. Sabloff (Eds.), *American archaeology, past and future* (pp. 415–38). Washington, DC: Smithsonian Institution Press.

Leone, Mark P. (Ed.)
(1972) *Contemporary archaeology: A guide to theory and contributions.* Southern Illinois University Press.

Leone, Mark P., Potter, Parker B., Jr., and Schackel, Paul A.
(1987) Toward a critical archaeology. *Current Anthropology, 28*(3), 283–302.

Leopold, Richard W.
(1954) *Elihu Root and the conservative tradition.* Boston: Little, Brown.

Levine, Joseph M.
(1977) *Dr. Woodward's shield: History, science, and satire in Augustan England.* Berkeley: University of California Press.
(1987) *Humanism and history: Origins of modern English historiography.* Ithaca: Cornell University Press.

Lewis, Thomas M. N., and Kneberg, Madeline
(1946) *Hiwassee Island: An archaeological account of four Tennessee Indian peoples.* Knoxville: The University of Tennessee Press.

Lewontin, Richard
(1985, October 24) An exchange on gender. *The New York Review of Books,* pp. 53–55.

Lilienfield, Robert
(1978) *The rise of systems theory.* New York: John Wiley and Sons.

Llobera, Josep R.
(1979) Techno-environmental determinism and the work of Marx on pre-capitalist societies. *Man 14*(2), 249–70.

Lloyd, Alan B.
(1983) The late period, 664–323 B.C. In Bruce G. Trigger, Barry J. Kemp, David O'Connor, and Alan B. Lloyd, *Ancient Egypt; a social history* (pp. 279–348). Cambridge: Cambridge University Press.

Locke, John
(1980) *Second treatise of government [1690].* C. B. MacPherson (Ed.). Indianapolis: Hackett Publishing Company.

Lothrop, Samuel K.
(1948) Julio C. Tello, 1880–1947. *American Antiquity, 14*(1), 50–56.

Lurie, Edward
(1988) *Louis Agassiz: A life in science [1960].* Baltimore: Johns Hopkins University Press.

Lyon, Edwin A., II
(1982) *New Deal archaeology in the Southeast: WPA, TVA, NPS, 1934–1942.* Unpublished doctoral dissertation, Louisiana State University and Agricultural and Mechanical College, Baton Rouge.

McCaughey, Robert A.
(1984) *International studies and academic enterprise: A chapter in the enclosure of American learning.* New York: Columbia University Press.

McCoy, Drew R.
(1978) *The elusive republic: Political economy in Jeffersonian America.* Chapel Hill: University of North Carolina Press.

McCune, Robert P.
(1971) *Origins and development of the National Science Foundation and its Division of Social Sciences, 1945–1961.* Unpublished doctoral dissertation, Ball State University, Muncie.

MacCurdy, George G.
(1913) On the relation of archeology to ethnology from the Quarternary viewpoint. *American Anthropologist, 15*(4), 567–73.
(1924) *Human origins* (Vols. 1–2). New York: D. Appleton and Company.

MacDonald, William K. (Ed.)
(1976) *Digging for gold: Papers on archeology for profit* (Tech. Rep. No. 5). Ann Arbor: University of Michigan, Museum of Anthropology.

McGuire, Randall H.
(1982) The study of ethnicity in historic archaeology. *Journal of Anthropological Archaeology, 1*(2), 159–78.
(1983) Breaking down cultural complexity: Inequality and heterogeneity. In Michael B. Schiffer (Ed.), *Advances in Archaeological Method and Theory* (Vol. 6, pp. 91–142). New York: Academic Press.
(1993) Archaeology and Marxism. In Michael B. Schiffer (Ed.), *Archaeological Method and Theory* (Vol. 5, pp 101–57). Tucson: University of Arizona Press.

McGuire, Randall H., and Paynter, Robert (Eds.)
(1991) *The archaeology in inequality.* Oxford: Basil Blackwell.

McKern, William C.
(1939) The Midwestern taxonomic method as an aid to archaeological culture study. *American Antiquity, 4*(4), 301–13.

McLuhan, H. Marshall
(1951) *The mechanical bride: Folklore of industrial man.* New York: The Vanguard Press.

McManamon, Francis P.
   (1992) Managing America's archaeological
         resources. In LuAnn Wandsnider (Ed.),
         *Quandaries and quests: Visions of
         archaeology's future* (Occasional Paper
         20, pp. 25–40).Carbondale: Southern Illi-
         nois University, Center for Archaeologi-
         cal Investigations.
McNall, Scott G.
   (1988) *The road to rebellion: Class formation
         and Kansas populism, 1865–1900.*
         Chicago: University of Chicago Press.
MacNeish, Richard S.
   (1964) Ancient Mesoamerican civilization. *Sci-
         ence, 143*(3606), 531–37.
   (1972) The evolution of community patterns in
         the Tehuacán Valley of Mexico and spec-
         ulations about the cultural processes. In
         Peter J. Ucko, Ruth Tringham, and G. W.
         Dimbleby (Eds.), *Man, settlement and
         urbanism* (pp. 67–93). London: Gerald
         Duckworth.
McVicker, Donald
   (1989) Prejudice and context: The anthropologi-
         cal archaeologist as historian. In Andrew
         L. Christenson (Ed.), *Tracing archaeolo-
         gy's past; The historiography of archae-
         ology* (pp. 113–26). Carbondale:
         Southern Illinois University, Center for
         Archaeological Investigations.
Malin, James C.
   (1921) Indian policy and westward expansion.
         *Bulletin of the University of Kansas
         Humanistic Studies, 2*(3), 101–08.
Maravall, José Antonio
   (1986) *Culture of the Baroque: Analysis of a his-
         torical structure.* Minneapolis: University
         of Minnesota Press.
Marchak, M. Patricia
   (1991) *The integrated circus: The New Right and
         the restructuring of global markets.* Mon-
         treal: McGill-Queen's University Press.
Mardock, Robert W.
   (1971) *The reformers and the American Indian.*
         Columbia: University of Missouri Press.
Mark, Joan
   (1980) *Four anthropologists: An American sci-
         ence in its early years.* New York: Sci-
         ence History Publications.
Marks, Russell
   (1980) Legitimating industrial capitalism: Phi-
         lanthropy and individual differences. In
         Robert F. Arnove (Ed.), *Philanthropy and
         imperialism: The foundations at home
         and abroad* (pp. 87–122). Boston: G.K.
         Hall.
Marsden, George M.
   (1980) *Fundamentalism and American culture:
         The shaping of twentieth-century evan-
         gelicalism, 1870–1925.* Oxford: Oxford
         University Press.
Martin, Julian
   (1992) *Francis Bacon, the state, and the reform
         of natural philosophy.* Cambridge: Cam-
         bridge University Press.
Martin, Paul S.
   (1936) Lowry ruin in southwestern Colorado.
         *Field Museum of Natural History,
         Anthropological Series, 23*(1). Chicago.

   (1938) Archaeological work in the Ackmen-
         Lowry area, southwestern Colorado,
         1937. *Field Museum of Natural History,
         Anthropological Series, 23*(2). Chicago.
   (1940) The SU Site: Excavations at a Mogollon
         village, western New Mexico, 1939. *Field
         Museum of Natural History, Anthropo-
         logical Series, 32*(1). Chicago.
Marx, Leo
   (1959) *The machine in the garden.* Oxford:
         Oxford University Press.
May, Lary (Ed.)
   (1989) *Recasting America: Culture and politics
         in the age of the Cold War.* Chicago: Uni-
         versity of Chicago Press.
Meade, Carroll W.
   (1969) *American Assyriology: Its growth and
         development.* Unpublished doctoral dis-
         sertation, University of Texas, Austin.
Meek, Ronald L.
   (1976) *Social science and the ignoble savage.*
         Cambridge: Cambridge University Press.
Meltzer, David J.
   (1983) The antiquity of man and the develop-
         ment of American archaeology. In
         Michael B. Schiffer (Ed.), *Advances in
         Archaeological Method and Theory* (Vol.
         6, pp. 1–52). New York: Academic Press.
Meltzer, David J., and Dunnell, Robert C.
   (1992) Introduction. In David J. Meltzer and
         Robert C. Dunnell (Eds.), *The archaeol-
         ogy of William Henry Holmes* (pp. vii–l).
         Washington, DC: Smithsonian Institution
         Press.
Menshikov, S.
   (1969) *Millionaires and managers: Structure of
         U.S. financial oligarchy.* Moscow:
         Progress Publishers.
Menzel, Dorothy
   (1959) The Inca occupation of the south coast of
         Peru. *Southwestern Journal of Anthropol-
         ogy, 15*(2), 125–42.
   (1976) *Pottery style and society in ancient Peru:
         Art as a mirror of history of the Ica Val-
         ley, 1350–1570.* Berkeley: University of
         California Press.
Merchant, Carolyn
   (1980) *The death of nature: Women, ecology,
         and the Scientific Revolution.* New York:
         Harper and Row.
Merk, Frederick
   (1950) *Albert Gallatin and the Oregon problem:
         A study in Anglo-American diplomacy.*
         Cambridge: Harvard University Press.
   (1966) *The Monroe Doctrine and American
         expansionism, 1843–1849.* New York:
         Alfred A. Knopf.
Meyer, Karl E.
   (1979) *The art museum: Power, money, ethics.*
         William Morrow and Company.
Miles, Edwin A.
   (1974) The young American nation and classical
         world. *Journal of the History of Ideas,
         35*(2), 259–74.
Miller, R. Berkeley
   (1975) Anthropology and institutionalization:
         Frederick Starr at the University of
         Chicago, 1892–1923. *Kroeber Anthropo-
         logical Society Papers, 51–52,* 49–60.

Millon, René
(1967) Teotihuacán. *Scientific American, 216*(6), 38–48.
(1976) Social relations in ancient Teotihuacán. In Eric R. Wolf (Ed.), *The Valley of Mexico: Studies in pre-hispanic ecology and society* (pp. 205–48). Albuquerque: University of New Mexico Press.

Moldow, Gloria
(1987) *Women doctors in Gilded-Age Washington: Race, gender, and professionalization.* Urbana: University of Illinois Press.

Montgomery, David
(1979) *Workers' control in America.* Cambridge: Cambridge University Press.

Moore, Frank G.
(1919) A history of the American Philological Association. *Transactions and Proceedings of the American Philological Association, 50,* 5–32.

Morgan, Lewis Henry
(1869) The "Seven Cities of Cibola." *North American Review, 108*(223), 457–98.
(1876) Montezuma's dinner. *North American Review, 122*(251), 265–308.
(1963) *Ancient society, or, researches in the lines of human progress from savagery through barbarism to civilization [1877]* Eleanor B. Leacock (Ed.). Cleveland: World Publishing Company.

Morgan, Will
(1977) *The effect of federal water projects on cultural resources: Implementation of the Historic Preservation Act of 1966 by the Army Corps of Engineers, Bureau of Reclamation, and TVA.* Washington, DC: Environmental Policy Institute.

Moseley, Michael E.
(1975) *The maritime foundations of Andean civilization.* Menlo Park: Cummings Publishing Company.

Mourt (pseud. George Morton)
(1622) *Relation or journal of the beginning and proceedings of the English plantation settled at Plimoth in New England, by certain English adventurers both merchants and others.* London: John Bellamie.

Murphy, Robert F.
(1976) Introduction: A quarter century of American anthropology. In Robert F. Murphy (Ed.), *Selected papers from the American Anthropologist 1946–1970* (pp. 1–22). Washington, DC: American Anthropological Association.

Nash, Gary B.
(1979) *The urban crucible: The Northern seaports and the origins of the American Revolution.* Cambridge: Harvard University Press.
(1986) *Race, class, and politics: Essays on American colonial and revolutionary society.* Urbana: University of Illinois Press.

Nash, Gerald D.
(1991) *Creating the West: Historical interpretations, 1890–1990.* Albuquerque: University of New Mexico Press.

Nash, Gerald D., and Etulain, Richard W. (Eds.).
(1989) *The twentieth-century West: Historical interpretations.* Albuquerque: University of New Mexico Press.

Nash, Roderick
(1982) *Wilderness and the American mind* (3rd ed.). New Haven, CT: Yale University Press.

Neale, R.S.
(1985) *Writing Marxist history: British society, economy and culture since 1700.* Oxford: Basil Blackwell.

Nell, Edward J.
(1979) Population pressure and methods of adaptation: A critique of classless theory. In Stanley Diamond (Ed.), *Towards a Marxist anthropology: Problems and perspectives* (pp. 457–68). The Hague: Mouton Publishers.

Noble, David F.
(1977) *America by design: Science, technology, and the rise of corporate capitalism.* New York: Alfred A. Knopf.
(1984) *Forces of production: A social history of industrial automation.* New York: Alfred A. Knopf.
(1992) *A world without women: The Christian clerical culture of Western science.* New York: Alfred A. Knopf.

Noelke, Virginia H. M.
(1974) The origin and early history of the Bureau of American Ethnology, 1879–1910. Unpublished doctoral dissertation, University of Texas. Austin.

Nonini, Don
(1988) Everyday forms of popular resistance. *Monthly Review, 40*(6), 25–36.

Norton, Charles E., Brimmer, Martin, Peabody, O.W., Greenleaf, E.H., Parkman, Francis, Haynes, H.W., Ware, W.R., Goodwin, W.W., and Agassi, Alexander
(1880) *First annual report of the executive committee, 1879–1880.* Cambridge: Archaeological Institute of America.

Nye, Russell B.
(1960) *The cultural life of the new nation, 1776–1830.* New York: Harper and Row.
(1974) *Society and culture in America, 1830–1860.* New York: Harper and Row.

Oakes, Guy
(1981) The epistemological foundations of cultural materialism. *Dialectical Anthropology, 6*(1), 1–21.

Ober, Frederick A.
(1894) Aborigines of the West Indies. *Proceedings of the American Antiquarian Society, 9*(2), 270–313.

O'Connor, James
(1973) *Fiscal crisis of the state.* New York: St. Martin's Press.

Oleson, Alexandra, and Brown, Sanborn C. (Eds.)
(1976) *The pursuit of knowledge in the early American Republic: American scientific and learned societies from colonial times to the Civil War.* Baltimore: Johns Hopkins University Press.

Olien, Michael D.
(1985) E. G. Squier and the Miskito: Anthropological scholarship and political propaganda. *Ethnohistory, 32*(2), 111–33.

Omi, Michael, and Winant, Howard
(1986) *Racial formation in the United States from the 1960s to the 1980s.* New York: Routledge and Kegan Paul.

Orser, Charles E., Jr.
   (1990) Archaeological approaches to New World
           plantation slavery. In Michael B. Schiffer
           (Ed.), Archaeological Method and Theory,
           (Vol. 2, pp. 111–54). Tucson: University
           of Arizona Press.
Padgen, Anthony
   (1982) The fall of natural man: The American
           Indians and the origins of comparative
           ethnology. Cambridge: Cambridge Univer-
           sity Press.
Parker, Franklin
   (1971) George Peabody: A biography. Nashville:
           Vanderbilt University.
Parrington, Vernon L.
   (1928–1930) Main currents in American thought
           (Vols. 1–3). New York: Harcourt Brace
           and World.
Patterson, Thomas C.
   (1986a) The last sixty years: Toward a social his-
           tory of Americanist archaeology in the
           United States. American Anthropologist,
           88(1), 7–26.
   (1986b) Some postwar theoretical trends in U.S.
           archaeology. Culture, 4(1), 43–54.
   (1987) Development, ecology, and marginal util-
           ity in anthropology. Dialectical Anthropol-
           ogy, 15(1), 15–31.
   (1989a) Political economy and a discourse called
           "Peruvian archaeology." Culture and His-
           tory, 4, 35–64.
   (1989b) History and the post-processual archaeolo-
           gies. Man 24(4), 555–66.
   (1990) Some theoretical tensions within and
           between the processual and postprocessual
           archaeologies. Journal of Anthropological
           Archaeology, 9(2), 189–200.
   (1991) The Inca empire: The formation and dis-
           integration of a pre-capitalist state. New
           York: Berg Publishers.
Patterson, Thomas C., and Gailey, Christine W. (Eds.)
   (1987) Power relations and state formation.
           Washington, DC: American Anthropolog-
           ical Association, Archeology Section.
Patterson, Thomas C., and Lanning, Edward P.
   (1964) Changing settlement patterns on the cen-
           tral coast of Peru. Ñawpa Pacha, 2,
           113–23.
Paynter, Robert
   (1988) Steps to an archaeology of capitalism:
           Material change and class analysis. In
           Mark P. Leone and Parker B. Potter, Jr.
           (Eds.), The recovery of meaning (pp.
           407–34). Washington, DC: Smithsonian
           Institution Press.
Peace, William J.
   (1993) Leslie White and evolutionary theory.
           Dialectical Anthropology, 18(2), 123–52.
Pearce, Roy Harvey
   (1965) The savages of America: A study of the
           Indian and the idea of civilization (rev.
           ed.). Baltimore: Johns Hopkins Press.
Peck, Harry T.
   (1970) William Hickling Prescott [1905]. New
           York: AMS Press.
Peebles, Christopher S., and Kus, Susan M.
   (1977) Some archaeological correlates of ranked
           societies. American Antiquity, 42(3),
           421–48.

Pels, Richard H.
   (1973) Radical visions and American dreams:
           Culture and social thought in the Depres-
           sion years. New York: Harper and Row.
Perkins, Dexter
   (1933) The Monroe Doctrine, 1826–1827. Balti-
           more: Johns Hopkins Press.
Perrett, Geoffrey
   (1974) Days of sadness, years of triumph: The
           American people, 1939–1945. Baltimore:
           Penguin Books.
Pessen, Edward
   (1985) Jacksonian America: Society, personal-
           ity, and politics (rev. ed.). Chicago: Uni-
           versity of Chicago Press.
Peters, Elizabeth
   (1989) Summer of the dragon [1979]. New York:
           TOR, A Tom Doherty Associates Book.
Phillips, Clifton J.
   (1969) Protestant America and the pagan world:
           The first half century of the American
           Board of Commissioners for Foreign Mis-
           sions, 1810–1860. Harvard East Asian
           Monographs, 32.
Phillips, Kevin P.
   (1982) Post-conservative America: People, poli-
           tics, and ideology in a time of crisis. New
           York: Random House.
   (1993) Boiling point: Democrats, Republicans,
           and the decline of middle-class prosperity.
           New York: Random House.
Pick, Daniel
   (1989) Faces of degeneration: A European disor-
           der, c. 1848–c. 1918. Cambridge: Cam-
           bridge University Press.
Piggott, Stuart
   (1937) Prehistory and the Romantic movement.
           Antiquity, 11(41), 31–38.
   (1976) Ruins in a landscape: Essays in antiquar-
           ianism. Edinburgh: Edinburgh University.
           Press.
Pike, Frederick B.
   (1992) The United States and Latin America:
           Myths and stereotypes of civilization and
           nature. Austin: University of Texas Press.
Pollock, Norman
   (1962) The populist response to industrial Amer-
           ica. New York: W.W. Norton.
Powell, Philip W.
   (1971) Tree of hate: Propaganda and prejudices
           affecting United States relations with the
           Hispanic world. New York: Basic Books.
Powell, Shirley, Garza, Christina E., and Hendricks,
           Aubrey
   (1993) Ethics and the ownership of the past: The
           reburial and repatriation controversy. In
           Michael B. Schiffer (Ed.), Archaeologi-
           cal Method and Theory, (Vol. 5, pp.
           1–42). Tucson: University of Arizona
           Press.
Prescott, William H.
   (1936) History of the conquest of Mexico [1843]
           and History of the conquest of Peru
           [1847]. New York: Random House.
Preucel, Robert W. (Ed.)
   (1991) Processual and postprocessual archaeolo-
           gies: Multiple ways of knowing the past
           (Occasional Paper No. 10). Carbondale:
           Center for Archaeological Investigations,

Southern Illinois University, Occasional Paper No. 10. Carbondale.

Price, Barbara J.
  (1978) Secondary state formation: An explanatory model. In Ronald Cohen and Elman R. Service (Eds.), *Origins of the state: The anthropology of political evolution* (pp. 161–86). Philadelphia: Institute for the Study of Human Issues.
  (1982) Cultural materialism: A theoretical view. *American Antiquity, 47*(4), 709–41.

Quimby, George I., Jr.
  (1979) A brief history of WPA anthropology. In Walter Goldschmidt (Ed.), The uses of anthropology *(Special Publication of the American Anthropological Association,* Vol. 11, 110–23). Washington, DC.

Raab, L. Mark, and Goodyear, Albert C.
  (1984) Middle-range theory in archaeology: A critical review of origins and applications. *American Antiquity, 49*(2), 255–68.

Rainey, Froelich
  (1992) *Reflections of a digger.* Philadelphia: University of Pennsylvania, The University Museum of Archaeology and Anthropology.

Rainger, Ronald
  (1991) *An agenda for antiquity: Henry Fairfield Osborn and vertebrate paleontology at the American Museum of Natural History, 1890–1935.* Tuscaloosa: University of Alabama Press.

Reidhead, Van
  (1980) The economics of subsistence change: A test of an optimization model. In Timothy Earle and A. Christenson (Eds.), *Modeling change in prehistoric subsistence strategies* (pp. 141–86). New York: Academic Press.

Reingold, Nathan
  (1979) National science policy in a private foundation: The Carnegie Institution of Washington. In Alexandra Oleson and John Voss (Eds.), *The organization of knowledge in modern America, 1860–1920* (pp. 313–41). Baltimore: The Johns Hopkins University Press.
  (1987) Graduate school and doctoral degree: European models and American realities. In Nathan Reingold and Marc Rothenberg (Eds.), *Scientific colonialism: A cross-cultural comparison* (pp. 129–50). Washington, DC: Smithsonian Institution.

Reinhold, Meyer
  (1984) *Classica Americana: The Greek and Roman heritage in the United States.* Detroit: Wayne State University Press.

Renfrew, Colin
  (1969) Trade and culture process in European prehistory. *Current Anthropology, 10*(2–3), 151–69.
  (1979) Systems collapse as social transformation: Catastrophe and anastrophe in early state societies. In Colin Renfrew and Kenneth L. Cooke (Eds.), *Transformations: Mathematical approaches to culture change* (pp. 481–506). New York: Academic Press.
  (1980) The great tradition versus the great divide: Archaeology as anthropology? *American*

Journal of Archaeology, 84(3), 287–98.
  (1984) Trade as action at a distance [1975]. In Colin Renfrew, *Approaches to social archaeology* (pp. 86–134). Edinburgh: Edinburgh University Press.

Resnick, Carl
  (1960) *Lewis Henry Morgan: American scholar.* Chicago: University of Chicago Press.

Riefstahl, Elizabeth
  (1962) The American Research Center in Egypt, Inc. *Bulletin of the Archaeological Institute of America, 53,* 33–35.
  (1963) The American Research Center in Egypt, Inc. *Bulletin of the Archaeological Institute of America, 54,* 23–25.

Rindos, David
  (1984) *The origins of agriculture: An evolutionary perspective.* New York: Academic Press.

Rippy, J. Fred
  (1926) *The United States and Mexico.* New York: Alfred A. Knopf.

Robertson, William
  (1778) *The history of America* (Vols. 1–2, 2nd ed.). London: A. Strahan.

Robinson, Cecil
  (1963) *With the ears of strangers: The Mexican in American literature.* Tucson: University of Arizona Press.

Roediger, David R.
  (1991) *The wages of whiteness: Race and the making of the American working class.* London: Verso.

Rogge, Allen E.
  (1983) Little archaeology, big archaeology: The changing context of archaeological research. Unpublished doctoral dissertation, University of Arizona, Tucson.

Rogin, Michael P.
  (1987) *Ronald Reagan, the movie and other episodes in political demonology.* Berkeley: University of California Press.

Rosen, Lawrence
  (1980) The excavation of American Indian burial sites: A problem of law and professional responsibility. *American Anthropologist, 82*(1), 5–27.

Rosenthal, Franz
  (1952) *A history of Muslim historiography.* Leiden, Netherlands: E.J. Brill.

Ross, Dorothy
  (1972) *G. Stanley Hall: The psychologist as prophet.* Chicago: University of Chicago Press.
  (1984) Historical consciousness in nineteenth-century America. *American Historical Review, 89*(4), 909–28.
  (1991) *The origins of American social science.* Cambridge: Cambridge University Press.

Rossiter, Margaret W.
  (1982) *Women scientists in America: Struggles and strategies to 1940.* Baltimore: Johns Hopkins University Press.

Rostovtzeff, Michael I.
  (1938) *Dura-Europos and its art.* Oxford: Oxford University Press.

Rostow, Walter W.
  (1960) *The stages of economic growth: A non-communist manifesto.* Cambridge: Cambridge University Press.

Rouse, B. Irving
  (1939) Prehistory in Haiti: A study in method. *Yale University Publications in Anthropology, 21.* New Haven, CT: Yale University.
Rowe, John H.
  (1954) Max Uhle, 1856–1944: A memoir of the father of Peruvian archaeology. *University of California Publications in American Archaeology and Ethnology, 46* (1). Berkeley, CA: University of California.
  (1962) Stages and periods in archaeological interpretation. *Southwestern Journal of Anthropology, 18*(1), 40–54.
  (1963) Urban settlements in ancient Peru. *Ñawpa Pacha, 1,* 1–27.
  (1964) Ethnology and ethnography in the sixteenth century. *Kroeber Anthropological Society Papers, 30,* 1–19.
  (1965) The Renaissance foundations of anthropology. *American Anthropologist, 67*(1), 1–20.
Rucker, Darnell
  (1969) *The Chicago pragmatists.* Minneapolis: University of Minnesota Press.
Rudwick, Martin J. S.
  (1985) *The great Devonian controversy: The shaping of scientific knowledge among gentlemanly specialists.* Chicago: University of Chicago Press.
Rumbaut, Rubén G.
  (1991) Passages to America: Perspectives on the new immigration. In Alan Wolfe (Ed.), *America at century's end* (pp. 208–44). Berkeley: University of California Press.
Ruskin, Michael
  (1991) *The good society and the inner world: Psychoanalysis, politics and culture.* London: Verso.
Russett, Cynthia E.
  (1976) *Darwin in America: The intellectual response, 1865–1912.* San Francisco: J. H. Freeman.
Rydell, Robert W.
  (1978) The World's Columbian Exposition of 1893: Racist underpinnings of a utopian artifact. *Journal of American Culture, 1*(2), 253–75.
  (1984) *All the world's a fair: Visions of empire at American international expositions, 1876–1916.* Chicago: University of Chicago Press.
Sacks, Karen B.
  (1992) *How did Jews become white folks?* Paper presented at the annual meeting of the American Anthropological Association, Washington, DC
Sahlins, Marshall
  (1969) Economic anthropology and anthropological economics. *Social Science Information, 8*(5), 13–33.
  (1976) *Culture and practical reason.* Chicago: University of Chicago Press.
Salmon, Merrilee H.
  (1982) *Philosophy and archaeology.* New York: Academic Press.
Sanders, Elizabeth
  (1987) The regulatory surge of the 1970's in historical perspective. In Elizabeth E. Bailey (Ed.), *Public regulation: New perspectives on institutions and policies* (pp. 117–50). Cambridge: MIT Press.
Sanders, William T., and Webster, David
  (1978) Unilinealism, multilinealism, and the evolution of complex societies. In Charles L. Redman, Mary J. Berman, Edward V. Curtin, William T. Langhorne, Jr., Nina M. Versaggi, and Jeffrey C. Wanser (Eds.), *Social archeology: Beyond subsistence and dating* (pp. 249–302). New York: Academic Press.
San Juan, Epifanio, Jr.
  (1992) *Race formations/critical transformations: Articulations of power in ethnic and racial studies in the United States.* Atlantic Highlands, NJ: Humanities Press International.
Sassoon, Ann S.
  (1983) Hegemony. In Tom Bottomore, Laurence Harris, V.G. Kiernan, and Ralph Miliband (Eds.), *A dictionary of Marxist thought* (pp. 201–03). Cambridge: Harvard University Press.
Satz, Ronald N.
  (1975) *American Indian policy in the Jacksonian era.* Lincoln: University of Nebraska Press.
Saxon, Alexander
  (1990) *The rise and fall of the white republic: Class politics and mass culture in nineteenth-century America.* London: Verso.
Sayres, Sohnya, Stephanson, Anders, Aronowitz, Stanley, and Jameson, Fredric (Eds.)
  (1984) *The 60s without apology.* Minneapolis: University of Minnesota Press.
Scaff, Lawrence A.
  (1989) *Fleeing the iron cage: Culture, politics, and modernity in the thought of Max Weber.* Berkeley: University of California Press.
Schiffer, Michael B., and Gumerman, George J.
  (1977) Cultural resource management. In Michael B. Schiffer and George J. Gumerman (Eds.), *Conservation archaeology: A guide for cultural resource management studies* (pp. 1–17). New York: Academic Press.
Schmidt, George P.
  (1936) Intellectual crosscurrents in American colleges, 1825–1855. *American Historical Review, 52*(4), 46–67.
Schnapp, Alain
  (1981) Archéologie, archélogues et nazisme. In Léon Poliakov (Ed.), *Le racisme; Mythes et sciences* (pp. 289–315). Brussels: Editions Complexes.
Schroeder, Albert H.
  (1979) History of archeological research. In William Sturtevant (Ed.), *Handbook of North American Indians* (Vol. 9, pp. 5–13). Washington, DC: Smithsonian Institution.
Schuyler, Robert L.
  (1970) Historical and historic sites archaeology as anthropology: Basic definitions and relationships. *Historical Archaeology, 4,* 83–89.
  (1976) Images of America: The contribution of historical archaeology to the national identity. *Southwestern Lore, 44*(4), 27–39.
Sellers, Charles
  (1991) *The market revolution: Jacksonian America, 1815–1846.* Oxford: Oxford University Press.

Service, Elman
(1962) *Primitive social organization: An evolutionary perspective.* New York: Random House.

Seymour, Thomas D.
(1897) American School of Classical Studies at Athens, 1896–1897: Report of the Managing Committee. *American Journal of Archaeology, 1*(1), 91–106.

Shanks, Michael, and Tilley, Christopher
(1987a) *Social theory and archaeology.* Oxford: Polity Press.
(1987b) *Re-constructing archaeology: Theory and practice.* Cambridge: Cambridge University Press.

Shapiro, Barbara J.
(1983) *Probability and certainty in seventeenth-century England: A study of the relationships between natural science, religion, history, law, and literature.* Princeton: Princeton University Press.

Shaw, Brent
(1983) "Eaters of flesh, drinkers of milk": The ancient Mediterranean ideology of the pastoral nomad. *Ancient Society, 13/14,* 5–31.

Shear, T. Leslie
(1936) The current excavations in the Athenian Agora. *American Journal of Archaeology, 33*(2), 188–203.

Sheehan, Bernard W.
(1973) *Seeds of extinction: Jeffersonian philanthropy and the American Indian.* New York: W.W. Norton.
(1980) *Savagism and civility: Indians and Englishmen in colonial Virginia.* Cambridge: Cambridge University Press.

Sheftel, Phoebe S.
(1979) The Archaeological Institute of America, 1879–1979: A centennial review. *American Journal of Archaeology, 83*(1), 3–17.

Shils, Edward
(1979) The order of learning in the United States: The ascendancy of the university. In Alexandra Oleson and John Voss (Eds.), *The organization of knowledge in modern America, 1860–1920* (pp. 19–47). Baltimore: The Johns Hopkins University Press.

Shipman, Pat
(1986) Scavenging or hunting in early hominids: Theoretical framework and tests. *American Anthropologist, 88*(1), 27–43.

Shorey, Paul
(1919) Fifty years of classical studies in America. *Transactions and Proceedings of the American Philological Association, 50,* 33–61.

Silberman, Neil A.
(1982) *Digging for God and country: Exploration, archeology, and the secret struggle for the Holy Land, 1799–1917.* New York: Alfred A. Knopf.
(1989) *Between past and present: Archaeology, ideology, and nationalism in the modern Middle East.* New York: Henry Holt and Company.

Silverberg, Robert
(1968) *Mound builders of ancient America: The archaeology of a myth.* Athens: Ohio University Press.

Sklar, Holly (Ed.)
(1980) *Trilateralism: The Trilateral Commission and elite planning for world management.* Boston: South End Press.

Skowronek, Stephen
(1982) *Building a new American state: The expansion of national administrative capacities, 1877–1902.* Cambridge: Cambridge University Press.

Slaughter, Sheila, and Silva, Edward T.
(1980) Looking backwards: How foundations formulated ideology in the Progressive Period. In Robert F. Arnove (Ed.), *Philanthropy and Imperialism: The Foundations at Home and Abroad* (pp. 55–86). Boston: G.K. Hall.

Slocum, Sally
(1975) Woman the gatherer: Male bias in anthropology [1971]. In Rayna R. Reiter (Ed.), *Toward an anthropology of women* (pp. 36–50). New York: Monthly Review Press.

Slotkin, Richard
(1973) *Regeneration through violence: The mythology of the American frontier, 1600–1860.* Middletown, CT: Wesleyan University Press.
(1985) *The fatal environment: The myth of the frontier in the age of industrialization, 1800–1870.* Middletown, CT: Wesleyan University Press.
(1992) *Gunfighter nation: The myth of the frontier in twentieth-century America.* New York: Atheneum.

Smith, Anthony D.
(1973) *The concept of change: A critique of the functionalist theory of change.* New York: Routledge and Kegan Paul.

Smith, Bruce L. R.
(1973) A new science policy in the United States. *Minerva 9,* 162–74.

Smith, Henry Nash
(1950) *Virgin land: The American West as symbol and myth.* New York: Vintage Books.

Smith, Jason
(1976) *Foundations of archaeology.* New York: Free Press.

Smith, Robert F.
(1972) *The United States and revolutionary nationalism in Mexico, 1916–1932.* Chicago: University of Chicago Press.

Snodgrass, Anthony M.
(1985) The new archaeology and the classical archaeologist. *American Journal of Archaeology, 89*(1), 31–37.

Society for American Archaeology
(1935) The Society for American Archaeology organizational meeting. *American Antiquity, 1*(2), 141–51.
(1942) Revised constitution. *American Antiquity, 8*(2), 206–08.

Sollors, Werner
(1986) *Beyond ethnicity: Consent and descent in American culture.* Oxford: Oxford University Press.

Solomon, Barbara M.
(1985) *In the company of educated women: A history of women and higher education in America.* New Haven, CT: Yale University Press.

South, Stanley
  (1977) *Method and theory in historical archaeology.* New York: Academic Press.
Spaulding, Albert C.
  (1953) Statistical techniques for the discovery of artifact types. *American Antiquity* 18(3), 305–13.
Spoehr, Luther W.
  (1973) Sambo and the Heathen Chinee: Californians' racial stereotypes in the late 1870's. *Pacific Historical Review,* 62(2), 185–204.
Springer, Carolyn
  (1987) *The marble wilderness: Ruins and representation in Italian romanticism, 1775–1850.* Cambridge: Cambridge University Press.
Squier, Ephraim George
  (1855) *Notes on Central America.* New York: Harper and Brothers.
Squier, Ephraim George, and Davis, Edwin H.
  (1848) Ancient monuments of the Mississippi Valley. *Smithsonian Contributions to Knowledge, 1.* Washington, DC.
Stansifer, Charles L.
  (1959) *The Central American career of E. George Squier.* Unpublished doctoral dissertation, Tulane University, New Orleans.
Stanton, William R.
  (1960) *The leopard's spots: Scientific attitudes toward race in America, 1815–1859.* Chicago: University of Chicago Press.
  (1975) *The great United States exploring expedition of 1838–1842.* Berkeley: University of California Press.
  (1991) *American scientific exploration, 1803–1860: Manuscripts in four Philadelphia libraries* (Library Publication No. 15). Philadelphia: American Philosophical Society.
Stegner, Wallace
  (1953) *Beyond the hundredth meridian: John Wesley Powell and the second opening of the West.* Lincoln: University of Nebraska Press.
Stepan, Nancy L.
  (1986) Race and gender: The role of analogy in science. *Isis, 77* (287), 261–77.
Stephens, John Lloyd
  (1839) *Incidents of travel in the Russian and Turkish empires* (Vols. 1–2). London: Richard Bentley.
  (1963) *Incidents of travels in Yucatán [1843]* (Vols. 1–2). New York: Dover Publications.
Stern, Bernhard
  (1931) *Lewis Henry Morgan: Social evolutionist.* Chicago: University of Chicago Press.
Steward, Julian H.
  (1937) Ecological aspects of Southwestern society. *Anthropos, 23,* 87–104.
  (1942) The direct historical approach to archaeology. *American Antiquity, 7*(4), 337–43.
  (1950) Area research: Theory and practice. *Social Science Research Council Bulletin, 63.*
  (1955) *Theory of culture change.* Urbana: University of Illinois Press.
Steward, Julian H., Adams, Robert M., Collier, Donald, Palerm, Angel, Wittfogel, Karl A., and Beals, Ralph L.
  (1960) Irrigation civilizations: A comparative study: A symposium on method and result in cross-cultural regularities. *Social Science Monographs, I.* Washington, DC: Pan American Union.
Steward, Julian H., and Seltzer, Frank M.
  (1938) Function and configuration in archaeology. *American Antiquity, 4*(1), 4–10.
Stirling, Matthew W.
  (1934) Smithsonian archeological projects conducted under the Federal Emergency Relief Administration, 1933–34. *Annual Report of the Board of Regents, Smithsonian Institution* (pp. 371–401). Washington, DC.
Stocking, George W., Jr.
  (1976) Ideas and institutions in American anthropology: Toward a history of the interwar period. In George W. Stocking, Jr. (Ed.), *Selected papers from the American Anthropologist 1921–1945* (pp. 1–50). Washington, DC: American Anthropological Association.
  (1982a) *Race, culture, and evolution: Essays in the history of anthropology [1968].* Chicago: University of Chicago Press.
  (1982b) The Santa Fe style in American anthropology: Regional interest, academic initiative, and philanthropic policy in the first two decades of the Laboratory of Anthropology, Inc. *The Journal of the History of the Behavioral Sciences, 18*(1), 3–19.
Stoneman, Richard
  (1987) *Land of lost gods: The search for classical Greece.* Norman: University of Oklahoma Press.
Story, Ronald
  (1980) *Harvard and the Boston upper class: The forging of an aristocracy, 1800–1870.* Middletown, CT: Wesleyan University Press.
Strong, William Duncan
  (1935) An introduction to Nebraska archeology. *Smithsonian Miscellaneous Collections, 93* (10). Washington, DC: Smithsonian Institution.
  (1936) Anthropological theory and archaeological fact. In Robert H. Lowie (Ed.), *Essays in honor of A. L. Kroeber* (pp. 359–70). Berkeley: University of California Press.
Sued-Badillo, Jalil
  (1992a) Facing up to Caribbean history. *American Antiquity, 57*(4), 599–607.
  (1992b) Christopher Columbus and the enslavement of the Amerindians in the Caribbean. *Monthly Review, 44*(3), 71–102.
Sullivan, Paul
  (1989) *Unfinished conversations: Mayas and foreigners between two wars.* Berkeley: University of California Press.
Susser, Ida
  (1993) Creating family forms: The exclusion of men and teenage boys from families in the New York City shelter system, 1987–1992. *Critique of Anthropology, 13*(3), 267–84.
Swann, Nancy Lee
  (1934) A woman among the rich merchants: The widow of Pa (3rd century B.C.). *Journal of*

the American Oriental Society, 54, 186–93.

Takaki, Ronald
  (1990) *Iron cages: Race and culture in 19th-century America.* Oxford: Oxford University Press.
  (1993) *A different mirror: A history of multicultural America.* Boston: Little, Brown and Company.

Tax, Thomas G.
  (1973) The development of American archaeology, 1800–1879. Unpublished doctoral dissertation, University of Chicago, Chicago.

Taylor, Charles
  (1992) *Multiculturalism and "the politics of recognition."* Princeton: Princeton University Press.

Taylor, Walter W.
  (1948) A study of archeology. *Memoirs of the American Anthropological Association, 69.* Menasha, WI.

Thomas, Cyrus
  (1894) Report on the mound explorations of the Bureau of Ethnology. *Twelfth Annual Report, Bureau of Ethnology, Smithsonian Institution 1890–1891* (pp. 3–730). Washington, DC.

Thomas, David H. (Ed.)
  (1989–1991) *Columbian consequences* (Vols. 1–3). Washington, DC: Smithsonian Institution Press.

Thoresen, Timothy H. H.
  (1975) Paying the piper and calling the tune: The beginnings of academic anthropology in California. *The Journal of the History of the Behavioral Sciences, 11*(3), 257–75.

Tisdall, Fitz Gerald
  (1894) Report of the Secretary of the New York Society. *Archaeological Institute of America fifteenth annual report, 1893–1894* (pp. 57–61). Boston, MA.

Tompkins, E. Berkeley
  (1970) *Anti-imperialism in the United States: The great debate, 1890–1920.* Philadelphia: University of Pennsylvania Press.

Trennert, Robert A., Jr.
  (1975) *Alternative to extinction: Federal Indian policy and the beginnings of the reservation system, 1846–1851.* Philadelphia: Temple University Press.

Trigger, Bruce
  (1980a) Archaeology and the image of the American Indian. *American Antiquity, 45*(4), 662–76.
  (1980b) *Gordon Childe: Revolution in archaeology.* London: Thames and Hudson.
  (1981) Anglo-American archaeology. *World Archaeology, 13*(2), 138–55.
  (1984) Alternative archaeologies: Nationalist, colonialist, imperialist. *Man, 19*(3), 355–70.
  (1989) *A history of archaeological thought.* Cambridge: Cambridge University Press.
  (1991) Constraint and freedom: A new synthesis for archaeological explanation. *American Anthropologist, 93*(3), 551–69.
  (1993) Marxism in contemporary Western archaeology. *Archaeological Method and Theory, 5,* 159–200.

Trumpbour, John
  (1989) Blinding them with science: Scientific

ideologies in the ruling of the modern world. In John Trumpbour (Ed.), *How Harvard rules: Reason in the service of empire* (pp. 221–241). Boston: South End Press.

Tsigakou, Fani-Maria
  (1981) *The rediscovery of Greece: Travellers and painters of the Romantic era.* London: Thames and Hudson.

Ucko, Peter
  (1987) *Academic freedom and apartheid: The story of the World Archaeological Congress.* London: Gerald Duckworth.

Utley, Robert M.
  (1984) *The Indian frontier of the American West, 1846–1890.* Albuquerque: University of New Mexico Press.

van Alstyne, Richard W.
  (1944) *American diplomacy in action: A series of case studies.* Stanford: Stanford University Press.
  (1960) *The rising American empire.* Oxford: Oxford University Press.

Vance, Carole
  (1975) Sexual stratification in academic anthropology 1974–1975. *Anthropology Newsletter, 16*(4), 10–13.

van der Pijl, Kees
  (1984) *The making of an Atlantic ruling class.* London: Verso.

von Hagen, Victor W.
  (1978) *Search for the Maya: The story of Stephens and Catherwood.* New York: Gordon and Cremonesi.

Wade, Edwin L.
  (1985) The ethnic art market in the American Southwest, 1880–1980. In George W. Stocking, Jr. (Ed.), *History of Anthropology,* (Vol. 3, pp. 167–91). Madison: University of Wisconsin Press.

Walde, Dale, and Willows, Noreen (Eds.)
  (1991) The archaeology of gender. *Proceedings of the 22nd Annual Chacmool Conference.* Calgary: University of Calgary, The Archaeology Association.

Wallace, Michael
  (1981) Visiting the past: History museums in the United States. *Radical History Review, 25,* 63–96.

Walters, Raymond, Jr.
  (1957) *Albert Gallatin: Jeffersonian financier and diplomat.* New York: Macmillan Company.

Washburn, Sherwood
  (1963) The study of race. *American Anthropologist, 65*(4), 521–32.

Watson, Patty Jo, LeBlanc, Steven A., and Redman, Charles L.
  (1971) *Archeological explanation: An explicitly scientific approach.* New York: Columbia University Press.
  (1984) *Archeological explanation: The scientific method in archeology.* New York: Columbia University Press.

Wauchope, Robert (Ed.)
  (1956) Seminars in archaeology: 1955. *Memoirs of the Society for American Archaeology, 11.*

Weinberg, Albert K.
  (1935) *Manifest destiny: A study of nationalist*

expansionism in American history. Baltimore: Johns Hopkins Press.

Weinstein, James
  (1968) *The corporate ideal in the liberal state, 1900–1918.* Boston: Beacon Press.

Weis, Lois
  (1990) *Working class without work: High school students in a de-industrializing economy.* New York: Routledge.

Weischadle, David E.
  (1980) The Carnegie Corporation and the shaping of American educational policy. In Robert F. Arnove, *Philanthropy and imperialism: The foundations at home and abroad* (pp. 385–412). Boston: G.K. Hall.

Weiss, Roberto
  (1988) *The Renaissance discovery of classical antiquity* (2nd ed.). Oxford: Basil Blackwell.

Wendorf, Fred
  (1979) Changing values in American archaeology. *American Antiquity, 44*(4), 641–43.

Wenke, Robert
  (1981) Explaining the evolution of cultural complexity: A review. *Advances in Archaeological Method and Theory, 4,* 79–128.

West, Cornel
  (1988) Marxist theory and the specificity of Afro-American oppression. In Cary Nelson and Lawrence Grossberg (Eds.), *Marxism and the interpretation of culture* (pp. 17–33). Urbana: University of Illinois Press.
  (1993) *Race matters.* Boston: Beacon Press.

Weston, Ruben F.
  (1972) *Racism in U.S. imperialism: The influence of racial assumptions on American foreign policy, 1893–1945.* Columbia: University of South Carolina Press.

Wetherell, Margaret, and Potter, Jonathan
  (1992) *Mapping the language of racism: Discourse and the legitimation of exploitation.* New York: Columbia University Press.

Whitehill, Walter M. (Ed.)
  (1967) *A cabinet of curiosities: Five episodes in the evolution of American museums.* Charlottesville: The University of Virginia Press.

Wiebe, Robert
  (1967) *The search for order, 1877–1920.* New York: Hill and Wang.
  (1985) *The opening of American society: From the adoption of the Constitution to the eve of disunion.* New York: Vintage Books.

Willey, Gordon R.
  (1946) The Chiclín conference for Peruvian archaeology. *American Antiquity, 12*(1), 49–56.
  (1953) Prehistoric settlement patterns in the Virú Valley, Peru. *Bureau of American Ethnology Bulletin 155.* Washington, DC.
  (1960a) New World prehistory. *Science, 131*(3393), 73–83.
  (1960b) Historical patterns and evolution in native New World cultures. In Sol Tax (Ed.), *Evolution after Darwin* (Vol. 2, pp. 111–41). Chicago: University of Chicago Press.
  (1984) Archaeological retrospect 6. *Antiquity, 58*(1), 5–14.
  (1988) *Portraits in American archaeology:*

Remembrances of some distinguished Americanists. Albuquerque: University of New Mexico Press.

Willey, Gordon R., and Phillips, Philip
  (1958) *Method and theory in American archaeology.* Chicago: University of Chicago Press.

Willey, Gordon R., and Sabloff, Jeremy A.
  (1993) *A history of American archaeology* (3rd ed.). New York: W. H. Freeman.

Williams, Raymond
  (1983) *Keywords: A vocabulary of culture and society* (rev. ed.). Oxford: Oxford University Press.

Williams, Stephen
  (1991) *Fantastic archaeology: The wild side of North American prehistory.* Philadelphia: University of Pennsylvania Press.

Williams, Walter L.
  (1980) United States Indian policy and the debate over Philippine annexation: Implications for the origins of American imperialism. *The Journal of American History, 66*(4), 810–31.

Williams, William A.
  (1961) *The contours of American history.* Cleveland: World Publishing Company.
  (1972) *The tragedy of American diplomacy* (2nd ed.). New York: Dell Publishers.

Willis, William S., Jr.
  (1980) Fusion and separation: Archaeology and ethnohistory in southeastern North America. In Stanley Diamond (Ed.), *Theory and practice: Essays presented to Gene Weltfish* (pp. 97–123). The Hague: Mouton Publishers.

Wilson, Edward O.
  (1975) *Sociobiology: The new synthesis.* Cambridge: Harvard University Press.
  (1978) *On human nature.* Cambridge: Harvard University Press.

Winegrad, Dilys P.
  (1993) *Through time, across continents: A hundred years of archaeology and anthropology at the University Museum.* Philadelphia: The University Museum, University of Pennsylvania.

Wish, Harvey
  (1966) *Contemporary America: The national scene since 1900* (4th ed.). New York: Harper and Row.

Wissler, Clark
  (1922) Notes on state archaeological surveys. *American Anthropologist, 24*(2), 233–42.

Wolfe, Alan
  (1977) *The limits of legitimacy: Political contradictions of contemporary capitalism.* New York: Free Press.
  (1981) *America's impasse: The rise and fall of the politics of growth.* New York: Pantheon Books.

Wolpoff, Milford H.
  (1989) Multiregional evolution: The fossil alternatives to Eden. In Paul Mellars and Chris Stringer (Eds.), *The human revolution* (pp. 62–108). Princeton: Princeton University Press.

Woodbury, Richard B.
  (1993) *60 years of Southwestern archaeology: A history of the Pecos Conference.* Albuquerque: University of New Mexico Press.

Woodward, C. Vann
  (1960)   *The Burden of Southern history.* Baton
          Rouge: Louisiana State University Press.
  (1966)   *Reunion and reaction: The Compromise of
          1877 and the end of Reconstruction.*
          Boston: Little, Brown and Company.
  (1974)   *The strange career of Jim Crow* (3rd ed.).
          Oxford: Oxford University Press.
Wright, G. Ernest
  (1975)   The "new" archaeology. *The Biblical
          Archaeologist, 38*(3–4, 104–15).
Wright, Henry T.
  (1969)   *The administration of rural production in
          an early Mesopotamian town.* (University
          of Michigan, Museum of Anthropology,
          Anthropological Paper No. 38). Ann Arbor.
  (1977)   Recent research on the origin of the state.
          Annual Review of Anthropology, 6,
          379–97.
  (1986)   The evolution of civilizations. In David J.
          Meltzer, Don D. Fowler, and Jeremy A.
          Sabloff (Eds.), *American archaeology past
          and future: A celebration of the Society for
          American Archaeology 1935–1985* (pp.
          323–65). Washington, DC: Smithsonian
          Institution Press.
Wuthnow, Robert
  (1988)   *The restructuring of American religion.*
          Princeton: Princeton University Press.
Wylie, M. Alison
  (1981)   *Positivism and the new archaeology.*
          Unpublished doctoral dissertation, State
          University of New York, Binghamton.
  (1991)   Gender theory and the archaeological
          record: Why is there no archaeology of gen-
          der? In Joan M. Gero and Margaret W.
          Conkey (Eds.), *Engendering archaeology:
          Women and prehistory* (pp. 31–56). Oxford:
          Basil Blackwell.
  (1993, January) *Invented lands/discovered pasts:
          The westward expansion of myth and his-
          tory.* Keynote address presented at the
          annual meeting of the Society for Histori-
          cal Archaeology, London.
Wynn, Neil
  (1976)   *The Afro-American and the Second World
          War.* London: Paul Elek.
Yale University, Office of Public Affairs
  (1991, April 17) "Yale University Receives $20 Mil-
          lion from Lee M. Bass to Support Teaching,
          Study of Western Civilization" (News
          Release). New Haven: Yale University.
Zilsel, Edgar
  (1942)   The sociological roots of science. *American
          Journal of Sociology, 47*(4), 544–62.
  (1957)   The genesis of the concept of scientific
          progress. In Philip J. Wiener and Aaron
          Noland (Eds.), *Roots of scientific thought: A
          cultural perspective* (pp. 251–75). New
          York: Basic Books.
Zimmerman, Larry J.
  (1989)   Made radical by my own: An archaeologist
          learns to accept reburial. In Robert Layton
          (Ed.), *Conflict in the archaeology of living
          traditions* (pp. 60–67). London: Unwin
          Hyman.
Zinn, Howard
  (1971)   *Postwar America: 1945–1971.* Indianapo-
          lis: The Bobbs-Merrill Company.

Zoraida Vásquez, Josefina, and Meyer, Lorenzo.
  (1985)   *The United States and Mexico.* Chicago:
          University of Chicago Press.

INDEX